SWITCH

CHIP HEATH is a professor in the Graduate School of Business at Stanford University. He lives in Los Gatos, California. DAN HEATH is a Senior Fellow at Duke University's Center for the Advancement of Social Entrepreneurship (CASE). Previously, he was a researcher and case writer at Harvard Business School, as well as the co-founder of a college textbook publishing firm called Thinkwell. Dan lives in Raleigh, NC. The Heath brothers write a monthly column for *Fast Company* magazine.

Also by Chip Heath and Dan Heath

Made to Stick: Why some ideas take hold and others come unstuck

SWITCH

HOW
TO
CHANGE
THINGS
WHEN
CHANGE
IS
HARD

CHIP HEATH and DAN HEATH

BUSINESS
BOOKS

Published by Random House Business Books 2010

8 10 9 7

First published in the United States in 2010 by Broadway Books, an imprint of the Crown Publishing Group, a division of Random House Inc., New York.

First published in Great Britain in 2010 by
Random House Business Books
Random House, 20 Vauxhall Bridge Road,
London SW1V 2SA

www.rbooks.co.uk

Addresses for companies within The Random House Group Limited can be found at:
www.randomhouse.co.uk/offices.htm

The Random House Group Limited Reg. No. 954009

A CIP catalogue record for this book
is available from the British Library

ISBN 9781847940315

The Random House Group Limited supports The Forest Stewardship Council (FSC), the leading international forest certification organisation. All our titles that are printed on Greenpeace approved FSC certified paper carry the FSC logo. Our paper procurement policy can be found at:
www.rbooks.co.uk/environment

Printed and bound in Great Britain by
CPI Mackays, Chatham, ME5 8TD

To our wives,

Susan and Amanda,

who changed everything

Contents

SWITCH

1

Three Surprises About Change

1.

One Saturday in 2000, some unsuspecting moviegoers showed up at a suburban theater in Chicago to catch a 1:05 p.m. matinee of Mel Gibson's action flick *Payback*. They were handed a soft drink and a free bucket of popcorn and were asked to stick around after the movie to answer a few questions about the concession stand. These movie fans were unwitting participants in a study of irrational eating behavior.

There was something unusual about the popcorn they received. It was wretched. In fact, it had been carefully engineered to be wretched. It had been popped five days earlier and was so stale that it squeaked when you ate it. One moviegoer later compared it to Styrofoam packing peanuts, and two others, forgetting that they'd received the popcorn for free, demanded their money back.

Some of them got their free popcorn in a medium-size bucket, and others got a large bucket—the sort of huge tub that looks like it might once have been an above-ground swimming pool. Every person got a bucket so there'd be no need to share. The researchers responsible for the study were interested in a simple question: Would the people with bigger buckets eat more?

Both buckets were so big that none of the moviegoers could finish their individual portions. So the actual research question was a bit more specific: Would somebody with a larger inexhaustible supply of popcorn eat more than someone with a smaller inexhaustible supply?

The sneaky researchers weighed the buckets before and after the movie, so they were able to measure precisely how much popcorn each person ate. The results were stunning: People with the large buckets ate 53 percent more popcorn than people with the medium size. That's the equivalent of 173 more calories and approximately 21 extra hand-dips into the bucket.

Brian Wansink, the author of the study, runs the Food and Brand Lab at Cornell University, and he described the results in his book *Mindless Eating:* "We've run other popcorn studies, and the results were always the same, however we tweaked the details. It didn't matter if our moviegoers were in Pennsylvania, Illinois, or Iowa, and it didn't matter what kind of movie was showing; all of our popcorn studies led to the same conclusion. People eat more when you give them a bigger container. Period."

No other theory explains the behavior. These people weren't eating for pleasure. (The popcorn was so stale it squeaked!) They weren't driven by a desire to finish their portion. (Both buckets were too big to finish.) It didn't matter whether they were hungry or full. The equation is unyielding: Bigger container = more eating.

Best of all, people refused to believe the results. After the movie, the researchers told the moviegoers about the two bucket sizes and the findings of their past research. The researchers asked,

Do you think you ate more because of the larger size? The majority scoffed at the idea, saying, "Things like that don't trick me," or, "I'm pretty good at knowing when I'm full."

Whoops.

2.

Imagine that someone showed you the data from the popcorn-eating study but didn't mention the bucket sizes. On your data summary, you could quickly scan the results and see how much popcorn different people ate—some people ate a little, some ate a lot, and some seemed to be testing the physical limits of the human stomach. Armed with a data set like that, you would find it easy to jump to conclusions. *Some people are Reasonable Snackers, and others are Big Gluttons.*

A public-health expert, studying that data alongside you, would likely get very worried about the Gluttons. *We need to motivate these people to adopt healthier snacking behaviors! Let's find ways to show them the health hazards of eating so much!*

But wait a second. If you want people to eat less popcorn, the solution is pretty simple: Give them smaller buckets. You don't have to worry about their knowledge or their attitudes.

You can see how easy it would be to turn an easy change problem (shrinking people's buckets) into a hard change problem (convincing people to think differently). And that's the first surprise about change: What looks like a people problem is often a situation problem.

3.

This is a book to help you change things. We consider change at every level—individual, organizational, and societal. Maybe you want to help your brother beat his gambling addiction. Maybe you need your team at work to act more frugally because of market conditions. Maybe you wish more of your neighbors would bike to work.

Usually these topics are treated separately—there is "change management" advice for executives and "self-help" advice for individuals and "change the world" advice for activists. That's a shame, because all change efforts have something in common: For anything to change, someone has to start acting differently. Your brother has got to stay out of the casino; your employees have got to start booking coach fares. Ultimately, all change efforts boil down to the same mission: Can you get people to start behaving in a new way?

We know what you're thinking—people resist change. But it's not quite that easy. Babies are born every day to parents who, inexplicably, welcome the change. Think about the sheer magnitude of that change! Would anyone agree to work for a boss who'd wake you up twice a night, screaming, for trivial administrative duties? (And what if, every time you wore a new piece of clothing, the boss spit up on it?) Yet people don't resist this massive change—they volunteer for it.

In our lives, we embrace lots of big changes—not only babies, but marriages and new homes and new technologies and new job duties. Meanwhile, other behaviors are maddeningly intractable. Smokers keep smoking and kids grow fatter and your husband can't ever seem to get his dirty shirts into a hamper.

So there are hard changes and easy changes. What distinguishes one from the other? In this book, we argue that successful changes share a common pattern. They require the leader of the change to do three things at once. We've already mentioned one of those three things: To change someone's behavior, you've got to change that person's situation.

The situation isn't the whole game, of course. You can send an alcoholic to rehab, where the new environment will help him go dry. But what happens when he leaves and loses that influence? You might see a boost in productivity from your sales reps when the sales manager shadows them, but what happens afterward when the situation returns to normal? For individuals' behavior to change, you've got to influence not only their environment but their hearts and minds.

The problem is this: Often the heart and mind disagree. Fervently.

4.

Consider the Clocky, an alarm clock invented by an MIT student, Gauri Nanda. It's no ordinary alarm clock—it has wheels. You set it at night, and in the morning when the alarm goes off, it rolls off your nightstand and scurries around the room, forcing you to chase it down. Picture the scene: You're crawling around the bedroom in your underwear, stalking and cursing a runaway clock.

Clocky ensures that you won't snooze-button your way to disaster. And apparently that's a common fear, since about 35,000 units were purchased, at $50 each, in Clocky's first two years on the market (despite minimal marketing).

The success of this invention reveals a lot about human psychology. What it shows, fundamentally, is that we are schizophrenic. Part of us—our rational side—wants to get up at 5:45 a.m., allowing ourselves plenty of time for a quick jog before we leave for the office. The other part of us—the emotional side—wakes up in the darkness of the early morning, snoozing inside a warm cocoon of sheets and blankets, and wants nothing in the world so much as a few more minutes of sleep. If, like us, your emotional side tends to win these internal debates, then you might be a potential Clocky customer. The beauty of the device is that it allows your rational side to outsmart your emotional side. It's simply impossible to stay cuddled up under the covers when a rogue alarm clock is rolling around your room.

Let's be blunt here: Clocky is not a product for a sane species. If Spock wants to get up at 5:45 a.m., he'll just get up. No drama required.

Our built-in schizophrenia is a deeply weird thing, but we don't think much about it because we're so used to it. When we kick off a new diet, we toss the Cheetos and Oreos out of the pantry, because our rational side knows that when our emotional side gets a craving, there's no hope of self-control. The only option is to remove the temptation altogether. (For the record, some MIT student will make a fortune designing Cheetos that scurry away from people when they're on a diet.)

The unavoidable conclusion is this: Your brain isn't of one mind.

The conventional wisdom in psychology, in fact, is that the brain has two independent systems at work at all times. First, there's what we called the emotional side. It's the part of you that is instinctive, that feels pain and pleasure. Second, there's the rational side, also known as the reflective or conscious system. It's the part of you that deliberates and analyzes and looks into the future.

In the past few decades, psychologists have learned a lot about these two systems, but of course mankind has always been aware of the tension. Plato said that in our heads we have a rational charioteer who has to rein in an unruly horse that "barely yields to horsewhip and goad combined." Freud wrote about the selfish id and the conscientious superego (and also about the ego, which mediates between them). More recently, behavioral economists dubbed the two systems the Planner and the Doer.

But, to us, the duo's tension is captured best by an analogy used by University of Virginia psychologist Jonathan Haidt in his wonderful book *The Happiness Hypothesis*. Haidt says that our emotional side is an Elephant and our rational side is its Rider. Perched atop the Elephant, the Rider holds the reins and seems to be the leader. But the Rider's control is precarious because the Rider is so small relative to the Elephant. Anytime the six-ton Elephant and the Rider disagree about which direction to go, the Rider is going to lose. He's completely overmatched.

Most of us are all too familiar with situations in which our Elephant overpowers our Rider. You've experienced this if you've ever slept in, overeaten, dialed up your ex at midnight, procrastinated, tried to quit smoking and failed, skipped the gym, gotten angry and said something you regretted, abandoned your Spanish or piano lessons, refused to speak up in a meeting because you were scared, and so on. Good thing no one is keeping score.

The weakness of the Elephant, our emotional and instinctive side, is clear: It's lazy and skittish, often looking for the quick payoff (ice cream cone) over the long-term payoff (being thin). When change efforts fail, it's usually the Elephant's fault, since the kinds of change we want typically involve short-term sacrifices for long-term payoffs. (We cut back on expenses today to yield a better balance sheet next year. We avoid ice cream today for a better body next year.) Changes often fail because the Rider simply can't keep the Elephant on the road long enough to reach the destination.

The Elephant's hunger for instant gratification is the opposite of the Rider's strength, which is the ability to think long-term, to plan, to think beyond the moment (all those things that your pet can't do).

But what may surprise you is that the Elephant also has enormous strengths and that the Rider has crippling weaknesses. The Elephant isn't always the bad guy. Emotion is the Elephant's turf—love and compassion and sympathy and loyalty. That fierce instinct you have to protect your kids against harm—that's the Elephant. That spine-stiffening you feel when you need to stand up for yourself—that's the Elephant.

And even more important if you're contemplating a change, the Elephant is the one who gets things done. To make progress toward a goal, whether it's noble or crass, requires the energy and drive of the Elephant. And this strength is the mirror image of the Rider's great weakness: spinning his wheels. The Rider tends to overanalyze and overthink things. Chances are, you know people with Rider problems: your friend who can agonize for twenty minutes about what to eat for dinner; your colleague who can brainstorm about new ideas for hours but can't ever seem to make a decision.

If you want to change things, you've got to appeal to both. The Rider provides the planning and direction, and the Elephant provides the energy. So if you reach the Riders of your team but not the Elephants, team members will have understanding without motivation. If you reach their Elephants but not their Riders, they'll have passion without direction. In both cases, the flaws can be paralyzing. A reluctant Elephant and a wheel-spinning Rider can both ensure that nothing changes. But when Elephants and Riders move together, change can come easily.

.

5.

When Rider and Elephant disagree about which way to move, you've got a problem. The Rider can get his way temporarily—he can tug on the reins hard enough to get the Elephant to submit. (Anytime you use willpower you're doing exactly that.) But the Rider can't win a tug-of-war with a huge animal for long. He simply gets exhausted.

To see this point more clearly, consider the behavior of some college students who participated in a study about "food perception" (or so they were told). They reported to the lab a bit hungry; they'd been asked not to eat for at least three hours beforehand. They were led to a room that smelled amazing—the researchers had just baked chocolate-chip cookies. On a table in the center of the room were two bowls. One held a sampling of chocolates, along with the warm, fresh-baked chocolate-chip cookies they'd smelled. The other bowl held a bunch of radishes.

The researchers had prepped a cover story: We've selected chocolates and radishes because they have highly distinctive tastes. Tomorrow, we'll contact you and ask about your memory of the taste sensations you experienced while eating them.

Half the participants were asked to eat two or three cookies and some chocolate candies, but no radishes. The other half were asked to eat at least two or three radishes, but no cookies. While they ate, the researchers left the room, intending, rather sadistically, to induce temptation: They wanted those poor radish-eaters to sit there, alone, nibbling on rabbit food, glancing enviously at the fresh-baked cookies. (It probably goes without saying that the cookie-eaters experienced no great struggle in resisting the radishes.) Despite the temptation, all participants ate what they were asked to eat, and none of the radish-eaters snuck a cookie. That's willpower at work.

At that point, the "taste study" was officially over, and another group of researchers entered with a second, supposedly unrelated study: We're trying to find who's better at solving problems,

college students or high school students. This framing was intended to get the college students to puff out their chests and
take the forthcoming task seriously.

The college students were presented with a series of puzzles that
required them to trace a complicated geometric shape without re-
tracing any lines and without lifting their pencils from the paper.
They were given multiple sheets of paper so they could try over
and over. In reality, the puzzles were designed to be unsolvable.
The researchers wanted to see how long the college students would
persist in a difficult, frustrating task before they finally gave up.

The "untempted" students, who had not had to resist eating
the chocolate-chip cookies, spent nineteen minutes on the task,
making thirty-four well-intentioned attempts to solve the problem.

The radish-eaters were less persistent. They gave up after only
eight minutes—less than half the time spent by the cookie-
eaters—and they managed only nineteen solution attempts. Why
did they quit so easily?

The answer may surprise you: They ran out of self-control. In
studies like this one, psychologists have discovered that self-
control is an exhaustible resource. It's like doing bench presses at
the gym. The first one is easy, when your muscles are fresh. But
with each additional repetition, your muscles get more exhausted,
until you can't lift the bar again. The radish-eaters had drained
their self-control by resisting the cookies. So when their Elephants, inevitably, started complaining about the puzzle task—*it's
too hard, it's no fun, we're no good at this*—their Riders didn't have
enough strength to yank on the reins for more than eight minutes. Meanwhile, the cookie-eaters had a fresh, untaxed Rider,
who fought off the Elephant for nineteen minutes.

Self-control is an exhaustible resource. This is a crucial realization, because when we talk about "self-control," we don't mean

the narrow sense of the word, as in the willpower needed to fight vice (smokes, cookies, alcohol). We're talking about a broader kind of self-supervision. Think of the way your mind works when you're giving negative feedback to an employee, or assembling a new bookshelf, or learning a new dance. You are careful and deliberate with your words or movements. It feels like there's a supervisor on duty. That's self-control, too.

Contrast that with all the situations in which your behavior doesn't feel "supervised"—for instance, the sensation while you're driving that you can't remember the last few miles of road, or the easy, unthinking way you take a shower or make your morning coffee. Much of our daily behavior, in fact, is more automatic than supervised, and that's a good thing because the supervised behavior is the hard stuff. It's draining.

Dozens of studies have demonstrated the exhausting nature of self-supervision. For instance, people who were asked to make tricky choices and trade-offs—such as setting up a wedding registry or ordering a new computer—were worse at focusing and solving problems than others who hadn't made the tough choices. In one study, some people were asked to restrain their emotions while watching a sad movie about sick animals. Afterward, they exhibited less physical endurance than others who'd let the tears flow freely. The research shows that we burn up self-control in a wide variety of situations: managing the impression we're making on others; coping with fears; controlling our spending; trying to focus on simple instructions such as "Don't think of a white bear"; and many, many others.

Here's why this matters for change: When people try to change things, they're usually tinkering with behaviors that have become automatic, and changing those behaviors requires careful supervision by the Rider. The bigger the change you're suggesting, the more it will sap people's self-control.

And when people exhaust their self-control, what they're exhausting are the mental muscles needed to think creatively, to focus, to inhibit their impulses, and to persist in the face of frustration or failure. In other words, they're exhausting precisely the mental muscles needed to make a big change.

So when you hear people say that change is hard because people are lazy or resistant, that's just flat wrong. In fact, the opposite is true: Change is hard because people wear themselves out. And that's the second surprise about change: What looks like laziness is often exhaustion.

6.

Jon Stegner believed the company he worked for, a large manufacturer, was wasting vast sums of money. "I thought we had an opportunity to drive down purchasing costs not by 2 percent but by something on the order of $1 billion over the next five years," said Stegner, who is quoted in John Kotter and Dan Cohen's essential book *The Heart of Change.*

To reap these savings, a big process shift would be required, and for that shift to occur, Stegner knew that he'd have to convince his bosses. He also knew that they'd never embrace such a big shift unless they believed in the opportunity, and for the most part, they didn't.

Seeking a compelling example of the company's poor purchasing habits, Stegner assigned a summer student intern to investigate a single item—work gloves, which workers in most of the company's factories wore. The student embarked on a mission to identify all the types of gloves used in all the company's factories and then trace back what the company was paying for them.

The intrepid intern soon reported that the factories were

purchasing 424 different kinds of gloves! Furthermore, they were using different glove suppliers, and they were all negotiating their own prices. The same pair of gloves that cost $5 at one factory might cost $17 at another.

At Stegner's request, the student collected a specimen of every one of the 424 different types of gloves and tagged each with the price paid. Then all the gloves were gathered up, brought to the boardroom, and piled up on the conference table. Stegner invited all the division presidents to come visit the Glove Shrine. He recalled the scene:

> What they saw was a large expensive table, normally clean or with a few papers, now stacked high with gloves. Each of our executives stared at this display for a minute. Then each said something like, "We really buy all these different kinds of gloves?" Well, as a matter of fact, yes we do. "Really?" Yes, really. Then they walked around the table. . . . They could see the prices. They looked at two gloves that seemed exactly alike, yet one was marked $3.22 and the other $10.55. It's a rare event when these people don't have anything to say. But that day, they just stood with their mouths gaping.

The gloves exhibit soon became a traveling road show, visiting dozens of plants. The reaction was visceral: *This is crazy. We're crazy. And we've got to make sure this stops happening.* Soon Stegner had exactly the mandate for change that he'd sought. The company changed its purchasing process and saved a great deal of money. This was exactly the happy ending everyone wanted (except, of course, for the glove salesmen who'd managed to sell the $5 gloves for $17).

7.

Let's be honest: Most of us would not have tried what Stegner did. It would have been so easy, so natural, to make a presentation that spoke only to the Rider. Think of the possibilities: the spreadsheets, the savings data, the cost-cutting protocols, the recommendations for supplier consolidation, the exquisite logic for central purchasing. You could have created a 12-tabbed Microsoft Excel spreadsheet that would have made a tax accountant weep with joy. But instead of doing any of that, Stegner dumped a bunch of gloves on a table and invited his bosses to see them.

If there is such a thing as white-collar courage, surely this was an instance.

Stegner knew that if things were going to change, he had to get his colleagues' Elephants on his side. If he had made an analytical appeal, he probably would have gotten some supportive nods, and the execs might have requested a follow-up meeting six weeks later (and then rescheduled it). The analytical case was compelling—by itself, it might have convinced Stegner's colleagues that overhauling the purchasing system would be an important thing to do . . . next year.

Remember that if you reach your colleagues' Riders but not their Elephants, they will have direction without motivation. Maybe their Riders will drag the Elephant down the road for a while, but as we've seen, that effort can't last long.

Once you break through to *feeling*, though, things change. Stegner delivered a jolt to his colleagues. First, they thought to themselves, *We're crazy!* Then they thought, *We can fix this.* Everyone could think of a few things to try to fix the glove problem— and by extension the ordering process as a whole. That got their Elephants fired up to move.

We don't expect potential billion-dollar change stories to come dressed up like this. The change effort was led by a single employee, with the able help of a summer intern. It focused on a single product. The scope of the presentation didn't correspond in any way to the scope of the proposal. Yet Stegner's strategy worked.

That's the power of speaking to both the Rider and the Elephant.

8.

It's true that an unmotivated Elephant can doom a change effort, but let's not forget that the Rider has his own issues. He's a navel-gazer, an analyzer, a wheel-spinner. If the Rider isn't sure exactly what direction to go, he tends to lead the Elephant in circles. And as we'll see, that tendency explains the third and final surprise about change: What looks like resistance is often a lack of clarity.

Two health researchers, Steve Booth-Butterfield and Bill Reger, professors at West Virginia University, were contemplating ways to persuade people to eat a healthier diet. From past research, they knew that people were more likely to change when the new behavior expected of them was crystal clear, but unfortunately, "eating a healthier diet" was anything but.

Where to begin? Which foods should people stop (or start) eating? Should they change their eating behavior at breakfast, lunch, or dinner? At home or in restaurants? The number of ways to "eat healthier" is limitless, especially given the starting place of the average American diet. This is exactly the kind of situation in which the Rider will spin his wheels, analyzing and agonizing and never moving forward.

As the two researchers brainstormed, their thoughts kept coming back to milk. Most Americans drink milk, and we all know that milk is a great source of calcium. But milk is also the single largest source of saturated fat in the typical American's diet. In fact, calculations showed something remarkable: If Americans switched from whole milk to skim or 1% milk, the average diet would immediately attain the USDA recommended levels of saturated fat.

How do you get Americans to start drinking low-fat milk? You make sure it shows up in their refrigerators. And that isn't an entirely facetious answer. People will drink whatever is around the house—a family will plow through low-fat milk as fast as whole milk. So, in essence, the problem was even easier than anticipated: You don't need to change *drinking* behavior. You need to change *purchasing* behavior.

Suddenly the intervention became razor-sharp. What behavior do we want to change? We want consumers to buy skim or 1% milk. When? When they're shopping for groceries. Where? Duh. What else needs to change? Nothing (for now).

Reger and Booth-Butterfield launched a campaign in two communities in West Virginia, running spots on the local media outlets (TV, newspaper, radio) for two weeks. In contrast to the bland messages of most public-health campaigns, the 1% milk campaign was punchy and specific. One ad trumpeted the fact that one glass of whole milk has the same amount of saturated fat as five strips of bacon! At a press conference, the researchers showed local reporters a tube full of fat—the equivalent of the amount found in a half-gallon of whole milk. (Notice the Elephant appeals: They're going for an "Oh, gross!" reaction.)

Reger and Booth-Butterfield monitored milk sales data at all eight stores in the intervention area. Before the campaign, the market share of low-fat milk was 18 percent. After the campaign, it was 41 percent. Six months later, it held at 35 percent.

This brings us to the final part of the pattern that characterizes successful changes: If you want people to change, you must provide crystal-clear direction.

By now, you can understand the reason this is so important:

It's so the Rider doesn't spin his wheels. If you tell people to "act healthier," think of how many ways they can interpret that—imagine their Riders contemplating the options endlessly. (Do I eat more grains and less meat? Or vice versa? Do I start taking vitamins? Would it be a good trade-off if I exercise more and bribe myself with ice cream? Should I switch to Diet Coke, or is the artificial sweetener worse than the calories?)

What looks like resistance is often a lack of clarity. Before this study, we might have looked at these West Virginians and concluded they were the kind of people who don't care about their health. But if they were indeed "that kind" of people, why was it so easy to shift their behavior?

If you want people to change, you don't ask them to "act healthier." You say, "Next time you're in the dairy aisle of the grocery store, reach for a jug of 1% milk instead of whole milk."

9.

Now you've had a glimpse of the basic three-part framework we will unpack in this book, one that can guide you in any situation where you need to change behavior:

- *Direct the Rider.* What looks like resistance is often a lack of clarity. So provide crystal-clear direction. (Think 1% milk.)

- *Motivate the Elephant.* What looks like laziness is often exhaustion. The Rider can't get his way by force for very long. So it's critical that you engage people's emotional side—get their Elephants on the path and cooperative. (Think of the cookies and radishes study and the boardroom conference table full of gloves.)

- *Shape the Path.* What looks like a people problem is often a situation problem. We call the situation (including the surrounding environment) the "Path." When you shape the Path, you make change more likely, no matter what's happening with the Rider and Elephant. (Think of the effect of shrinking movie popcorn buckets.)

We created this framework to be useful for people who don't have scads of authority or resources. Some people can get their way by fiat. CEOs, for instance, can sell off divisions, hire people, fire people, change incentive systems, merge teams, and so on. Politicians can pass laws or impose punishments to change behavior. The rest of us don't have these tools (though, admittedly, they would make life easier: "Son, if you don't take out the trash tonight, you're fired"). In this book, we don't talk a lot about these structural methods.

As helpful as we hope this framework will be to you, we're well aware, and you should be, too, that this framework is no panacea. For one thing, it's incomplete. We've deliberately left out lots of great thinking on change in the interests of creating a framework that's simple enough to be practical. For another, there's a good reason why change can be difficult: The world doesn't always want what you want. You want to change how others are acting, but they get a vote. You can cajole, influence, inspire, and motivate—but sometimes an employee would rather lose his job than move out of his comfortable routines. Sometimes the alcoholic will want another drink no matter what the consequences.

So we don't promise that we're going to make change easy, but at least we can make it *easier.* Our goal is to teach you a framework, based on decades of scientific research, that is simple enough to remember and flexible enough to use in many different situations—family, work, community, and otherwise.

To change behavior, you've got to direct the Rider, motivate the Elephant, and shape the Path. If you can do all three at once, dramatic change can happen even if you don't have lots of power or resources behind you. For proof of that, we don't need to look beyond Donald Berwick, a man who changed the face of health care.

10.

In 2004, Donald Berwick, a doctor and the CEO of the Institute for Healthcare Improvement (IHI), had some ideas about how to save lives—massive numbers of lives. Researchers at the IHI had analyzed patient care with the kinds of analytical tools used to assess the quality of cars coming off a production line. They discovered that the "defect" rate in health care was as high as 1 in 10—meaning, for example, that 10 percent of patients did not receive their antibiotics in the specified time. This was a shockingly high defect rate—many other industries had managed to achieve performance at levels of 1 error in 1,000 cases (and often far better). Berwick knew that the high medical defect rate meant that tens of thousands of patients were dying every year, unnecessarily.

Berwick's insight was that hospitals could benefit from the same kinds of rigorous process improvements that had worked in other industries. Couldn't a transplant operation be "produced" as consistently and flawlessly as a Toyota Camry?

Berwick's ideas were so well supported by research that they were essentially indisputable, yet little was happening. He certainly had no ability to force any changes on the industry. IHI had only seventy-five employees. But Berwick wasn't deterred.

On December 14, 2004, he gave a speech to a room full of

hospital administrators at a large industry convention. He said, "Here is what I think we should do. I think we should save 100,000 lives. And I think we should do that by June 14, 2006—18 months from today. Some is not a number; soon is not a time. Here's the number: 100,000. Here's the time: June 14, 2006—9 a.m."

The crowd was astonished. The goal was daunting. But Berwick was quite serious about his intentions. He and his tiny team set out to do the impossible.

IHI proposed six very specific interventions to save lives. For instance, one asked hospitals to adopt a set of proven procedures for managing patients on ventilators, to prevent them from getting pneumonia, a common cause of unnecessary death. (One of the procedures called for a patient's head to be elevated between 30 and 45 degrees, so that oral secretions couldn't get into the windpipe.)

Of course, all hospital administrators agreed with the goal to save lives, but the road to that goal was filled with obstacles. For one thing, for a hospital to reduce its "defect rate," it had to acknowledge having a defect rate. In other words, it had to admit that some patients were dying needless deaths. Hospital lawyers were not keen to put this admission on record.

Berwick knew he had to address the hospitals' squeamishness about admitting error. At his December 14 speech, he was joined by the mother of a girl who'd been killed by a medical error. She said, "I'm a little speechless, and I'm a little sad, because I know that if this campaign had been in place four or five years ago, that Josie would be fine. . . . But, I'm happy, I'm thrilled to be part of this, because I know you can do it, because you have to do it."

Another guest on stage, the chair of the North Carolina State Hospital Association, said: "An awful lot of people for a long time have had their heads in the sand on this issue, and it's time to do the right thing. It's as simple as that."

IHI made joining the campaign easy: It required only a one-page form signed by a hospital CEO. By two months after Berwick's speech, over a thousand hospitals had enrolled. Once a hospital enrolled, the IHI team helped the hospital embrace the new interventions. Team members provided research, step-by-step instruction guides, and training. They arranged conference calls for hospital leaders to share their victories and struggles with one another. They encouraged hospitals with early successes to become "mentors" to hospitals just joining the campaign.

The friction in the system was substantial. Adopting the IHI interventions required hospitals to overcome decades' worth of habits and routines. Many doctors were irritated by the new procedures, which they perceived as constricting. But the adopting hospitals were seeing dramatic results, and their visible successes attracted more hospitals to join the campaign.

Eighteen months later, at the exact moment he'd promised to return—June 14, 2006, at 9 a.m.—Berwick took the stage again to announce the results: "Hospitals enrolled in the 100,000 Lives Campaign have collectively prevented an estimated 122,300 avoidable deaths and, as importantly, have begun to institutionalize new standards of care that will continue to save lives and improve health outcomes into the future."

The crowd was euphoric. Don Berwick, with his 75-person team at IHI, had convinced thousands of hospitals to change their behavior, and collectively, they'd saved 122,300 lives—the equivalent of throwing a life preserver to every man, woman, and child in Ann Arbor, Michigan.

This outcome was the fulfillment of the vision Berwick had articulated as he closed his speech eighteen months earlier, about how the world would look when hospitals achieved the 100,000 lives goal:

> And, we will celebrate. Starting with pizza, and ending with champagne. We will celebrate the importance of what we have undertaken to do, the courage of honesty, the joy of companionship, the cleverness of a field operation, and the results we will achieve. We will celebrate ourselves, because the patients whose lives we save cannot join us, because their names can never be known. Our contribution will be what did not happen to them. And, though they are unknown, we will know that mothers and fathers are at graduations and weddings they would have missed, and that grandchildren will know grandparents they might never have known, and holidays will be taken, and work completed, and books read, and symphonies heard, and gardens tended that, without our work, would have been only beds of weeds.

11.

Big changes can happen.

Don Berwick and his team catalyzed a change that saved 100,000 lives, yet Berwick himself wielded no power. He couldn't change the law. He couldn't fire hospital leaders who didn't agree with him. He couldn't pay bonuses to hospitals that accepted his proposals.

Berwick had the same tools the rest of us have. First, he directed his audience's Riders. The destination was crystal clear: *Some is not a number; soon is not a time. Here's the number:*

100,000. Here's the time: June 14, 2006—9 a.m. But that wasn't enough. He had to help hospitals figure out how to get there, and he couldn't simply say, "Try harder." (Remember "act healthier" versus "buy 1% milk.") So he proposed six specific interventions, such as elevating the heads of patients on ventilators, that were known to save lives. By staying laser-focused on these six interventions, Berwick made sure not to exhaust the Riders of his audience with endless behavioral changes.

Second, he motivated his audience's Elephants. He made them *feel* the need for change. Many of the people in the audience already knew the facts, but knowing was not enough. (Remember, knowing wasn't enough for executives at Jon Stegner's company. It took a stack of gloves to get their Elephants engaged.) Berwick had to get beyond knowing, so he brought his audience face-to-face with the mother of the girl who'd been killed by a medical error: "I know that if this campaign had been in place four or five years ago, that Josie would be fine." Berwick was also careful to motivate the people who hadn't been in the room for his presentation. He didn't challenge people to "overhaul medicine" or "bring TQM to health care." He challenged them to save 100,000 lives. That speaks to anyone's Elephant.

Third, he shaped the Path. He made it easier for the hospitals to embrace the change. Think of the one-page enrollment form, the step-by-step instructions, the training, the support groups, the mentors. He was designing an environment that made it more likely for hospital administrators to reform. Berwick also knew that behavior was contagious. He used peer pressure to persuade hospitals to join the campaign. *(Your rival hospital across town just signed on to help save 100,000 lives. Do you really want them to have the moral high ground?)* He also connected people—he matched up people who were struggling to implement the changes with people who had mastered them, almost like the "mentors" found in Alcoholics Anonymous. Berwick was creating a support group for health care reform.

In this book, you'll learn about people like Berwick who've created sweeping change despite having few resources and little structural authority. You'll learn about an entrepreneur who saved his small company by turning his skeptical employees into customer-service zealots; a student fresh out of college who saved an endangered species from extinction; a manager who plotted a way to get his colleague to stop acting like a jerk; and a therapist who reformed a group of child abusers.

Whether the switch you seek is in your family, in your charity, in your organization, or in society at large, you'll get there by making three things happen. You'll direct the Rider, motivate the Elephant, and shape the Path.

DIRECT
THE
RIDER

2

Find the Bright Spots

1.

In 1990, Jerry Sternin was working for Save the Children, the international organization that helps children in need. He'd been asked to open a new office in Vietnam. The government had invited Save the Children into the country to fight malnutrition. But when Sternin arrived, the welcome was rather chilly. The foreign minister let him know that not everyone in the government appreciated his presence. The minister told Sternin, "You have six months to make a difference."

Sternin was traveling with his wife and 10-year-old son. None of them spoke Vietnamese. "We were like orphans at the airport when we arrived in Vietnam," he recalled. "We had no idea what we were going to do." Sternin had minimal staff and meager resources.

Sternin had read as much as he could about the malnutrition problem. The conventional wisdom was that malnutrition was the result of an intertwined set of problems: Sanitation was poor. Poverty was nearly universal. Clean water was not readily available. The rural people tended to be ignorant about nutrition.

In Sternin's judgment, all of this analysis was "TBU"—true but useless. "Millions of kids can't wait for those issues to be addressed," he said. If addressing malnutrition required ending poverty and purifying water and building sanitation systems, then it would never happen. Especially in six months, with almost no money to spend.

Sternin had a better idea. He traveled to rural villages and met with groups of local mothers. The mothers divided into teams and went out to weigh and measure every child in their village. They then pored over the results together.

Sternin asked them, "Did you find any very, very poor kids who are bigger and healthier than the typical child?" The women, scanning the data, nodded and said, *"Có, có, có."* (Yes, yes, yes.)

Sternin said, "You mean it's possible today in this village for a very poor family to have a well-nourished child?"

"Có, có, có."

"Then let's go see what they're doing."

Sternin's strategy was to search the community for *bright spots*— successful efforts worth emulating. If some kids were healthy despite their disadvantages, that meant malnourishment was not inevitable. Furthermore, the mere existence of healthy kids provided hope for a practical, short-term solution. Sternin knew he couldn't fix the thorny "root causes." But if a handful of kids were staying healthy against the odds, why couldn't every kid be healthy?

Notice that Sternin was trying to focus the mothers' Riders. The overall topic—what can you do to make your child healthier?—is simply too big and loaded to take on at once. The mothers needed direction, not motivation. After all, every mother's

Elephant is going to be motivated to make her child healthier. But how?

Remember the power of the 1% milk campaign, which made an abstract idea ("eat healthier") practical. Sternin was saying: Let's not sit around analyzing "malnutrition." Let's go study what these bright-spot mothers are doing.

As a first step, Sternin and the mothers had to eliminate any bright spots who weren't "typical." For example, a boy might have an uncle in the government who could send extra food his way. Other families wouldn't be able to replicate that.

In order to recognize what the bright-spot mothers were doing differently, the group had to synthesize the "conventional wisdom" about feeding kids. So they talked to dozens of people—mothers, fathers, older brothers and sisters, grandparents— and discovered that the community norms were pretty clear: Kids ate twice a day along with the rest of their families. They ate food that was appropriate for kids—soft, pure foods like the highest-quality rice.

Armed with an understanding of the norms, Sternin and the mothers went into the homes of the bright-spot kids and observed the way the homes were run, alert for any deviations. Their observation yielded some unexpected insights. For one thing, bright-spot moms were feeding their kids four meals a day (using the same amount of food as other moms but spreading it across four servings rather than two). The larger twice-a-day meals eaten by most families turned out to be a mistake for children, because their malnourished stomachs couldn't process that much food at one time.

The style of eating was also different. Most parents believed that their kids understood their own needs and would feed themselves appropriately from the communal bowl. But the healthy kids were fed more actively—hand-fed by parents if necessary.

They were even encouraged to eat when they were sick, which was not the norm.

Perhaps most interesting, the healthy kids were eating different kinds of food. The bright-spot mothers were collecting tiny shrimp and crabs from the rice paddies and mixing them in with their kids' rice. Shrimp and crabs were eaten by adults but generally weren't considered appropriate food for kids. The mothers also tossed in sweet-potato greens, which were considered a low-class food. These dietary improvisations, however strange or "low class," were doing something precious: adding sorely needed protein and vitamins to the children's diet.

As an outsider, Sternin never could have foreseen these practices. He knew nothing about sweet-potato greens. The solution was a native one, emerging from the real-world experience of the villagers, and for that reason it was inherently realistic and inherently sustainable. But knowing the solution wasn't enough. For anything to change, lots of mothers needed to adopt the new cooking habits.

Most people in Sternin's situation would have been itching to make an announcement, to call the village together and unveil a set of recommendations. *Gather 'round, everyone: I've studied your problem and now I have the answer! Here are Sternin's 5 Rules for Fighting Malnutrition.*

But Sternin refused to make a formal announcement. "Knowledge does not change behavior," he said. "We have all encountered crazy shrinks and obese doctors and divorced marriage counselors." He knew that telling the mothers about nutrition wouldn't change their behavior. They'd have to practice it.

The community designed a program in which fifty malnourished families, in groups of ten, would meet at a hut each day and prepare food. The families were required to bring shrimp, crabs, and sweet-potato greens. The mothers washed their hands with soap and cooked the meal together. Sternin said that the moms were "acting their way into a new way of thinking." Most important, it was *their* change, something that arose from the local wisdom of the village. Sternin's role was only to help them see that they could do it, that they could conquer malnutrition on their own.

By organizing these cooking groups, Sternin was addressing both the Rider and the Elephant. The mothers' Riders got highly specific instructions: *Here's how to cook a tasty lunch with shrimp and sweet-potato greens.* And their Elephants got a feeling: hope. *There really is a way to make my daughter healthier. And it's not very hard—it's something I can do!* Notice that the Path played a role, too. When so many of the mothers were doing something, there was strong social pressure to go along. The cooking classes, in effect, were changing the culture of the village.

Best of all, bright spots solve the "Not Invented Here" problem. Some people have a knee-jerk skeptical response to "imported" solutions. Imagine the public outcry if an American politician proposed that the United States adopt the French health care system. (Or vice versa.) We all think our group is the smartest.

By looking for bright spots within the very village he was trying to change, Sternin ensured that the solution would be a native one. He would have faced a much more difficult quest if he'd brought in a plan from a different village. The local mothers would have bristled: *Those people aren't like us. Our situation is more complicated than that. Those ideas wouldn't work here.*

Finding bright spots, then, solves many different problems at once. That's no surprise; successful change efforts involve connecting all three parts of the framework: Rider, Elephant, and Path. (Although in this book we explain one part of the framework at a time, we'll continue to remind you that even an example in the "Rider" chapters will influence the Elephant and Path. Concepts are rarely exclusive.)

Six months after Sternin had come to the Vietnamese village, 65 percent of the kids were better nourished and stayed that way. Later, when researchers from Emory University's School of Public Health came to Vietnam to gather independent data, they found that even children who hadn't been born when Sternin left the villages were as healthy as the kids Sternin had reached directly. That discovery provided proof that the changes had stuck.

Sternin's success began to spread. "We took the first 14 villages in different phases of the program and turned them into a social laboratory. People who wanted to replicate the nutrition model came from different parts of Vietnam. Every day, they would go to this living university, to these villages, touching, smelling, sniffing, watching, listening. They would 'graduate,' go to their villages, and implement the process until they got it right. . . . The program reached 2.2 million Vietnamese people in 265 villages. Our living university has become a national model for teaching villagers to reduce drastically malnutrition in Vietnam," Sternin said.

Stories don't come much more heroic than this. Sternin and his small team of believers, working with a shoestring budget, managed to make a big dent in malnutrition. What makes it more remarkable is that they weren't experts. They didn't walk in with the answers. All they had was a deep faith in the power of bright spots.

2.

The Rider part of our minds has many strengths. The Rider is a thinker and a planner and can plot a course for a better future. But as we've seen, the Rider has a terrible weakness—the tendency to spin his wheels. The Rider loves to contemplate and analyze, and, making matters worse, his analysis is almost always

directed at problems rather than at bright spots. (You can probably recall a conversation with a friend who agonized for hours
over a particular relationship problem. But can you remember an
instance when a friend spent even a few minutes analyzing why
something was working so well?)

These analytical qualities can be extremely helpful, obviously—
many problems get solved through analysis—but in situations
where change is needed, too much analysis can doom the effort.
The Rider will see too many problems and spend too much time
sizing them up. Look again at Jerry Sternin and the Vietnam
story: Dozens of experts had analyzed the situation in Vietnam.
Their Riders had agonized over the problems—the water supply,
the sanitation, the poverty, the ignorance. They'd written position papers and research documents and development plans. But
they hadn't changed a thing.

In tough times, the Rider sees problems everywhere, and
"analysis paralysis" often kicks in. The Rider will spin his wheels
indefinitely unless he's given clear direction. That's why to make
progress on a change, you need ways to *direct* the Rider. Show him
where to go, how to act, what destination to pursue. And that's
why bright spots are so essential, because they are your best hope
for directing the Rider when you're trying to bring about change.

3.

"School stinks," said Bobby, a ninth grader who'd just reported
for his first school counseling session. John J. Murphy, the school
psychologist, was surprised Bobby had shown up at all.

Several teachers had referred Bobby for counseling, frustrated
by his bad behavior. He was constantly late, rarely did his work,
was disruptive in class, and sometimes made loud threats to other
kids in the hallways.

Bobby's home life was just as chaotic. He'd been shuffled in and out of foster homes and special facilities for kids with behavioral problems. He and his father were on the waiting list for family counseling. The local social service agency in Covington, Kentucky, was keeping tabs on Bobby. By the time he showed up for his session with Murphy, he was in danger of being placed in another special facility because of his problems at school.

Murphy was almost powerless in the situation. The counselor had no way to improve Bobby's situation at home, and time was working against him—at best, he'd see Bobby for an hour here, an hour there. Murphy couldn't reward Bobby if he behaved well or punish him if he behaved poorly. (Not that punishment would have worked. Bobby usually ended up in the principal's office by mid-morning for disciplinary issues, but his behavior never changed.)

Ignoring the "school stinks" comment, Murphy began talking to Bobby and posed a series of unusual questions. So began the first of a handful of conversations between Murphy and Bobby.

Now, fast-forward to three months later: A dramatic change had occurred. The number of days Bobby was sent to the principal's office had declined by 80 percent. Bobby hadn't become an Eagle Scout, mind you, but the improvement was strong enough to keep social services from having to transfer him to the school for troubled kids. Bobby, a chronic offender, had become an occasional offender. And it happened because of a few hours of talking with a counselor.

What, exactly, happened in those conversations?

4.

John Murphy is a practitioner of solutions-focused brief therapy ("solutions-focused therapy" for short). Solutions-focused therapy was invented in the late 1970s by a husband-and-wife therapist team, Steve de Shazer and Insoo Kim Berg, and their colleagues at the Brief Family Therapy Center in Milwaukee. Solutions-focused therapy is radically different from traditional therapy. In classical psychotherapy (think Tony Soprano and Dr. Melfi), you and your therapist explore your problem. What are its roots? Does it trace back to something in your childhood? There's a sense of archaeological excavation: You're digging around your mind for a buried nugget of insight, something that may explain why you behave the way you do. Excavating the past takes time. A standard Freudian psychoanalysis might take five years of work, with sessions once or twice a week. (And after five years and $50,000, you discover it's all your mom's fault.)

Solutions-focused therapists, in contrast, couldn't care less about archaeology. They don't dig around for clues about why you act the way you do. They don't care about your childhood. All they care about is the solution to the problem at hand.

Marriage therapist Michele Weiner-Davis was initially trained as a classical psychoanalyst. Like all psychoanalysts, she believed that childhood experiences created unresolved traumas that fed current problems, and she tried to help her clients understand how their upbringing had shaped their behavior in relationships. But she was often unhappy with the outcomes her clients achieved through psychoanalysis. In her book *Divorce Busting*, she explained why: "My clients would frequently plead, 'Now I see that we are reenacting our parents' marriages, but what do we do about it? We can't stop fighting.'" She learned that under-standing a problem doesn't necessarily solve it—that knowing is not enough.

Weiner-Davis was initially skeptical about solutions-focused brief therapy: "It seemed too simple. . . . Most people, including most therapists, believe the change process has to be complicated and arduous. 'No pain, no gain' is the general rule of thumb." To describe how her thinking about solutions-focused therapy changed, she used an analogy from golf.

At one point, her golf swing started misfiring, so she went to a golf pro, thinking her technique needed a major overhaul. She noted that the golf pro didn't do any archaeology. He never said, "You obviously have a fear of winning. Did your father intimidate you as a little girl?" Instead, all he did was suggest a minor modification: relaxing her tight grip on the club. At first, she was a little peeved by this advice. It didn't seem profound enough to justify his fee. But later, on the course, her balls were going straighter and farther. *Maybe small adjustments can work after all,* she thought.

5.

Solutions-focused therapists use a common set of techniques for discovering potential solutions. Early in the first session, after hearing the patient explain his or her problem, the therapist poses the Miracle Question: "Can I ask you a sort of strange question? Suppose that you go to bed tonight and sleep well. Sometime, in the middle of the night, while you are sleeping, a miracle happens and all the troubles that brought you here are resolved. When you wake up in the morning, what's the *first small sign* you'd see that would make you think, 'Well, something must have happened—the problem is gone!'?"

Here's how one couple in marital therapy answered the Miracle Question posed by their therapist, Brian Cade of Sydney, Australia:

> WIFE: I'd be happy, feeling at ease at last. I'd be more pleasant to Bob, not jumping down his throat all the time.

CADE: What will you do instead?

WIFE: Well, there would be more understanding between us. We'd listen to what each other was saying.

HUSBAND: Yes. At the moment, we don't really listen to each other. We just can't wait to get our own point in.

CADE: How could you tell that the other was really listening?

WIFE: In the face, I think. We'd perhaps make more eye contact. (*Pauses, then laughs.*) We'd nod in the right places.

HUSBAND: Yes. We'd both respond to what the other was saying rather than just attacking or ignoring it.

Notice that Cade prods the couple for specifics: "What will you do instead?" "How could you tell the other person was really listening?" The Miracle Question doesn't ask you to describe the miracle itself; it asks you to identify the tangible signs that the miracle happened.

Here's another example from a therapist's session with a man with a drinking problem: *If a miracle solved your drinking problem, what would you be doing differently the next morning?* "I don't know, I can't imagine." *Try.* "Well, all my friends drink, so what do you expect me to do?" *I know it's not easy, but think about it.* "Well, there are all sorts of things." *Name one.* "Maybe I would go to the library and look at the newspapers." *How would your day be different if you went to the library?*

Solutions-focused therapists learn to focus their patients on the first hints of the miracle—"What's *the first small sign* you'd see that would make you think the problem was gone"—because they want to avoid answers that are overly grand and unattainable: "My bank account is full, I love my job, and my marriage is great."

Once they've helped patients identify specific and vivid signs of progress, they pivot to a second question, which is perhaps even more important. It's the Exception Question: "When was the last time you saw a little bit of the miracle, even just for a short time?"

An alcoholic would be asked: "When was the last time you stayed sober for an hour or two?" Or the wife in the dialogue quoted above would be asked: "When was the last time you felt like your husband was truly listening to you?"

It's an ingenious tactic. What the therapist is trying to demonstrate, in a subtle way, is that the client is capable of solving her own problem. As a matter of fact, the client is offering up proof that she's *already solved it,* at least in some circumstances. For instance, Brian Cade worked with a mother whose children were out of control. He asked her the Exception Question: "What was different about the last time your kids obeyed you? In what circumstances do they seem to behave better?"

MOM: (*after a pause*) I guess it's when they realize they have pushed me too far.

CADE: How could they tell that?

MOM: You know, it's funny. I think it's when I stop ranting and raving at them and my voice goes very, very calm. . . . I think I'm able to do that when I feel generally less harassed, when I feel I've got things done rather than spent the whole day worrying about getting things done. When I feel I've not been able to get on top of the housework, I tend to panic.

Cade asks her what the kids might notice on good days.

MOM: I think I just look calmer.

CADE: What else?

MOM: I probably greet them more enthusiastically and smile more.

Solutions-focused therapists believe that there are exceptions to every problem and that those exceptions, once identified, can be carefully analyzed, like the game film of a sporting event. *Let's replay that scene, where things were working for you. What was happening? How did you behave? Were you smiling? Did you make eye contact?* And that analysis can point directly toward a solution that is, by definition, workable. After all, it worked before.

These "exceptions" are just like Jerry Sternin's bright spots. Just as there were some kids in the Vietnamese village who managed to stay healthy despite the poverty, there are some moments in an alcoholic's life when he is sober despite the cravings. Those bright spots are gold to be mined. (Notice again that bright spots provide not only direction for the Rider but hope and motivation for the Elephant.)

What does this mean for you? You may not fight malnutrition, and you may not need therapy. But if you're trying to change things, there are going to be bright spots in your field of view, and if you learn to recognize them and understand them, you will solve one of the fundamental mysteries of change: What, exactly, needs to be done differently?

Suppose you're a human relations manager, and you've been encouraging line managers to give feedback to their employees more frequently, rather than storing it up for their once-a-year performance reviews. You hosted an offsite training program for ten managers so they could practice the recommended new style of in-the-moment feedback, and they all left the program pledging to experiment with it.

After four weeks, you start to hear back from some of the managers, and their results have been mixed. Two of the managers seem genuinely transformed—excited about the way the faster feedback has improved their relationships with team members. Five of the managers are weakly positive, saying they tried it a few times. Two of the managers say, regretfully, that they've been too busy to try. One is an outright skeptic and thinks the whole initiative is hogwash.

What now? The bright spots give you an action plan: Go investigate the two successful managers. First, see if either situation is an anomaly. For instance, in your follow-up, you might discover that one of the successful managers had not been giving any more feedback to his team—he'd simply been approaching individuals more often to make small talk. The extra social contact made him feel good but annoyed team members (who were constantly interrupted). That manager is not a real bright spot.

The other success might be legitimate. Maybe the manager, Debbie, devised a tracking sheet that reminds her to provide feedback to every employee every week. Maybe she set a goal for herself that her "quick feedback" will never last longer than two minutes and will apply only to a specific project—it won't be a referendum on an employee's overall performance. Maybe she set up open-door "office hours" so that employees can drop by for quick feedback on ongoing projects.

Now that you've defined your bright spot, you can try to clone it. Have the other managers spend an hour or two shadowing Debbie, seeing firsthand how she incorporated the new style into her workday. Get Debbie to attend your next offsite training program so she can coach other managers on the mechanics of quick feedback. Talk to IT and see if there's a way to roll out a more polished version of Debbie's impromptu tracking sheet.

Bottom line: You are spending 80 percent of your time exploring Debbie's success and finding ways to replicate it. You aren't obsessing about the manager who was skeptical. You aren't planning another training program with the same managers to review the material. You are simply asking yourself, "What's working and how can we do more of it?" That's the bright-spot philosophy in a single question.

6.

Focusing on bright spots can be counterintuitive for businesses. Richard Pascale, one of Jerry Sternin's collaborators, discovered this in 2003 when he accepted a consulting assignment with Genentech. The company had recently launched a drug called Xolair, which had been regarded as a "miracle drug" for asthma. It had proved effective in preventing asthma attacks for many patients. Yet six months after launch, sales of Xolair remained well below expectations.

Pascale and his team were asked to help figure out why Xolair was underperforming. They immediately started looking for bright spots and soon found one: Two saleswomen who worked the Dallas–Fort Worth area were selling twenty times more Xolair than their peers. Further investigation revealed that the women were using a fundamentally different kind of sales pitch. Rather than selling the health benefits of the drug—which doctors largely understood—they were helping doctors understand how to *administer* the drug. Xolair was not a pill or an inhaler; it required infusion via an intravenous drip. This technique was unfamiliar (and therefore Elephant-spooking) to the allergists and pediatricians who would be prescribing the drug.

Here was a classic bright-spot situation. Like the Vietnamese mothers who mixed sweet-potato greens into their kids' rice, these saleswomen were achieving radically different results with the same set of resources everyone else had. Having discovered the bright spot, Genentech's managers could help spread the innovation across their entire sales force.

But that didn't happen. And here is where a cautionary tale intrudes on our success story. What actually happened was this: The superior results of the Dallas–Fort Worth reps were viewed with suspicion! Managers speculated that the saleswomen had an unfair advantage, and their initial assumption was that the pair's sales territories or quotas needed to be revisited. (Later investigation established that the two women had the same type of client base as the other reps.)

To be fair to the Genentech managers, let's acknowledge that there was indeed a chance that those two reps were simply an anomaly. But the managers' *first reaction* to the good news was that it must be bad news! That reaction is a good reminder that the Rider's capacity for analysis is endless. Even successes can look like problems to an overactive Rider.

7.

Let's circle back to Bobby, the troubled student, because now we can start to understand his rather abrupt transformation. Here's a brief exchange from one of Bobby's counseling sessions. Notice how Murphy, the school counselor, starts by popping the Exception Question:

MURPHY: Tell me about the times at school when you don't get in trouble as much.

BOBBY: I never get in trouble, well, not a lot, in Ms. Smith's class.

MURPHY: What's different about Ms. Smith's class?

BOBBY: I don't know, she's nicer. We get along great.

MURPHY: What exactly does she do that's nicer?

Murphy wasn't content with Bobby's vague conclusion that Ms. Smith is "nicer." He kept probing until Bobby identified several things about Ms. Smith and her class that seemed to help him behave well. For instance, Ms. Smith always greeted him as soon as he walked into class. (Other teachers, understandably, avoided him.) She gave him easier work, which she knew he could complete (Bobby has a learning disability). And whenever the class started working on an assignment, she checked with Bobby to make sure he understood the instructions.

Ms. Smith's class was a bright spot, and as we've seen, anytime you have a bright spot, your mission is to clone it. Using Ms. Smith's class as a model, Murphy gave Bobby's other teachers very practical tips about how to deal with him: Greet Bobby at the door. Make sure he's assigned work he can do. Check to make sure he understands the instructions.

What Murphy had avoided, of course, was archaeology. He didn't dig into Bobby's troubled childhood, and he didn't try to excavate the sources of his anger and willfulness. For Murphy, all that information would have been TBU, as Sternin would say: true but useless. The other thing Murphy avoided was Genentech's knee-jerk skepticism. The mental quibbles could have come so easily: *Ms. Smith is just a nicer person than the other teachers* or *Her class is easier* or *Teachers shouldn't have to adapt their approach to a problem student.* Instead, Murphy found a bright spot, and he trusted it.

Bobby's teachers were pleased when Murphy approached them with such specific guidance, and they promised to give his recommendations a try. Murphy asked the teachers to help him track whether the solutions were working by recording Bobby's performance on three metrics: (1) arriving to class on time, (2) completing assignments in class, and (3) behaving acceptably in class. Over the next three months, as reported earlier, Bobby's rate of being sent to the principal's office for a major infraction decreased by 80 percent. Bobby also made striking progress on day-to-day behavior as measured by the three metrics. Before solutions-focused therapy, his teachers typically rated his performance as acceptable in only 1 or 2 out of 6 class periods per day. After solutions-focused therapy, he was rated as acceptable in 4 or 5 of the 6 periods. Bobby is still not a model student. But he's a lot better.

8.

Notice something remarkable about both the Vietnam and the Bobby case studies. In each one, relatively small changes—cooking with sweet-potato greens, greeting Bobby at the door—had a big impact on a big problem. There is a clear asymmetry between the scale of the problem and the scale of the solution. Big problem, small solution.

This is a theme you will see again and again. Big problems are rarely solved with commensurately big solutions. Instead, they are most often solved by a sequence of small solutions, sometimes over weeks, sometimes over decades. And this asymmetry is why the Rider's predilection for analysis can backfire so easily.

When the Rider analyzes a problem, he seeks a solution that befits the scale of it. If the Rider spots a hole, he wants to fill it, and if he's got a round hole with a 24-inch diameter, he's gonna go looking for a 24-inch peg. But that mental model is wrong. For instance, in analyzing malnutrition in Vietnam, the experts had exhaustively analyzed all the big systemic forces that were responsible for it: lack of sanitation, poverty, ignorance, lack of water. No doubt they also concocted big systemic plans to address those forces. But that was fantasy. No one, other than Sternin, thought to ask, "What's working right now?"

In reviewing Bobby's situation at high school, the teachers and administrators whispered about all the things that were broken: broken home, learning disability, uncontrollable impulses. Any normal person, analyzing Bobby's situation, would have craved an intensive, complex solution to match the intensive, complex problem. But no one, other than the counselor Murphy, thought to ask, "What's working right now?"

To pursue bright spots is to ask the question "What's working, and how can we do more of it?" Sounds simple, doesn't it? Yet, in the real world, this obvious question is almost never asked. Instead, the question we ask is more problem focused: "What's broken, and how do we fix it?"

This problem-seeking mindset is a shortcoming of the Rider in each of us. Psychologists who have studied this phenomenon— our predilection for the negative—have reached some fascinating conclusions. As an illustration of what they've found, take a look at the following words taken from a "Learn English at home" website. They're all words for emotions. We've excerpted the first twenty-four of them from an alphabetical list. See if you notice any patterns:

ANGRY	DELIGHTED
ANNOYED	DISAPPOINTED
APPALLED	ECSTATIC
APPREHENSIVE	EXCITED

ASHAMED	EMOTIONAL
BEWILDERED	ENVIOUS
BETRAYED	EMBARRASSED
CONFUSED	FURIOUS
CONFIDENT	FRIGHTENED
CHEATED	GREAT
CROSS	HAPPY
DEPRESSED	HORRIFIED

Those are 24 of the most common "emotion" words in English, and only 6 of them are positive! In a more exhaustive study, a psychologist analyzed 558 emotion words—every one that he could find in the English language—and found that 62 percent of them were negative versus 38 percent positive. That's a pretty shocking discrepancy. According to an old urban legend, Eskimos have 100 different words for snow. Well, it turns out that negative emotions are our snow.

This negative focus is not confined to emotions. Across the board, we seem wired to focus on the negative. A group of psychologists reviewed over two hundred articles and concluded that, for a wide range of human behavior and perception, a general principle holds true: "Bad is stronger than good."

Exhibit A: People who were shown photos of bad and good events spent longer viewing the bad ones.

Exhibit B: When people learn bad stuff about someone else, it's stickier than good stuff. People pay closer attention to the bad stuff, reflect on it more, remember it longer, and weigh it more heavily in assessing the person overall. This pattern is so robust that researchers who study how we perceive one another have a label for it—"positive-negative asymmetry."

Exhibit C: A researcher reviewed seventeen studies about how people interpret and explain events in their lives—for example, how sports fans interpret sporting events or how students describe their days in their journals. Across multiple domains—work and politics and sports and personal life—people were more likely to spontaneously bring up (and attempt to explain) negative events than positive ones.

We could present plenty more exhibits, but for now we'll give the study's authors the last (disappointed) word on the subject: "When we began this review we anticipated finding some exceptions that would demarcate the limits of the phenomenon . . . [but] *we were unable to locate any significant spheres in which good was consistently stronger than bad*" (emphasis added).

Bad is stronger than good. As Leslie Fiedler once said, lots of novelists have achieved their fame by focusing on marital problems, but there's never been a successful novel about a happy marriage.

9.

A particular strain of this "bad is stronger than good" bias is critical when it comes to tackling change. Let's call it a *problem focus*. To see it, consider this situation: Your child comes home one day with her report card. She got one A, four B's, and one F. Where will you spend your time as a parent?

This hypothetical comes from author Marcus Buckingham, who says that nearly all parents will tend to fixate on the F. It's easy to empathize with them: *Something seems broken—we should fix it. Let's get her a tutor. Or maybe she should be punished—she's grounded until that grade recovers*. It is the rare parent who would say, instead, "Honey, you made an 'A' in this one class. You must really have a strength in this subject. How can we build on that?" (Buckingham has a fine series of books on making the most of your strengths rather than obsessing about your weaknesses.)

When the Rider sees that things are going well, he doesn't

think much about them. But when things break, he snaps to attention and starts applying his problem-solving skills. So when your kids are making A's and B's, you don't think much about their grades. But when they make a D or an F, you spring into action. It's weird when you think about, isn't it?

What if the Rider had a more positive orientation? Imagine a world in which you experienced a rush of gratitude every single time you flipped a light switch and the room lit up. Imagine a world in which after a husband forgot his wife's birthday, she gave him a big kiss and said, "For thirteen of the last fourteen years you remembered my birthday! That's wonderful!"

This is not our world.

But in times of change, it needs to be. Our Rider has a problem focus when he needs a *solution focus*. If you are a manager, ask yourself: "What is the ratio of the time I spend solving problems to the time I spend scaling successes?"

We need to switch from archaeological problem solving to bright-spot evangelizing. There's no question that it's possible to do. Take Jerry Sternin. He came into an environment riddled with failure. The opportunities for analysis were endless. He could have stayed in Vietnam for twenty years, writing position papers on the malnutrition problem. But what he knew was this: Even in failure there is success.

An alcoholic goes an hour without a drink. Three sales reps out of fifty sell like crazy. A few Vietnamese mothers, with no more money than any others, manage to raise healthy kids.

These flashes of success—these bright spots—can illuminate the road map for action and spark the hope that change is possible.

3

Script the Critical Moves

1.

A doctor was asked to consider the medical records of a 67-year-old patient who had chronic hip pain from arthritis. In the past, the patient had been given drugs to treat his pain, but they'd been ineffective, so the doctor was forced to consider a more drastic option: hip-replacement surgery, which involves slicing open the thigh, wrenching the bone out of the socket, sawing off the arthritic end, and replacing it with an implant. Recovery from hip-replacement surgery is long and painful.

Then came an unexpected break in the case: A final check with the patient's pharmacy uncovered one medication that hadn't been tried. Now the doctor faced a dilemma: Should he prescribe the untried medication, even though other medications had failed, or should he go ahead and refer the patient for surgery?

This dilemma, based on real medical cases, was created by physician Donald Redelmeier and psychologist Eldar Shafir, who used it to study the way doctors make decisions. When doctors were presented with this case history, 47 percent of them chose to try the medication, in hopes of saving the patient from going under the knife.

In a variation on the dilemma, another group of doctors were presented with almost exactly the same set of case facts—except this time, the patient's pharmacy discovered *two* untried medications. If you were the patient with the arthritic hip, you'd be thrilled—certainly two nonsurgical options are better than one. But when the doctors were presented with two medications, *only 28 percent chose to try either one.*

This doesn't make sense. The doctors were acting as though having more medication options somehow made medication a worse bet than surgery. But if 47 percent of doctors thought medication A was preferable to surgery, the mere *existence* of a second medication shouldn't have tipped them toward surgery.

What happened here is *decision paralysis.* More options, even good ones, can freeze us and make us retreat to the default plan, which in this case was a painful and invasive hip-replacement surgery. This behavior clearly is not rational, but it is human.

Decisions are the Rider's turf, and because they require careful supervision and self-control, they tax the Rider's strength. (Remember the radish/chocolate-chip cookie study from Chapter 1.) The more choices the Rider is offered, the more exhausted the Rider gets. Have you ever noticed that shopping is a lot more tiring than other kinds of light activity? Now you know why—it's all those choices. This is important, because we encounter excess choice all around us. Consider three real examples of decision paralysis:

Scene 1: A gourmet food store. The store managers have set up a table where customers can sample imported jams for free. One day, the table showcases 6 different jams. Another day,

24 jams. As you'd expect, the 24-jam display attracts more customers to stop by for a sample—but when it comes time to buy, they can't make a decision. Shoppers who saw only 6 jams on display are *10 times* more likely to buy a jar of jam!

Scene 2: The office. The employees of a large company read over their 401(k) materials, ready to start saving for retirement. The human resources department has thoughtfully provided many investment options: domestic growth stock funds, domestic value stock funds, municipal bond funds, real estate investment trusts, emerging market funds, developed market funds, money market accounts, and more. Each category might have several choices within it. (Really complete 401(k) plans might offer dozens of options.) The extra options backfire, however, because for every 10 options offered, the employees' rate of participation goes *down by 2 percent.* Decision paralysis deters people from saving for their own retirement! And because many companies match employees' contributions, employees may also be walking away from free money.

Scene 3: A local bar. It's speed-dating night. Singles meet a series of other singles one-on-one, spending perhaps five minutes with each person, in hopes of making a romantic connection. But decision paralysis thwarts even Cupid. Young adults who meet eight other singles make more "matches" than those who meet twenty.

Bottom line: Decision paralysis disrupts medical decisions and retail decisions and investment decisions and dating decisions. Let's go out on a limb and suggest that it might affect decisions in your job and life, too.

Think about the sources of decision paralysis in your organization. Every business must choose among attractive options. Growing revenue quickly versus maximizing profitability. Making perfect products versus getting products to market faster.

Being innovative and creative versus optimizing efficiency. If you fold together lots of those tensions, you create a surefire recipe for paralysis. It took only two medications to fuzz the doctors' brains. How many options do your people have?

Think about your local school board. Every year, the problems and solutions multiply. You can just imagine the mental conversation: "Property tax revenue is falling, but the teachers need a 3 percent cost-of-living raise, and we can't forget about extracurriculars (cutting the marching band last year was a killer), but we must continue to invest in our new science magnet school—if it doesn't work, there will be egg on our face—yet it's ridiculous to consider any of this until we fix our crumbling infrastructure and address our overcrowded classrooms." For the frazzled school board member, it suddenly looks a lot more attractive to roll over last year's budget with a 1.5 percent increase on every line item.

As Barry Schwartz puts it in his book *The Paradox of Choice*, as we face more and more options, "we become overloaded. Choice no longer liberates, it debilitates. It might even be said to tyrannize."

2.

The status quo feels comfortable and steady because much of the choice has been squeezed out. You have your routines, your ways of doing things. For most of your day, the Rider is on autopilot. But in times of change, autopilot doesn't work anymore, choices suddenly proliferate, and autopilot habits become unfamiliar decisions. When you're on a diet, the habitual daily trip for Nachos Bell Grande is disqualified, and in its place is left a decision. When you've got a new manager, the way you communicate stops being second nature and starts being a choice.

Change brings new choices that create uncertainty. Let's be clear: It's not only options that yield decision paralysis—like picking one donut from 100 flavors. Ambiguity does, too. In times of change, you may not know what options are available. And this uncertainty leads to decision paralysis as surely as a table with 24 jams.

Ambiguity is exhausting to the Rider, because the Rider is tugging on the reins of the Elephant, trying to direct the Elephant down a new path. But when the road is uncertain, the Elephant will insist on taking the default path, the most familiar path, just as the doctors did. Why? Because uncertainty makes the Elephant anxious. (Think of how, in an unfamiliar place, you gravitate toward a familiar face.) And that's why decision paralysis can be deadly for change—because *the most familiar path is always the status quo.*

Many leaders pride themselves on setting high-level direction: *I'll set the vision and stay out of the details.* It's true that a compelling vision is critical (as we'll see in the next chapter). But it's not enough. Big-picture, hands-off leadership isn't likely to work in a change situation, because the hardest part of change—the paralyzing part—is precisely in the details.

In Chapter 1, we explained why what looks like resistance is often a lack of clarity. The citizens of two West Virginia communities, unhealthy in their eating habits, underwent a major change when a couple of professors coached them to buy 1% milk. They didn't need a big-picture vision—no one needs convincing that "eating healthy" is an admirable goal. What they needed was someone who could bring a noble goal within the realm of everyday behavior, someone who could cut through the bewildering array of potentially healthy choices and suggest a good place to start.

Ambiguity is the enemy. Any successful change requires a

translation of ambiguous goals into concrete behaviors. In short, to make a switch, you need to *script the critical moves.*

3.

In 1995, Brazilian president Fernando Henrique Cardoso decided to privatize Brazil's railroads. He split the system into seven different branches (shades of Ma Bell) and auctioned off the rights to run them. Previous administrations had not invested much in the rail system, and at the time of the auction, it was a deteriorating mess. A study concluded that 50 percent of the network's bridges needed repair and 20 percent of them were on the verge of collapse. The technologies used in Brazil were far behind those in other developed countries. In fact, the rail system was still using twenty locomotives powered by *steam engines.*

A private firm, GP Investimentos Limited, decided to bid for the branch known as the "southern line," which ran through Brazil's three southernmost states. GP was high bidder in the auction in December 1996. After an interim period of management, the firm put one of its own executives, Alexandre Behring, in charge of the company, which was later renamed America Latina Logistica (ALL). When Behring took charge, he was in his early 30s—just four years out of business school.

Behring didn't have much to work with. ALL had only 30 million Brazilian reals in cash on its balance sheet. At one of Behring's first meetings, a mid-level manager beseeched him for 5 million reals to repair a single bridge. Though sympathetic, Behring knew that fixing everything that was broken would require hundreds of millions of reals. The needs were profound, but he faced an unyielding constraint: ALL's depleted bank account.

The railroad purchased by GP was in chaos, and when Behring and his team took charge, with new personnel and new priorities, more chaos was whipped into the preexisting chaos. The resulting decision paralysis should have been inescapable. And it likely would have been if Behring hadn't made clear exactly what needed to be done.

His top priority was to lift ALL out of its precarious, cash-strapped financial state. To accomplish this, he and his 35-year-old CFO, Duilio Calciolari, developed four rules to govern the company's investments:

> Rule 1: Money would be invested only in projects that would allow ALL to earn more revenue in the short term.

> Rule 2: The best solution to any problem was the one that would cost the least money up front—even if it ended up costing more in the long term, and even if it was a lower-quality solution.

> Rule 3: Options that would fix a problem quickly were preferred to slower options that would provide superior long-term fixes.

> Rule 4: Reusing or recycling existing materials was better than acquiring new materials.

The four rules were clear: (1) Unblock revenue. (2) Minimize up-front cash. (3) Faster is better than best. (4) Use what you've got. These rules, taken together, ensured that cash wouldn't be consumed unless it was being used as bait for more cash. Spend a little, make a little more.

This is what we mean by "scripting" the critical moves.

Change begins at the level of individual decisions and behaviors, but that's a hard place to start because that's where the friction is. Inertia and decision paralysis will conspire to keep people doing things the old way. To spark movement in a new direction, you need to provide crystal-clear guidance. That's why scripting is important—you've got to think about the specific behavior that you'd want to see in a tough moment, whether the tough moment takes place in a Brazilian railroad system or late at night in your own snack-loaded pantry.

You can't script every move—that would be like trying to foresee the seventeenth move in a chess game. It's the *critical* moves that count. Recall that, in West Virginia, the researchers decided to focus their campaign on milk because it was the source of the most saturated fat in the average diet. The researchers didn't offer suggestions about bread or soda or butter or potato chips. They scripted the *critical* move: Switch to 1% milk.

Similarly, Behring's four rules were focused on financial triage. He didn't have the luxury of long-term planning. He needed his people to move, immediately, in a new direction, in hopes that they could buy ALL enough time to make a fuller transformation. (Notice that he didn't say a word about other important issues such as employee morale or marketing or R&D.) By staying focused on the *critical* moves, he made it easier for his people to change direction.

In 1998, for instance, the company had to turn down business hauling grain because it didn't have enough locomotives. While its competitors were negotiating for new locomotives, ALL's engineers worked around the clock repairing old locomotives. *(Faster is better than best. Minimize up-front cash.)*

Also, ALL's engineers figured out a way to boost the locomotives' fuel capacity so they could operate longer without refueling. This reduced downtime, allowing more routes per locomotive, just as Southwest Airlines gets more flights per plane than its competitors because of its quick turnarounds at the gate. *(Unblock revenue.)* Engineers also found a creative solution to the nagging problem of damaged tracks, which limited a train's speed. Rather than purchasing new metal rails, which cost US$400 per ton, they ripped up tracks at abandoned stations and installed them on active routes. *(Use what you've got.)*

Three years later, Behring's discipline was paying off. ALL's performance improved from a net loss of 80 million reals in 1998 to a net profit of 24 million reals in 2000.

Knowing what we know about the Rider, it's no surprise that Behring's strategy worked. Behring had scripted the moves that helped his people make hard decisions. What tires out the Rider—and puts change efforts at risk—is ambiguity, and Behring eliminated it. For every investment decision, his rules suggested the correct choice.

To see the power of this, let's return to the doctors and the patient with the arthritic hip. Imagine that the leaders of the hospital had scripted their critical moves, and that one of those moves was this: *Use invasive options only as a last resort.* Does anyone doubt that this guideline would have caused a big shift in the doctors' decisions?

4.

In the shaded area that follows, we present a feature that we call a "Clinic." In each Clinic, we describe a real-world situation and challenge you to think about how to apply the *Switch* framework to create change. At the end of each Clinic, we give our own suggestions, but we encourage you to generate your own game plan before you look at ours. The Clinic is intended to be a kind of pause button, a chance to step outside the text and think about how to apply what you've read. We hope you find this a useful way to practice applying the framework. The Clinics are written to be sidebars—if you prefer to plow through the prose uninterrupted, you can return to them later.

CLINIC

Can You Get People to File Their Expense Reports on Time?

SITUATION Barbara, the controller of a consulting firm, is fuming again about expense reports. Why do people *always* turn them in late? The monthly due date was yesterday, and she's still missing 38 percent of the reports. That puts pressure on members of her team—especially on Maria, the "expense czar"— because they're expected to close the company's monthly books on time and the expense reports are a necessary input to the close. Frustrated, Barbara starts composing a reminder e-mail, full of underlined words and exclamation points. (The "nag" e-mail has become a monthly tradition.) Why does she have to "shout" before people do what they're supposed to? [This is a fictional situation that is inspired by a true story. *Many* true stories.]

WHAT'S THE SWITCH AND WHAT'S HOLDING IT BACK? The behavior Barbara wants is clear: Employees need to file their expense reports by the deadline. It's not obvious what the barrier is. Maybe the process is sufficiently complicated that it paralyzes the Rider. Maybe the process is perfectly clear, but the Elephant always finds things it would rather be doing. Or maybe the reporting systems are so antiquated that the Path is one giant speed bump. Let's attack on all three fronts.

HOW DO WE MAKE THE SWITCH?
• *Direct the Rider.* **1. Find the bright spots.** Barbara should investigate her bright spots—the 62 percent of employees who file their expense reports on

time every month. What are they doing differently? Maybe they've handcrafted a set of techniques for logging expenses as they occur, so there's not a big pile at the end of the month. Once Barbara figures out the bright spots' tricks, she can get them to share their system with others. **2. Script the critical moves.** It's possible that parts of the reporting process are confusing enough to cause decision paralysis. Maybe there's ambiguity about how to code particular expenses or how to allocate certain costs between clients. Barbara should observe a few laggards as they complete their reports. She won't know how to script the critical moves until she sees the confusion firsthand.

• *Motivate the Elephant.* **1. Find the feeling.** Nobody who misses an expense-report deadline "feels" anything. Sure, Barbara chastises laggards via e-mail, but after they've received the nag note for the sixth consecutive month, it loses its sting. Barbara needs to find something people can care about. Or *someone*: After all, the company depends on people like Maria to close the books every month, and they'll be held accountable if they blow the deadline. So, in essence, the goal is not to file the report; it's to do Maria a favor, once a month. It may be easy to rationalize missing an administrative deadline, but it's harder to rationalize letting down a coworker who's counting on you.

• *Shape the Path.* **1. Tweak the environment.** How easy are the expense-report forms to fill out? The accounting department should be obsessive about simplifying them, to the point of preloading people's names in their reports and distributing empty envelopes for loose receipts. Think Amazon's 1-Click ordering. Every barrier that's removed makes the Path clearer. **2. Rally the herd.** Many people may conclude, falsely, that *everyone* turns in the reports late, that lateness is accepted behavior. (Barbara's nagging e-mails may actually reinforce this perception. Why would she send them unless lots of people are slacking?) People are sensitive to social norms, so Barbara's e-mail should highlight the fact that almost two-thirds of reports are turned in on time. No one likes to hear that they're underperforming relative to their peers.

5.

When Alexandre Behring set up four simple rules for ALL employees to follow, they changed quickly. So did the West Virginians who were urged to drink 1% milk. But why did these changes need to be scripted? Wasn't it obvious to the West Virginians that they should be drinking 1% milk instead of whole milk?

Well, no, it wasn't. Not many people know that a glass of whole milk has the same amount of saturated fat as five bacon strips. That's not intuitive knowledge. Nor was it intuitive for any of Behring's employees at ALL to decide, "Yep, let's rip up old, abandoned tracks instead of purchasing new ones." When you want someone to behave in a new way, explain the "new way" clearly. Don't assume the new moves are obvious.

To see why this is so important, consider a campaign that is essentially the "antimatter" version of the 1% milk campaign—a campaign that, while well intentioned, systematically ignores or reverses every smart component of the 1% milk intervention. What would such an antimatter campaign look like? It might look very much like the U.S. government's Food Pyramid.

The Food Pyramid, which specifies the types and quantities of food that make up a healthy diet, is the perfect example of how *not* to change people's behavior. It's worth considering for a moment, because what dooms the Pyramid could doom your efforts to create change in your life, as well.

Let's start with the pyramid shape. A pyramid signifies hierarchy, yet no hierarchy is evident in the Food Pyramid. The first version of it displayed rows of food, one row on top of the next, with grains at the bottom and oils at the top. Some people interpreted this arrangement to mean that oils were the most important food group. (Whoops.) The revised version, shown here, abandoned that construct for vertical-ish streaks of color intended to eliminate any implied ranking. What this means is that the pyramid structure itself *has no meaning whatsoever.* The Food Pyramid might as well be a Food Rhombus or a Food Rooster.

Look at it again—its meaning is almost completely opaque. What do the streaks mean? The only meaning that can be gleaned quickly comes from the stick figure dashing up the side. The meaning is clear enough: "You should exercise." The answers to more meaningful questions—How much? How often? What kind?— aren't as easy to infer, which of course adds more ambiguity.

To learn what the Food Pyramid has to say about food, you must be willing to decipher the Pyramid's markings. If you make the effort, you'll find that each streak of color represents a class of food. For instance, the yellow streak (the tiny one near the middle) is "oils," and the orange streak (on the far left) is "grains." If you dig even further, you'll find that with every color streak comes a recommendation. For instance, the USDA advises that adults consume about 5 to 7 teaspoons of oil each day.

Quick, how many teaspoons of oil did you consume today?

Quick, how many "ounce equivalents" of grain did you have today?

Can you imagine any message that would be less effective in changing people's eating behavior? The language and concepts here are so hopelessly abstracted from people's actual experience with food—which consists of things like buying groceries and ordering hamburgers at restaurants, not tabulating grain portions—that the message confuses and demoralizes: *I can't understand this stuff.*

As an analogy, most of us have internalized the rule of thumb to get the oil in our cars changed every 3 months or 3,000 miles. It's transparent and actionable, like the 1% milk campaign. What if, instead, the auto industry publicized its version of the disastrous Food Pyramid—say, a Car Rainbow, where each color of the rainbow represents a different diagnostic test. (Pink would warn you not to let your engine oil exceed a certain "sludge threshold.") Jiffy Lube would be out of business in months.

OK, the Food Pyramid is almost too easy to pick on. But the lessons here are serious and practical. If you are leading a change effort, you need to remove the ambiguity from your vision of change. Granted, this is asking a lot. It means that you'll need to understand how to script the critical moves, to translate aspirations into actions. It's not good enough to ask your team to "be more creative" or to "tighten up on the purse strings." That's like telling the American public to "be healthier."

In a pioneering study of organizational change, described in the book *The Critical Path to Corporate Renewal,* researchers divided the change efforts they'd studied into three groups: the most successful (the top third), the average (the middle third), and the least successful (the bottom third). They found that, across the spectrum, almost everyone set goals: 89 percent of the top third and 86 percent of the bottom third. A typical goal might be to improve inventory turns by 50 percent. But the more successful change transformations were more likely to set *behavioral* goals: 89 percent of the top third versus only 33 percent of the bottom third. For instance, a behavioral goal might be that project teams would meet once a week and each team would include at least one representative of every functional area.

Until you can ladder your way down from a change idea to a specific behavior, you're not ready to lead a switch. To create movement, you've got to be specific and be concrete. You've got to emulate 1% milk and flee from the Food Pyramid.

6.

How far does this theory go? How much difference can specific instructions make? Let's subject the idea to the toughest possible test: Can you change child abusers by scripting some critical parenting moves for them?

In 2004, a study was conducted of 110 parents who had abused their children. Seventy-three percent of them had assaulted their kids—hitting or punching them with their fists. Twenty percent had engaged in even more violent assaults, resulting in broken bones or severe lacerations.

The parents tended to blame their abusive behavior on their kids. "They'll say, 'I had to discipline my child this way because he's so rotten and he won't listen,'" said Beverly Funderburk, a research professor at the University of Oklahoma's Health Sciences Center. The parents believed that they'd gotten a "bad kid," or a stubborn one, and that violence was the only way they could get their kids to obey.

The mission of Funderburk's team was to change these parents, to stop their abuse. If you think that sounds naive and even hopeless, you're in good company. That's also what Funderburk worried about when she first began the work.

She practices what's called parent-child interaction therapy (PCIT), which tries to disrupt the escalating cycles of coercion and frustration that characterize abusive situations. In the first step of PCIT, parents are given an assignment: "We want you to play with your child for five minutes a day. Here are the rules: You're going to devote 100% of your attention to them, you're not going to answer the phone, you are not going to teach them their ABCs. You're just going to enjoy them." The parents are incredulous that five minutes will accomplish anything. "For goodness' sake," said one parent, "I spend every minute of every day on this child."

At first, these five-minute play periods take place in a laboratory setting. The parent and child sit in an empty room with only a table and chairs. Three or four toys are put on the tabletop. The parents are instructed to let the child lead the play session, and they're forbidden to give commands, to criticize, even to ask questions. Letting their child direct the action is incredibly difficult for them.

During the play session, a therapist watches the parents through a one-way mirror and gives real-time coaching by means of an earpiece. Funderburk describes a typical interaction:

> The parent and child might start coloring, and the parent tries to play along by coloring on the child's paper. The child objects. So we tell the parent, "Okay, get a separate piece of paper and imitate what your child is doing."
>
> If the child is coloring a rainbow, the parent colors a rainbow too, saying, "I'm coloring a rainbow just like you. You're using green, I'm going to use green."
>
> And some kids, if they're particularly oppositional, might reach over and grab the parent's green crayon yelling, "I want that." And we teach the parents to say, "Okay, I'd be *happy* to share that crayon with you . . . in

fact let me put all the crayons over by you so you can reach them all."

Or perhaps the parent says, "I'm going to color my rainbow with pink now." And the child says, "Pink is ugly, don't do pink!" If the child has been particularly nasty we may just ask the parents to ignore the comment, but otherwise we coach the parents to agree with their child, "You're right! Pink is not a good color for the rainbow! I think I'll do red."

We try to get the parents to bend like a reed. Whatever the child is doing, the parent offers no resistance, so the child has nothing to fight against.

An abusive parent typically finds the five-minute exercise utterly exhausting. (And you understand why—the parent's Rider has to supervise every single moment.) Funderburk and her colleagues demand that the parents practice the same set of behaviors (called "child-directed interaction") every day, whether in the lab or at home, so that the behaviors gradually become instinctive. The more instinctive a behavior becomes, the less self-control from the Rider it requires, and thus the more sustainable it becomes.

Parents are taught skills that feel unnatural at first. They are taught to look for opportunities to praise their kids' behavior. ("I like how hard you're working." "Good job. You're being very kind to that doll.") They are taught to simply *describe* their child's behavior, so that the child feels noticed. ("Oh, look, now you're putting the car in the garage.")

Later in the program, after parents have become better at having short positive interactions with their kids, they are taught how to give commands so that their kids will listen and obey. They are taught a very specific formula for a command—

combining a command with a reason so the command doesn't feel arbitrary. ("Johnny, it's almost time for the bus to come, so please put your shoes on now.")

Funderburk and her team at the University of Oklahoma studied 110 parents who had abused their children. Half of them were randomly assigned to take 12 sessions of PCIT, and the other half were assigned to take 12 sessions of a form of anger-management therapy, focused on helping them control their emotions—the standard treatment for abusive parents. After the therapy sessions concluded, the parents were tracked for 3 years. Across 3 years, 60 percent of the anger-management-therapy group committed another act of child abuse. In contrast, only 20 percent of the PCIT parents re-offended.

PCIT did not eliminate the problem: One in five parents abused his or her kids again. But, from the perspective of behavior change, the results are staggering. Most of us believe in our hearts that child abusers are irredeemably flawed. Who could hit a child other than someone who is disturbed in some basic way? It simply boggles the mind to think that the behavior of child abusers could be altered by only twelve sessions of therapy concentrating on such simple instructions.

Funderburk said, "In my experience, the physically abusive parent has the same goals as a normal parent; it's their method and their ideas that are wrong. They think that their child is woeful, because they told their 3-year-old to just play in the front yard, and then he wandered off into the street. And they don't understand that a 3-year-old might forget an instruction, or might not have that kind of impulse control, so they think they have to punish the child *for his own good* because he was disobedient and dangerous."

Earlier, we said that what looks like stubbornness or opposition may actually be a lack of clarity. The PCIT intervention suggests that child abuse, too, may be partly the result of a lack of understanding, a lack of clear instruction or guidance on what to do. This is not to excuse the parents' behavior, of course. It is simply to point out that simple scripting has power beyond what any of us could have predicted. Even child abusers become pliable in its presence.

7.

In 1995, the same year Brazil's president Cardoso announced the privatization of the railroads, a group of high school students in Howard, South Dakota, started plotting a revival. They wanted to do something, anything, that might revive their dying community.

Howard and surrounding Miner County had been shrinking for decades. Farm and industrial jobs had slowly dried up, and nothing replaced them. The median price of houses in Howard was only $26,500. The population was about 3,000 and shrinking. The county had the highest elderly population per capita in South Dakota, and it also had the highest rate of youth out-migration in South Dakota, meaning that when young people got old enough, they left and didn't return.

"We'd been in decline for ninety years," said Randy Parry, a longtime resident who taught a business class at the local high school, coached the varsity basketball team, and ran an ice cream parlor on the side.

At Howard High School, the students had just finished reading a book about the death of rural communities in Iowa. The students said, "That's us, it's just seventy years from now," according to Parry. "So in class they started asking, 'How could we change this?'"

Imagine the decision paralysis in this situation. Think of how many factors influence a town's health: its history, its demographics, its location, its economic base, its weather, among countless others. The problem was simply too complex for anyone to solve. And it wasn't for lack of motivation—there wasn't one person in Miner County who wouldn't have jumped at the chance to help rejuvenate the community. The Elephant herd was ready to move. But where? What can a few people do to restore an entire *county*?

The students started investigating the situation, designing a survey and distributing it to a sample of Miner County's 1,000 registered voters. One finding in particular disturbed them: They discovered that half of the residents were shopping outside the county, driving an hour to Sioux Falls to shop in larger stores.

If Miner County was going to be reborn, its economy would need a boost. Most of the things that would boost an economy— investment, entrepreneurship, immigration—were out of the students' control. But they had uncovered one thing that was very much in their control: spending money locally. They had found their first rallying cry: Let's keep Miner dollars in Miner County.

Parry urged the students to present their findings to the community. The students accepted the challenge and began to put together a presentation.

The students' newfound interest in revitalization dovetailed with the efforts of others in the community. A group of other Miner County citizens had been hosting a series of meetings intended to get county residents talking about the future. They held five gatherings, some in the high school and some in people's homes, and they invited a cross section of residents: farmers and businesspeople and ministers and retirees. They challenged each other: What can we do to energize Miner County?

The issues raised were all over the map: *Why does our town look so shabby, with rusty cars on the street? Why should a farmer get a subsidy when a businessperson doesn't get a subsidy? Why don't we have a more thriving Main Street?* Many of the issues were TBU, unsolvable by the community. Many required investment, but with a limited pool of tax dollars to draw from, it wasn't clear where they'd find the money. But there were a few things they knew they could take into their own hands.

A gas station owner in the town of Fedora, population 150, complained that residents years ago had cut down a lot of diseased trees—stumps were still littering the area, making Fedora look run-down and sad. The group of concerned citizens decided to deal with the stumps in Fedora. One Saturday, farmers carrying chain saws rode into Fedora on their tractors and loaders. Other residents made sandwiches and cookies for the workers. In a single day, the group dug up four hundred stumps.

Kathy Callies, who was heading up the kitchen crew that day, said it was amazing to see fifty people, ages ranging from 5 to 95, come together to do something for their community. Callies recalled that by the end of the day, "People felt like, 'Look at what we did in a day.' And when you've dug up stumps together and you start to realize you have shared ideas about what you want the community to be, then things start to happen." (Notice that the log-clearing day had powerful Elephant and Path elements, as well. The flush of victory—of making a difference—gave the Elephant strength to continue. And the strong support of the community made the Path feel less difficult. It's easier to make a long journey when you've got a herd around you.)

The community began to rally around the movement. Callies remembered the day that Phyllis, a civic-minded woman in her 80s, dropped by the office where the community boosters were meeting. Phyllis announced, "I've been waiting for you to call me. I thought if you needed my help, you would call. But then I realized that 'Oh, they're all too busy to call!' So here I am." On her refrigerator at home, Phyllis had posted a cross-stitch that said "Screw the Golden Years."

When the high school students were ready to unveil their recommendations, eighty-five residents gathered in the high school gym to hear the presentation. Among them were the top leaders of the towns in Miner County: the school boards, the city councils, and the county commissioners.

The crowd listened attentively to the high school students. Parry said, "You could hear a pin drop. . . . People said, 'I can't say no because I want to make this a place where these kids can come home someday.' Because the other option is we sit here and keep watching things decline, so pretty soon all that will be left is the dust."

The students had prepared an impressive array of spreadsheets and charts and graphs. But they'd also simplified the complex data into one simple, surprising fact: They'd calculated that if Howard residents spent just 10 percent more of their disposable income at home, they would boost the local economy by $7 million.

The audience was impressed, and the presentation worked better than anyone expected. The students had scripted the first critical move for Miner County, and the locals responded immediately, consciously spending more of their money in the county. A year later, South Dakota's Department of Revenue released an astonishing number: The amount of money spent in Miner County had increased by $15.6 million, more than twice the increase the kids had expected.

The change began to snowball. Suddenly, because the county was collecting more taxes, money was available to fund the other proposals the local groups had considered. And in the years following the students' presentation, the tax receipts kept climbing, which enabled the community to tackle even more ambitious problems. Later, Howard and Miner County received $6 million in grants from various foundations to fuel the transformation. Randy Parry left his teaching job and became a full-time revitalizer-in-chief. The town of Howard became the host to twenty-first-century businesses such as an organic beef producer and a wind-turbine repair shop.

"It all started small," said Parry. "It's like when I took over the basketball team at the high school. They were just coming off of a losing season and you couldn't get people to come into the gym. But then you start to win and a few people come, and then more people come. And then we started winning a lot." To date, Parry has discussed the rebirth of Miner County with community leaders from thirty-three different states.

8.

A railroad and a South Dakota small town. Both crumbling. Both with a dense thicket of problems and no real resources to use in untangling them. In each situation, an unlikely leader emerged—a young man fresh out of business school and a high school basketball coach. And both succeeded by formulating solutions that were strikingly smaller than the problems they were intended to solve. (We've seen this asymmetry before, in the stories of Jerry Sternin in Vietnam and Bobby the troubled teenager.)

The challenges facing Miner County were big and sprawling: the decline of an industrial base, the aging of a population. The citizens understood these challenges well, but the knowledge was TBU—true but useless. It was paralyzing knowledge.

To the Rider, a big problem calls for a big solution. But if you seek out a solution that's as complex as the problem, you'll get the Food Pyramid and nothing will change. (The Rider will just spin his wheels trying to make sense of it.) The Rider has to be jarred out of introspection, out of analysis. He needs a script that explains how to act, and that's why the successes we've seen have involved such crisp direction. *Buy 1% milk. Don't spend cash unless it makes cash. Shop a little more in Miner County.*

We all hear a lot of "common sense" wisdom about change: People don't like to change; people resist change; people are set in their ways; people are stubborn. But here we've seen something else entirely: railroads made profitable, towns reborn, diets changed, and child abusers reformed.

Clarity dissolves resistance.

4

Point to the Destination

1.

Crystal Jones joined Teach For America in 2003. She was assigned to teach the first-grade class at an elementary school in Atlanta, Georgia. The school had no kindergarten, so for many of the kids, Jones would be their first teacher.

At the beginning of the year, the skill gaps among her students were daunting. She said, "I had two or three students who could recognize kindergarten sight words, and I also had some that couldn't even hold their pencils. The ones who had never been to school—their basic behavior wasn't where it needed to be for them to be in the classroom. I had students that, of course, didn't know their alphabet or their numbers. . . . They were all on different levels, and no one was really where they needed to be for first grade."

Jones felt confident that she could elevate the kids' abilities. She could create great lesson plans and activities (she could script the critical moves). But to what end? How do you show a room-ful of first graders where they're headed and why going there is worth the effort—in terms they can understand?

Well, here's a way *not* to do that, from another Teach For America teacher, who reported her goals for the year as follows:

> With respect to reading for the school year, I adminis-tered three diagnostics: CWT, Assessment of Compre-hension, and Monster Test. Using the CWT, I identified my classes' average as grade level 1.5 in September. My goal is to increase my students' word identification so as to ensure a class average of 3.0. Upon analyzing the re-sults of the Assessment of Comprehension, I identified my classes' average as a 41% in September. My goal is to increase my students' comprehension so as to ensure a class average of 80%. Using the Monster Test, I identi-fied my classes' average score as Semiphonetic/Phonetic. My goal is to increase my students' phonics and spelling skills to Transitional.

That ambitious and specific set of goals was probably quite use-ful to the teacher in her planning. But it obviously won't be use-ful in lighting a fire in the hearts of first graders.

Crystal Jones, in contrast, knew that if she wanted to moti-vate the kids, she had to speak their language. At the beginning of the school year, she announced a goal for her class that she knew would captivate every student: By the end of this school year, you're going to be *third graders*. (Not literally, of course, but in the sense that they would be at third-grade skill levels.)

That goal was tailor-made for the first-grade psyche. First graders know very well what third graders look like—they are bigger, smarter, and cooler. You know the feeling you get when you're admiring the grace and power of an Olympic athlete? That's the feeling first graders get about third graders.

Jones chose the goal carefully. She knew exactly what the third-grade standards in Georgia required, and she knew where her kids were starting. She genuinely thought she could close the gap.

One of her first efforts was to cultivate a culture of learning in her classroom, calling her students "scholars" and asking them to address one another that way. When people visited her classroom, she introduced her class as a group of scholars and asked them to define the term for the guest. They would shout, "A scholar is someone who lives to learn and is good at it." The scholars were encouraged to go home and share what they learned with their families.

One day, a scholar was called out of the classroom for administrative reasons, and some of the others in the room started groaning. In most classrooms it would have been a groan of jealousy—*Get me out of here, too.* Jones realized, to her surprise, that it was a groan of pity—*That kid is going to miss some "scholar work."* At that moment, Jones said, "I knew I had them."

By springtime, the kids' test scores had reached second-grade level. So Jones threw a graduation ceremony right before spring break. For the rest of the year, the kids took great pleasure in referring to themselves as "second graders." And by the end of the year, over 90 percent of the kids were reading at or above a third-grade level.

These were some of the same kids who, nine months earlier, didn't know the alphabet.

Crystal Jones's challenge is reminiscent of what Jim Collins and Jerry Porras, in *Built to Last,* their great study of long-lived business organizations, memorably called a BHAG: a Big, Hairy,

Audacious Goal. Henry Ford's BHAG early in the twentieth century was to "democratize the automobile"; Wal-Mart, in 1990,
set the goal of quadrupling in size to be a $125 billion company
by the year 2000. Collins and Porras defined a BHAG as "an
audacious 10-to-30-year goal to progress towards an envisioned
future," and their research showed that setting these big, motivating goals was a practice that distinguished lasting companies
from less successful ones.

In creating change, though, we're interested in goals that are
closer at hand—the kinds of things that can be tackled by parents
or middle managers or social activists. We want a goal that can be
tackled in months or years, not decades.

We want what we might call a *destination postcard*—a vivid
picture from the near-term future that shows what could be possible. That's the missing piece of what we've discussed so far.
We've seen the importance of pursuing bright spots, and we've
discussed ways of instructing the Rider *how* to behave, but we
haven't answered a very basic question: Where are we headed in
the end? What's the destination?

Crystal Jones provided a great destination postcard: *You'll be
third graders soon!* Notice that the goal she set for her students
didn't only direct the Rider; it also motivated the Elephant. It
was inspirational. It tapped into feeling. Collins and Porras knew
that goals should have an emotional component—a BHAG
shouldn't just be big and compelling; it should "hit you in the
gut." To a first grader, becoming a third grader in nine months is
a gut-smacking goal.

2.

Women with breast cancer flew to San Francisco to be treated by
Laura Esserman, a surgeon and an associate professor of surgery

at the University of California at San Francisco (UCSF). Patients loved Esserman for her warmth and empathy. She gave out her personal cell phone number to her patients, and she sometimes sang patients to sleep in the operating room as their anesthesia took effect.

Esserman's human touch was in sharp contrast to the usual treatment afforded women diagnosed with breast cancer. As if the diagnosis itself weren't frightening enough, women were often bounced around from place to place during the treatment cycle, adding stress. In a typical progression, described by a Stanford case study, a woman first notices a lump on her breast during a monthly self-exam. Anxious, she calls a doctor and waits a few days (or weeks) for an appointment. The doctor confirms that the lump should be examined, so the patient is referred to a radiologist at another facility to get a mammogram. Getting the results of the scan takes another agonizing few days.

The mammogram shows something suspicious, so she is referred to a surgeon, who meets her and again verifies that the lump is present. Unfortunately, the mammogram images didn't arrive at the surgeon's office before the visit, so there's another delay while radiology is contacted. The surgeon conducts a biopsy, which is sent to the pathology department to determine whether the growth contains cancerous cells. The woman is sent home to wait by the phone for the answer.

If cancer is detected, she undergoes surgery, and then the surgeon refers her to a radiation therapist for radiation treatment and to a medical oncologist for chemotherapy. Radiation and chemotherapy are conducted at different sites with different booking procedures and delays. In an attempt to smooth the process, a patient might have to collect her own records, films, and pathology slides and carry them around herself, sometimes even within the same hospital. The sequence might take weeks to unfold, and all while the woman is wondering, *Am I going to live through this?*

This anxiety-filled process appalled Laura Esserman, and she had a vision of how it could be different. What if there were a breast care clinic where a woman worried about a lump in her breast could walk in at the beginning of the day and walk out at the end of the day with an answer—either knowing that the lump was no problem, or if it was a problem, having a treatment plan already in hand?

The main barrier to this vision was the lack of coordination among medical departments. If they could be integrated more tightly, then weeks of agonizing waiting could be eliminated, the patient would not have to leave the building, and the experience would be designed around the patient's needs, not the departments'. That was Esserman's destination postcard, and it was an admirable one.

But as an associate professor at a large university medical center, Esserman was far down the totem pole, with few resources at her disposal. Even if she could start a breast care clinic, she would never be able to hire or fire the people who might work for it, and she couldn't even set their salaries. The medical departments, such as radiology and pathology, controlled the purse strings and the resources. The two most commonly used descriptions of the medical school at UCSF were "bureaucratic" and "political." "The departments have money, and the departments have turf, and you can't bring them together," said Meredithe Mendelsohn, who became Esserman's chief administrative director.

Esserman said, "The radiation oncologists report to radiation oncology. The surgeons report to the School of Medicine. The medical oncologists report to medical oncology. The nurses and staff report to the medical center. The psychologists and social workers report someplace else. So it's an organizational challenge to make people feel like they belong to something." Because Esserman wielded so little institutional power, her best assets for creating change were her own tenacity and her ability to sell a vision of what breast cancer care could be.

Esserman and Mendelsohn started small. They set up the Breast Care Center to operate for four hours one day per week. They cajoled the medical departments to start working together in more integrated ways. It took practice, and it took persistence. "Radiology, which does the mammographies, works like a train station," says Mendelsohn. "If your appointment's at 12:15, you're seen at 12:15 and that's how they operate." But Esserman's goal was to build treatment around the patients' needs, and those needs weren't always predictable enough to conform to radiology's schedule. Esserman worked with the radiologists to figure out how to create some flexibility in their traditionally rigid processes.

"We couldn't take up too much of radiology's time," said Mendelsohn, so they figured out how to improvise. "Dr. Esserman would see the patient in the morning, and she was the only doctor that would do it—she was the guinea pig—and then she would send them off, say 'Go have lunch. Go shopping. Come back at 1:00.' And during lunch time she would go to radiology, where she and the radiologist would sit and look through all of the images and decide what needed to happen next."

For the first year, the Center stuck with the one-day-per-week model. Then, once the work was going smoothly, Esserman expanded to two days per week. More surgeons started to get involved, and then nurses, and counselors, and support staff, and the snowball began.

Eventually, the Breast Care Center achieved enough success that it was offered an entire floor in a new cancer center being constructed by UCSF. "Where's radiology?" asked Esserman when she saw the layout. The cancer center master plan assumed that the radiology department would remain in its old building. But that would have made Esserman's "everything under one roof" vision impossible. So she agreed to give up one-third of the Breast Care Center's space to make room for a mammography unit on the same floor. (Onlookers were shocked—academic departments usually fought hard to secure space, and Esserman was giving up some of hers!)

Now Esserman had two powerful assets: a proper home for the Center and a staff who increasingly embraced her vision for a new kind of care. Patients flocked to the Breast Cancer Center. From 1997 to 2003, the number of patients seen per month skyrocketed from 175 to 1,300. In time, the Center became a major source of revenue for UCSF and a recognized national leader in breast cancer care and research. The Center evolved to be the place that Esserman described in her destination postcard.

Here's how Esserman describes the way the patient's experience looks today:

> When a patient comes into the Breast Care Center, I can walk around the corner and look at her films that day. While she's in the room, we can do a biopsy and get the diagnosis in five minutes. We have a gynecologist on staff that specializes in fertility issues for women with breast cancer, and I have a psychologist and genetic counselor on staff that is one of the nurse practitioners. The patient stays in the same place and doesn't need to go anywhere.

The Breast Care Center also has a relaxing healing garden and a café that serves coffee. The boutique sells not only the usual flowers and gifts but also wigs and scarves for patients undergoing chemo.

"For the first time," said Esserman, "we put the woman at the center."

3.

When you describe a compelling destination, you're helping to correct one of the Rider's great weaknesses—the tendency to get lost in analysis. Our first instinct, in most change situations, is to offer up data to people's Riders: *Here's why we need to change. Here are the tables and graphs and charts that prove it.* The Rider loves this. He'll start poring over the data, analyzing it and poking holes in it, and he'll be inclined to debate with you about the conclusions you've drawn. To the Rider, the "analyzing" phase is often more satisfying than the "doing" phase, and that's dangerous for your switch.

Notice what happens, though, when you point to an attractive destination: The Rider starts applying his strengths to figuring out *how to get there.* For instance, after Esserman announced her "under one roof" vision, her team could start thinking through the implications of that: *Let's see, we'll never pull that off unless we have access to radiology, so we'll need to give up square footage to them . . .*

You have a choice about how to use the Rider's energy: By default, he'll obsess about which way to move, or whether it's necessary to move at all. But you can redirect that energy to helping you navigate toward the destination. For that to happen, you need a gut-smacking goal, one that appeals to both Rider and Elephant. Think of Esserman's "under one roof" vision or of Crystal Jones's challenge to her kids to become third graders.

Goals in most organizations, however, lack emotional resonance. Instead, SMART goals—goals that are Specific, Measurable, Actionable, Relevant, and Timely—have become the norm. A typical SMART goal might be "My marketing campaign will generate 4,500 qualified sales leads for the sales group by the end of Q3'09."

The specificity of SMART goals is a great cure for the worst sins of goal setting—ambiguity and irrelevance ("We are going to *delight* our customers every day in every way!"). But SMART goals are better for steady-state situations than for change situations, because the assumptions underlying them are that the goals are worthwhile. If you accept that generating 4,500 leads for the sales force is a great use of your time, the SMART goal will be effective. But if a new boss, pushing a new direction, assigns you the 4,500-leads goal even though you've never handled lead generation before, then there might be trouble. SMART goals *presume* the emotion; they don't generate it.

In looking for a goal that reaches the Elephant—that hits people in the gut—you can't bank on SMART goals. (There are some people whose hearts are set aflutter by goals such as "improving the liquidity ratio by 30 percent over the next 18 months." They're called accountants.) In the 1980s, a major study of corporate change efforts found that financial goals inspired successful change less well than did more emotional goals, such as the goal to provide better service to customers or to make more useful products. According to the researchers, "Effective visions expressed values that allow employees to identify with the organization. . . . One manager at a glass company suggested, 'it's hard to get excited about 15% return on equity.'"

Destination postcards do double duty: They show the Rider where you're headed, and they show the Elephant why the journey is worthwhile.

CLINIC

How Can You Get Corporations to Avoid
Short-Term Thinking?

SITUATION Judy Samuelson heads a policy think tank within the Aspen Institute called the Business and Society Program. It's committed to fighting "short-termism" in the business world. Samuelson points out that it's hard to solve global problems (global warming, poverty, energy needs) without the help of the business sector. After all, some businesses have more resources than entire countries. But businesses with a short-term focus can't afford to tackle long-term problems. Samuelson recounts a conversation with the CEO of a huge financial services firm. He tells her that he would like to be involved with the big issues of the day, but he points to the 90-day calendar posted on his wall and admits, "This is my reality." Translation: The public markets are forcing him to adopt a quarter-by-quarter focus. How can Samuelson—the leader of a small nonprofit—possibly influence such massive forces? How can she fight "short-termism"? [This is an actual situation, ongoing as of 2009. We'll discuss some of Samuelson's strategy along with some of our own thinking.]

WHAT'S THE SWITCH AND WHAT'S HOLDING IT BACK? We want executives to act with a longer-term mindset. So what's stopping them? First, there's a big Rider problem here. We hope your radar went off when you read the phrase "short-termism." It's useful as a one-word summary of the problems that Samuelson is fighting, but to provoke change, we've got to script the critical moves. (A "long-term mindset" isn't a behavior.) Second, there's a Path problem: The culture of the stock market encourages short-term thinking. Interestingly, the Elephant probably isn't the villain here. Most execs would probably prefer, all things being equal, to have a longer-term focus. That means motivation probably isn't our obstacle. Finally, let's be realistic: Samuelson is seeking a *massive* change. We can't expect to generate a magic-bullet solution. But big changes can start with small steps. How can we improve Samuelson's odds?

HOW DO WE MAKE THE SWITCH?

• *Direct the Rider.* **1. Script the critical moves.** Samuelson finds a way to translate her big-picture goal into specific behaviors. One insight: Let's convince executives to stop giving quarterly earnings guidance. Backstory: Investors know the bizarre Kabuki dance of earnings guidance, but other people may not. Each quarter, a public company "sets expectations" for the earnings per share it will deliver in its next quarterly financial report. Then, when the company files its report, a miracle occurs: The company announces that it beat the expectations by a penny per share! Oh, glory! The markets find this little game inspiring, but none of it is required by law. A company could simply file its quarterly financial reports without any advance expectation-setting. In other words, Samuelson has located a *specific behavior that's within the control of the executive.* The expectations dance is the perfect symbol of short-term thinking. **2. Point to the destination.** Samuelson should sell the vision here. How will life be different for the progressive CEO who rids himself of the burden of managing to the quarter rather than to the long term? What's the destination postcard?

• *Motivate the Elephant.* **1. Shrink the change.** Note that by focusing on quarterly earnings guidance, Samuelson shrinks the change. It's an attainable first step on the road to long-term thinking. **2. Appeal to identity.** Samuelson should play up the fact that the CEOs of some well-respected companies—GE, Microsoft, Coca-Cola, Google, and others—have already made this change. If other CEOs want to act like "forward-thinking CEOs," this is the step they need to take.

• *Shape the Path.* **1. Build a habit.** Remember the story of Donald Berwick and the campaign to save 100,000 lives? Berwick made it easy for hospitals to join the campaign. They simply submitted the hospital CEO's signature on a one-page form. At that point, Berwick's team swooped in to help the hospital build the new habits. What if Samuelson could make it that easy to join a "No Earnings Guidance" campaign? Her team should offer a simple checklist of things to address (including legal, PR, and operational issues) and support the companies as they change. **2. Rally the herd.** Some CEOs are reluctant to discontinue earnings guidance. They worry that investors will think it's a signal that the company is in trouble and will hurry to sell off their stock. Samuelson could help CEOs counter this perception by organizing a "Drop the Guidance" day on a certain date. That way, the timing of the announcement would be less conspicuous. Also, by linking together business leaders who are intrigued by the idea, Samuelson could encourage a bandwagon effect. As we'll see later, behavior is contagious.

4.

Destination postcards—pictures of a future that hard work can make possible—can be incredibly inspiring. The first graders dreamed of being third graders. Laura Esserman's team imagined a new kind of breast care clinic that would cater to the needs of the patient.

But what if your team isn't inspired?

What if, in fact, members of your team are secretly or not-so-secretly resistant to the vision of the future you've articulated? This introduces a new enemy: rationalization. For instance, surely we've all made a New Year's resolution to "Be healthier." We conjure up a mental image of our future selves—fit and svelte—and we like what we see. But, deep inside us, the commitment isn't there. A few days after January 1, we get hungry, and we see that gorgeous bag of Cheetos in the pantry.

There's no question what the Elephant wants: a big mouthful of Cheetoian goodness. And when the Elephant wants something badly, the Rider can be trusted to go along—what choice does he have?—and he may actually begin to formulate rationalizations to excuse the breach. *Well, we did eat that salad last Thursday. And for Pete's sake, we bought 1% milk at the grocery store! We don't want to go overboard on this diet. A few Cheetos is a reasonable reward for good behavior.* And presto! We eat the Cheetos! Even more impressive than that, we'll still be convinced, in our heart of hearts, that we're being healthier.

A big-picture goal like "Be healthier" is necessarily imprecise, and that ambiguity creates wiggle room for the Elephant. It makes it easy to rationalize failure. One response to this dilemma is to set super-prescriptive goals. Your firm might announce, "We will boost revenue by 14.2 percent this year." Certainly, that's much better than just urging employees to do their best. But although numbers themselves are wiggle-proof, the way we deal with numbers isn't. For instance, if your firm achieved a 12.3 percent increase in revenue, do you really think anyone would get fired? Or is it more likely that a compelling rationalization would smooth over the discrepancy? *Team, in this economic climate, we should consider 12.3 percent a huge victory!*

The danger is present in our personal lives, too. Imagine that, in hopes of reining in your alcohol consumption, you set a goal of drinking no more than one glass of wine per night. Well, let's face it, there will come a night when your Elephant is going to crave more than one, and that's when the boundaries are going to get fuzzy. You'll "honor" your one-glass rule—by filling your glass all the way to the brim. Or you'll mentally trade an extra drink now for a zero-drink night in the (speculative) future. We're all loophole-exploiting lawyers when it comes to our own self-control.

If you're worried about the possibility of rationalization at home or at work, you need to squeeze out the ambiguity from your goal. You need a black-and-white (B&W) goal. A B&W goal is an all-or-nothing goal, and it's useful in times when you worry about backsliding. Maybe your B&W goal for your alcohol consumption could be "No wine ever." No wiggle room there. And what if we changed our New Year's resolution from "Be healthier" to "Gym every day" or even "No more Cheetos"? Those goals leave nowhere to hide. Either you've got damning orange Cheeto dust on your fingers or you don't.

Note that B&W goals—"No more Cheetos," "No wine ever"—are not inspiring at all. They're 100 percent restrictive. Furthermore, they are scripting critical behaviors rather than painting a picture of a destination. Is it possible to combine the emotional power of a destination postcard with the rationalization-squashing strength of a B&W goal? Yes, and to see how, consider the case of British Petroleum (BP). In 1991, BP announced a B&W goal that shocked its employees who had spent years in the oil industry. It was the multibillion-dollar equivalent of "No more Cheetos."

5.

For most of the twentieth century, oil explorers had trusted their gut, which worked out well, because their gut was pretty smart and oil reserves were largely untapped. In the 1960s, Jim Vanderby, one of the great BP explorers, went to Egypt. The first four or five holes he drilled there were dry. His superiors at BP sent him a telegram and told him to stop trying. He didn't get the telegram, or so he claimed. Regardless, he drilled again, and on his next try in the Gulf of Suez, he tapped into the world's first multibillion-barrel oil field.

BP's good fortune continued in the 1960s and 1970s, with huge discoveries such as Prudhoe Bay in Alaska (1968) and Montrose in the North Sea (1971), among others. Toward the late eighties, though, the mega-hits slowed down. "What was changing was that fields were getting more difficult to find," said Pete Callagher, a senior leader at Amoco, which merged with BP in the late 1990s. "The older fields were *huge,* visible on 2-D seismic technology. Targets became smaller and more difficult to see. So the skill sets changed."

As the landscape changed, BP's strategy evolved. In 1989, its leaders locked onto the exploration doctrine that would guide them for the next fifteen years. They would focus only on *big* fields and stop competing for the smaller ones, thereby avoiding competition with hundreds of smaller competitors. They also decided to attack costs. At that time, BP was considered by many to be the world's most effective exploration company. Even so, BP's leaders believed it was spending far too much on exploration. They committed to slash exploration costs from $5 per barrel to $1. People inside the company thought this goal was outrageous.

To reduce costs so drastically, BP needed to minimize the number of "dry holes" it drilled. The historical success rate for drilling a new well was roughly 1 out of 8. BP's rate was much better: 1 out of 5. To cut exploration costs from $5 to $1 per barrel, though, it would have to go from "good" performance to unprecedented performance. (Some said *impossible* performance.)

Researchers at BP began to investigate past explorations. One thing they studied was whether explorers were good at predicting the success of their wells. They reviewed wells that had been drilled over a 10-year period and found that, on average, explorers' predictions were extraordinarily accurate. Their average prediction was that a well had a 20 percent chance of hitting, and on average, 20 percent of wells actually hit.

But the averages concealed some fascinating biases. For instance, when the explorers gave the well a 20 to 70 percent probability of hitting, their predictions were pretty accurate. But when the explorers predicted a greater than 75 percent chance of success, the wells hit nearly all the time. Also, wells that had been given a 10 percent chance of success actually had more like a 1 percent chance. So the explorers' instincts about the wells were correct—they knew the good ones from the bad ones. But there was information, especially for high- and low-probability wells, that they weren't using.

Traditionally, the explorers had been salesmen for their wells, pressing top management for the green light to drill. In the 1980s, they had learned that the way to sell management was to use the tools of risk economics—in particular, the concept of *expected value*.

Expected-value calculations are bulletproof in situations where the risks and returns are well understood. If I flip a coin, you can feel confident that you have a 50 percent probability of winning. But what are the odds of hitting a gusher? And if you hit one, what's the payoff? Those are subjective estimates. When you feed subjective estimates into an expected-value calculation, a precise number pops out, giving the illusion of scientific certainty. ("Our expected value for this well is $112.8 million. It's a no-brainer—let's drill it.")

It didn't go unnoticed among explorers that if they really wanted to drill a well, they could simply tinker around with the math in a spreadsheet. If they jacked up the hit rate or the payoff, the expected value obediently inflated. (This tinkering probably wasn't malicious or even *conscious*. Remember, when the Elephant really wants something, the Rider can be trusted to find rationalizations for it.)

More subtly, the use of expected value made people think about drilling as a numbers game. As Jim Farnsworth, a top leader in BP's exploration unit, said, "Explorers think in terms of risk probabilities. People get so caught up in the numbers that they think, 'Well, if we drill ten of these 1-in-10 wells, we'll hit at least one of them and we'll all make a lot of money. But when you do the analysis, you realize that something that is 1 in 10 *never* works, so it's a false sense of statistical clarity."

The odds-playing gave everyone a false sense of comfort. *Hey, if we drill some dry holes, one of the other holes will hit and make up for it.* Explorers were like venture capitalists, hoping for an eBay or a Google to bail them out of an otherwise lousy portfolio.

If you were an executive at BP, hoping to cut your exploration costs by 80 percent, your first mission would be to remove this false sense of comfort. The ambiguity in the goal is allowing rationalization to creep in. So how could you change your team's behavior so that every single drilling operation is taken seriously? How could you leave your team's Riders with nowhere to hide?

Consider the alternatives for your new strategic rallying cry: "We'll double our strikes!" "No more dumb holes!" "Let's maximize expected value!" Some of them sound promising, but notice the fudge room in all of them. "No more dumb holes" would be easy for any competent Rider to dodge. Would any self-respecting explorer think he was drilling a *dumb* hole? "Doubling strikes" is better, but there's still room to rationalize a lot of dry holes. And as for "maximize expected value," well, let's just move on.

Ian Vann, BP's head of exploration at the time, figured out a way to eliminate the fudge room. He announced his new vision: "No dry holes."

None.

Explorers were irate. They thought the goal was preposterous. Their leaders were asking the impossible. Dry holes had always been a normal and acceptable part of doing business. Remember, the number of dry holes outnumbered successes by a factor of 4. Now Vann was defining them as failure.

"No dry holes" was a painful B&W goal. Probabilistic predictions had always provided a cover for failure. As Jim Farnsworth said, "We wanted to get away from the language of probability, from people hiding behind a notion that if a 1-in-5 well didn't work, 'I told you it was 1 in 5 so I was right.' 'No dry holes' was an attempt to make people go to the absolute extreme limit, to make sure they'd looked at every piece of data and done the right analysis."

As explorers began talking about "No dry holes," they started taking off their explorer hats and putting on their geologist hats. Lots of things had to go right to create a productive oil field, and geologists had previously devised different tests to evaluate every geologic feature: Was the right carbon-rich substrate available to form oil? Was there a harder, impermeable base layer underneath the oil to capture and contain it if it formed? Even if the oil had formed at some point in geologic history, could subsequent underground pressures or temperatures have degraded the oil?

The idea of eliminating dry holes prompted geologists to become more systematic about mapping and aggregating the information they had. They color-coded maps—green for aspects that might support an oil field, amber for areas where information was missing, and red for clear counter indications. Then they overlaid the color-coded maps on top of one another, each layer representing a different geologic test. They decided to drill only in regions that were green on every conceivable dimension.

"No dry holes" was effective in stamping out two kinds of rationalizations for poorly conceived drilling operations. One was "learning"—the convenient notion that even if a particular well doesn't hit, the team will learn so much from the process that future operations will be more successful. Vann said, "I can give you a hundred examples where people made a mistake because they didn't use knowledge they already had, for every one example where we learn something that is valuable for next time." The other common rationalization was that certain wells had "strategic value." Callagher said, "The last defense of the charlatan is always that something is 'strategic.' 'This is a strategic well, so we have to drill it.'" "No dry holes" removed the fudge room. A well might be strategic, or it might not be, but either way, it better not be dry.

David Bamford, BP's chief geophysicist during much of this period, said, "I can think of several examples of where technical teams knew a proposed well would be dry and yet senior management wanted to drill it because of pressure from government or business partners." Previously it was hard for frontline people to object to these decisions. When your manager is the only one who knows what the "partner pressure" consists of, how can you possibly raise a credible objection?

The "No dry holes" goal boosted the confidence of the frontline employees. The Exploration Forum—the peer group accountable for exploration decisions—became more outspoken and pushed back on "strategic reasons" to engage in low-probability explorations. After all, the strategy was "No dry holes," not "No dry holes unless drilling helps to placate an important partner." The strategy had changed in a way that gave lower-level employees an equally credible voice in the decision.

The B&W goal worked exactly as the management team had intended. When BP left nowhere for people to hide, its people stopped trying to hide. They tightened up their analyses, and they made fewer "play-the-odds" decisions. They got serious about using every available scrap of data in their decisions. And they toughened up their resistance to governmental and partner pressure.

By 2000, BP's hit rate was an industry-leading 2 in 3. That's *triple* the success rate of 1989. BP was still hitting dry holes, but the goal had stirred improvements that many had considered impossible. BP transformed itself when it eliminated its own wiggle room. *When we drill a hole, it better not be dry.*

Note that the leaders at BP didn't say, "Two out of three—

that's close enough. Let's celebrate!" Every dry hole was a failure, and there was no dodging it. Because they couldn't easily excuse failure—*It was strategic! It was a learning opportunity!*—they were left with only one choice: Drill smarter next time.

6.

If you worry about the potential for inaction on your team, or if you worry that silent resistance may slow or sabotage your change initiative, B&W goals may be the solution. But, to be clear, you won't always need a goal that's so unyielding. Crystal Jones's call to become a third grader was not a B&W goal. Let's face it, if kids got third-grade-level scores on math and science but not on vocabulary, we'd all let them "graduate." Laura Esserman's vision for the Breast Care Center wasn't B&W, and it didn't need to be.

What is essential, though, is to marry your long-term goal with short-term critical moves. Esserman's vision was compelling, but it would have been empty talk without lots of behavior-level execution.

You have to back up your destination postcard with a good behavioral script. That's a recipe for success. What you *don't* need to do is anticipate every turn in the road between today and the destination. It's not that plotting the whole journey is undesirable; it's that it's impossible. To think that you can plot a turn-by-turn map to the end, like a leader's version of Mapquest, is almost certainly hubris.

When you're at the beginning, don't obsess about the middle, because the middle is going to look different once you get there. Just look for a strong beginning and a strong ending and get moving.

7.

The average investor might make stock-picking decisions by listening to Jim Cramer or reading news reports or compulsively watching CNBC. But big institutional investors, such as philanthropic foundations or teachers' retirement funds, get special attention from Wall Street. Historically, investment banks sponsored research departments as a free service to institutional investors. The exchange was clear: The bank hoped that if it made good recommendations, then the investors would use the bank's traders to buy and sell stocks, bringing in revenue for the bank.

Because research is, in essence, a lure for big investment dollars, it is taken very seriously on Wall Street. Every year, *Institutional Investor* magazine asks big investors to assess the research they've received. Based on those responses, the magazine ranks the research analysts in each industry and also provides an overall ranking for the research departments on Wall Street. These *Institutional Investor* rankings are treated like holy writ. They drive (huge) bonuses to individual analysts, and they attract customers to the banks with the best research departments.

In 1986, Shearson Lehman's research department ranked a humiliating fifteenth. Top executives at Shearson wanted a new leader, so they recruited Jack Rivkin, who had built Paine Webber's research department into a powerhouse. The execs' expectations for Rivkin were clear: Get us into the Top 5.

Rivkin's first impressions of the department were not promising. "When I got to Lehman, the research department was a mess. It got no respect." One of Shearson's top analysts, Elaine Garzarelli, said, "The department wasn't disciplined. . . . People did whatever they wanted to do. They didn't have to talk at regular meetings; they didn't have to submit reports at certain times. Absolutely no mention was ever made of the *Institutional Investor* All-America team."

Rivkin made many formal changes to the department: He hired a number two, Fred Fraenkel. He successfully petitioned Shearson for a much larger staff and budget. He fired deadwood on the team. He changed the compensation system for the team.

These changes were vital, but ultimately, Rivkin had to influence the day-to-day behavior of the analysts on his team. As an analogy, consider a general manager (GM) running a baseball team. If you have more money at your disposal, you can sign more talented players. You can trade underperformers. You can offer your team a bonus for making the playoffs. These changes are important, but they don't directly influence the way players play. To do that, you need a coach.

Rivkin was both GM and coach. As a coach, he knew he needed members of his team to improve their work dramatically, and that meant he needed to script some of their early moves. He started by announcing that he expected analysts to initiate at least 125 client conversations per month. He required them to take notes on their conversations and post them to the internal network. Both the quantity and the quality of analysts' contacts became a matter of public record. One newly hired analyst said, "Once the report card on analyst contacts was electronically pinned up on a board, all the analysts began trying to get to the front section of the rankings; no one wanted to be near the end. . . . The analysts started asking one another: 'How do you make so many calls? Where do you find the time?'"

The 125-call benchmark jolted the department, snapped it out of its lackadaisical attitude. Most of the analysts began working 12 to 15 hours per day, nearly every day of the year. (Note the clarity of the instructions—this is Rivkin's 1% milk campaign.)

Rivkin also sought to build a team mentality in the department, fighting against the traditional culture of self-interested cowboys. He demanded that, when analysts were making presentations to clients, they cite their colleagues' work at least twice. "I don't want to hear 'I—I—I' in the presentation. I want to hear 'we,' and I want to hear other people's names." The forced (at first) sharing of ideas and credit made the team as a whole better, but it also benefited the individual analysts by exposing them to information they otherwise wouldn't have encountered.

Rivkin didn't just script the critical moves—*Make 125 calls, and cite your colleagues' work*—he also pointed to the destination: *We're going to crack the* I.I. *(*Institutional Investor*) Top 5.* That was something everyone in his department understood and aspired to.

In fact, there was a joke that circulated in the department: "*I.I.* or Die." But the aspiration was serious. Within eighteen months of the turnaround, a full 95 percent of one group of newly minted analysts broke onto the individual *I.I.* analyst rankings for their industry. Customers were noticing the extra attention they got from Shearson analysts, and for the first time, Shearson analysts were top-of-mind when *Institutional Investor* magazine called investors to ask who they relied on most.

The direction set by Rivkin prepared the department for a contrarian bet that left the department alone on Wall Street. It was a bet that would cement Shearson's place in the *I.I.* rankings.

In 1988, a Shearson analyst began investigating a drug called Epogen, made by Amgen and distributed by Johnson & Johnson. Epogen is a synthetic version of a hormone called erythropoietin, which increases the body's production of red blood cells. Red blood cells are responsible for ferrying oxygen to all the cells of the body. Epogen would give them a boost, making the drug the perfect treatment for various types of serious anemia—for example, in patients whose blood cells were damaged by chemotherapy. At the time, the drug was winding its way through the drug approval process. With its release imminent, stock investors began to make their bets on how the drug would sell, which would in turn drive Amgen's stock price.

Other research departments had identified one major market for the drug, but Shearson analysts thought there might be others. Surely, they reasoned, there'd be other uses for a drug that increased red blood cell production. So they dived into the research process. Fred Fraenkel said, "Every analyst and every assistant made calls. They called about 100 hospitals and pharmacies around the world, estimating the market potential for the drug. Once they had the data together, they knew Amgen had a multibillion-dollar drug on its hands. No research department could have possibly made this estimation with just one analyst and an assistant."

Shearson's analysts defied the conventional wisdom by predicting that Amgen had a blockbuster on its hands. Shearson's team was so confident, in fact, that it published ads touting its findings in the *New York Times* and *Wall Street Journal*.

They were right. Epogen became Amgen's first blockbuster drug and, at that time, was the most successful drug of the whole biotech industry. In 1990, Shearson was ranked at the top of the *Institutional Investor* All-America Research Team. In just three years, Shearson had leapfrogged from fifteenth to first.

The call on Amgen was something that Rivkin never could have anticipated, and it would have been pointless to try. He focused on what he could control: He provided a destination postcard ("*I.I.* or Die"), and he scripted some moves that would give his people a head start. He had the beginning right and the ending right, and when the Amgen situation popped up in the middle, the team was ready.

8.

So far we've learned a great deal about the Rider and his many strengths and weaknesses. On the plus side of the ledger, the Rider is a visionary. He's willing to make short-term sacrifices for long-term payoffs (which is why he fights so often with the Elephant, who generally prefers immediate gratification). He's a clever tactician, too—give him a map and he'll follow it perfectly. But we've also seen plenty of evidence of the Rider's flaws—his limited reserves of strength, his paralysis in the face of ambiguity and choice, and his relentless focus on problems rather than solutions.

Here's the good news: The Rider's strengths are substantial, and his flaws can be mitigated. When you appeal to the Rider inside yourself or inside others you are trying to influence, your game plan should be simple.

First, *follow the bright spots.* Think of the Vietnamese children who stayed well nourished against the odds, or the Genentech sales reps who racked up sales against the odds. As you analyze your situation, you're sure to find some things that are working better than others. Don't obsess about the failures. Instead, investigate and clone the successes.

Next, *give direction to the Rider*—both a start and a finish. Send him a destination postcard ("You'll be a third grader soon!"), and script his critical moves ("Buy 1% milk").

When you do these things, you'll prepare the Rider to lead a switch. And you'll arm him for the ongoing struggles with his reluctant and formidable partner, the Elephant.

**MOTIVATE
THE
ELEPHANT**

5

Find the Feeling

1.

In 1992, Target was a $3 billion regional retailer, a pip-squeak compared to its competitors Kmart ($9 billion) and Wal-Mart ($30 billion). But it aspired to be different. Even in those days, the chain's advertising was hip and fashionable. Unfortunately, the store's merchandise didn't deliver on the advertising's promise. Customers complained: *I see all these great ads, but when I come to the store, you've got the same boring stuff as Wal-Mart.*

You already know how this movie ends. Over the following fifteen years, Target became "Tar-ZHAY," the $63 billion giant, the Apple of the retailing world, the keeper of the beloved bull's-eye, the champion of design. The new era started with the iconic Michael Graves teakettle and expanded over the years to Todd Oldham bedding and Isaac Mizrahi shower curtains and Mossimo sweaters and countless other products that combined the holy duo of hip and cheap.

The beginning and end points of the Target tale are pretty well known. But we suspect you don't know much about the middle, and that's a shame, because what happened in the middle was *the change*. It didn't happen in the boardroom. It happened because of people like Robyn Waters.

Waters had no intention of working for Target. She was a self-described fashion snob, and she'd vowed not to come back to Minnesota, where she was raised, and where winter takes over much of fall and spring. She certainly had no intention of working for a *discounter*. She had an enviable job at the posh Jordan Marsh department store and was living in high style: "I was going to Italy and attending meetings with Armani and Versace and rubbing shoulders with all the fashionistas, and that was really cool when you're in your mid-thirties. But then one day we all got laid off. So that's how I came to be open-minded."

She joined Target in 1992 as the "ready-to-wear" trend manager, which made her responsible for black stirrup pants, sweats, and Looney Tunes T-shirts. She'd wondered how she'd managed to slip from Versace to Tweety Bird.

The company was at an important inflection point when she joined. Bob Ulrich had just retired as CEO, and he'd become chairman of the board. He had a very clear vision of Target as an "upscale discounter" that would differentiate itself through design. He dreamed that Target's bull's-eye would become a "lovemark," as respected and well loved as Coca-Cola or the Beatles or Lego. He wanted the bull's-eye to be as ubiquitous as McDonald's golden arches.

At the time, though, Target was a long way from realizing that vision. The merchants at Target—the people who select the merchandise that will show up for sale in various departments—had traditionally been copycats. Waters said the mindset among the clothing merchants had been to "find the best seller this year, take it to Asia, knock it off, and sell it next year at half the price." For Target to become a design powerhouse, the company had to stop lagging the trends and start riding the trends. That was Waters's mandate in the trend department.

The problem was that Waters had almost no power to advance this "trend-right" vision. The merchants didn't have to deal with her. "I had to win them over. I could never mandate, 'We have to have purple this year because that's the trend,'" she recalled.

Waters slowly built up believers. An early convert was the merchant responsible for turtlenecks. She was fed up with using the same tired patterns each year—you know, the cutesy snowflake-and-reindeer prints used by every discount retailer. So, at Waters's urging, she hired a designer to create some fresh patterns, and as they both predicted, sales improved dramatically.

These early-adopter experiments gave Waters much-needed success stories. Since Target had an analytical, numbers-driven culture, publicizing the early results was critical. Waters could point to "heroes" in the organization who'd taken a risk and succeeded. ("Check out what the turtleneck merchant did.")

For a time in retail, trendy clothing was neutral in color. Everything was gray, white, khaki, tan, or black. Then, one season, color exploded at the fabric shows and in the retailers in London and Paris. It wasn't an obscure trend; it was a big wave. So, as the design champion at Target, Waters needed to get her merchants excited about color. But the merchants, being numbers driven, would review the past few years' sales and see that color hadn't sold. (In this situation, a Rider appeal couldn't possibly succeed because the data contradicted Waters's position.)

Waters had to get creative. She went to the candy store at FAO Schwarz, where you could buy M&Ms in whatever color you wanted, and brought huge bags full of bright-colored M&Ms

to her internal meetings. She poured the candy into a glass bowl, creating cascades of turquoise and hot pink and lime green. "People would go 'Wow,' and I'd say, 'See, look at your reaction to color.'"

She brought in samples of Apple's recently released iMac computers—in lime, strawberry, grape, and tangerine—which had been a sensation. For the first time, consumers were choosing the color of their computers with the same seriousness they used to choose the color of their cars. And she constantly brought in photographs from boutiques around the world. She'd show a merchant the photo of a polo assortment and say, "See how they have three neutrals, and a mild yellow, and then they add the bright blue for a pop." Then she'd create a mock-up display with actual clothing samples so the merchants could see for themselves, *Yup, that blue color pops*. And, soon after, that blue polo shirt would show up on the floor of Target, for one clothing line, for one season.

This is how organizational change happens.

When Waters talks about this period, she is emphatic that she's not the "hero" of the Target story. She says she was one person among many who managed to transform the company. However you assess her contribution, the remarkable thing is that her successes came despite a lack of authority and resources. Waters said, "I had no head count at the time. I was always borrowing people, and my budgets never balanced. But I kept getting support from merchants who would say, 'Oh, I've got an extra head count over here. And you can hire this designer, but she's only going to work on our stuff.' And in the next division they'd say, 'Wow, I want one, too.'"

Not only did Waters lack control over the merchants, she didn't even speak their language. Indeed, the biggest mystery of Waters's success might well be this: In the analytical culture of

Target, where numbers were the lingua franca, why did a bunch of demonstrations seem to make the difference?

2.

In *The Heart of Change,* John Kotter and Dan Cohen report on a study they conducted with the help of a team at Deloitte Consulting. The project team interviewed over 400 people across more than 130 companies in the United States, Europe, Australia, and South Africa, in hopes of understanding why change happens in large organizations. Summarizing the data, Kotter and Cohen said that in most change situations, managers initially focus on strategy, structure, culture, or systems, which leads them to miss the most important issue:

> . . . the core of the matter is always about changing the behavior of people, and behavior change happens in highly successful situations mostly by speaking to people's feelings. This is true even in organizations that are very focused on analysis and quantitative measurement, even among people who think of themselves as smart in an MBA sense. In highly successful change efforts, people find ways to help others see the problems or solutions in ways that influence emotions, not just thought.

In other words, when change works, it's because leaders are speaking to the Elephant as well as to the Rider.

Most of us, in Robyn Waters's shoes, would create a "business case" for the power of design. We'd compile a PowerPoint presentation with charts and graphs and strategically selected quotes from the chairman who'd embraced the design-forward vision.

When we finished our presentation, everyone in the room would understand what we meant. They might even agree! But would they change their behavior? Kotter's research suggests no.

Kotter and Cohen say that most people think change happens in this order: ANALYZE-THINK-CHANGE. You analyze, then you think, and then you change. In a normal environment, that might work pretty well. If you need to reduce duplication costs in your print shop by 6 percent, or if you need to shave off 5 minutes from your daily commute, then that process will serve you well. Kotter and Cohen note that analytical tools work best when "parameters are known, assumptions are minimal, and the future is not fuzzy."

But big change situations don't look like that. In most change situations, the parameters aren't well understood, and the future is fuzzy. Because of the uncertainty that change brings, the Elephant is reluctant to move, and analytical arguments will not overcome that reluctance. (If someone is unsure about whether to marry her significant other, you're not going to tip her by talking up tax advantages and rent savings.)

Kotter and Cohen observed that, in almost all successful change efforts, the sequence of change is not ANALYZE-THINK-CHANGE, but rather SEE-FEEL-CHANGE. You're presented with evidence that makes you feel something. It might be a disturbing look at the problem, or a hopeful glimpse of the solution, or a sobering reflection of your current habits, but regardless, it's something that hits you at the emotional level. It's something that speaks to the Elephant.

In staging demos for her colleagues at Target, Robyn Waters was honoring the SEE-FEEL-CHANGE philosophy. She set up displays that let the merchants see what was possible: *See how that blue polo shirt pops? See how it catches your attention and draws your attention?* She brought in iMacs and M&Ms and let people ooh and aah over them—"See, look at your reaction to color." *(And, by the way, wouldn't it be nice to be part of the same movement as Steve Jobs and Apple?)*

Waters thought carefully about what her colleagues would *see* because she knew what she wanted them to *feel*: energized, hopeful, creative, competitive. They took the bait.

Let's remember, too, the story about Jon Stegner from Chapter 1, the man who created the Glove Shrine. He knew his colleagues weren't enthused about his idea for centralized purchasing, so he didn't bother talking about the numbers. Instead, he showed them something that made them feel something. *(We really buy all these different kinds of gloves?)* SEE-FEEL-CHANGE.

Trying to fight inertia and indifference with analytical arguments is like tossing a fire extinguisher to someone who's drowning. The solution doesn't match the problem.

It can sometimes be challenging, though, to distinguish why people don't support your change. Is it because they don't understand or because they're not enthused? Do you need an Elephant appeal or a Rider appeal? The answer isn't always obvious, even to experts.

3.

Pam Omidyar, the founder of HopeLab, knew the struggles of teenagers with cancer. They endured weeks of brutal chemotherapy in the hospital and went home a mess—sapped of energy, their hair falling out, their throats raw and tender, their immune system wrecked. But when they finally walked out of the hospital to return home, there was one silver lining: The worst was likely over. Going forward, their obligations would be relatively simple: They'd need to immediately report any symptoms they developed, such as a fever, and take their medicine faithfully, which might include a regimen of antibiotics and low-dosage chemotherapy pills for two years.

But many teens simply failed to comply, partly because following the medication regimen wasn't easy. The side effects of chemotherapy, even at low doses, were rough—nausea, skin breakouts, tiredness, irritability. The side effects of the home regimen, though, were nothing compared to the horror of intensive chemotherapy, and by missing their doses, kids were risking a recurrence of their cancer. Steve Cole, the research director for HopeLab, says, "If you skip 20 percent of your doses, you don't just have a 20 percent higher chance of getting cancer again. Your odds go up 200 percent."

How could teens take such a terrible risk? Omidyar was convinced that teens simply weren't getting the message. She sought a new way of influencing their behavior—something unconventional, something that spoke in their language. Her inspiration: We'll make a video game.

After months of effort, HopeLab developed a game called Re-Mission. In the game, teens became Roxxi, a silver-suited nanobot who charged through the bloodstream zapping tumor cells with electric-green chemo-rays. In between rounds of gameplay, teens watched short "briefing" videos featuring Smitty, a mentor robot, who provided additional information about chemotherapy and recovery.

Re-Mission featured twenty levels of play, each lasting an hour and packed with information. The team at HopeLab was convinced that if it could get kids to play the whole game, any misunderstandings that could lead to noncompliance would be wiped out.

Eventually the team launched the first clinical trial for Re-Mission. In 2008, the results were announced in the medical journal *Pediatrics*. To the team's delight, the game had increased kids' adherence to their medication plans. The amount of chemotherapy drugs circulating in the blood of kids who played the game went up by 20 percent. That may not sound like much, but small differences in adherence make a big difference in health. The odds of surviving cancer double if you can bump up chemotherapy adherence by 20 percent.

But there was a surprise buried in the evidence of success. A lot of the kids didn't actually play the game all that much, attempting only one or two levels instead of the twenty that had been designed into the game. Yet even those early quitters ended up taking their medications more regularly. In fact, the teens who played only two levels were changing their behavior as much as the kids who played all twenty.

At first glance, that finding seemed as absurd as if you'd discovered that students got comparable scores on their algebra finals whether they took only one week of classes or a whole semester. Research director Cole acknowledged, "Clearly, in one or two levels we're not teaching them a whole lot, since the bulk of that time is spent flying around the body blowing things up." Why had the underutilized game been so effective at changing the kids' behavior?

Cole started asking around, trying to understand the puzzling result. One of his friends, a marketing professor at Stanford, said, "Think about this from a marketing perspective. We can change behavior in a short television ad. We don't do it with information. We do it with identity: 'If I buy a BMW, I'm going to be this kind of person. If I take that kind of vacation, I'm that kind of eco-friendly person.'"

And it dawned on Cole: When teens didn't comply with their drug regimen, the problem wasn't knowledge, it was emotion. He said, "It boils down to an identity thing. After you have gone through intensive chemo, you've had your life stolen from you by cancer. So the kids think, 'I just want to get back to being the original me.' They don't want to be 'the sick kid' anymore."

The game was making a gut-level emotional connection. You are Roxxi, the nanobot, boldly defeating cancer. You fuel your ray gun by taking chemotherapy and antibiotics. Medicine means power. And the educational videos that pop up occasionally, with the mentor-robot lecturing you about the importance of compliance, are completely irrelevant to the change that's going on. The change is not one of understanding but one of feeling. It's realizing that *I can do this. I'm in charge.* Chemo isn't a reminder of the sickness; it's how you get your life back—how you steal back the real you from cancer. Take the pills, and you can stop being a cancer kid forever.

CLINIC
How Can You Make Developers Care About the End-User?

SITUATION At many software companies, the developers—who are responsible for writing new software programs—fall in love with their code. When their programs are tested by customers, they can be skeptical of the customer feedback. At Microsoft, for instance, one test of a new feature showed that six out of ten users couldn't figure out how to use it. When the test lab shared the data with the developers, their reaction was, "Where'd you find six dumb people?" Many companies experience a form of this problem. Is it possible to convince developers to be more responsive to customer feedback?

WHAT'S THE SWITCH AND WHAT'S HOLDING IT BACK? Ultimately, companies need developers to tweak their software in response to feedback from customers; otherwise, the programs won't be successful. But sometimes developers resist or dismiss customer feedback and make only "token" revisions rather than trying to empathize with customers' difficulties. This is probably an Elephant problem—the developers understand what's being asked of them but resent being forced to change their beautiful code for the dummies in their audience. But let's not be too quick to treat developers as a "type" (e.g., as arrogant technologists). Character judgments like that reflect a psychological bias that we explore in Chapter 8. Let's focus on providing developers with more motivation and a smoother path.

HOW DO WE MAKE THE SWITCH?

• *Direct the Rider.* **1. Point to the destination.** We should paint a picture of the group glory that will result from a successful product launch. The developers will be software heroes, and they'll have a line on their résumés that will always be impressive. Listening carefully to the customer is simply a way to accelerate that glory. **2. Script the critical moves.** Are we being specific enough about what's needed from the developers? Imagine that we tell them that their program's "ease of use" is rated as "poor." What in the world can they do with that? Their Riders will spin for hours, trying to decide among dozens of possible improvements. It's our responsibility to define the critical moves—along the lines of, "We need to give people a quicker way to rotate these objects."

• *Motivate the Elephant.* **1. Find the feeling.** At Microsoft, the developers were invited to visit the usability testing lab. There, from behind a one-way mirror, they could watch real users struggling with their programs. It made all the difference. The test lab manager says that when developers see a user live, "Twenty ideas just immediately come to mind. First of all, you immediately empathize with the person. The usual nonsense answers—'Well, they can just look in the manual if they don't know how to use it,' or 'My idea is brilliant; you just found six stupid people' . . . that kind of stuff just goes out the door." **2. Grow your people.** Developers may worry that, if their code needs revising, it reflects negatively on their abilities. (We'll talk about more about this in Chapter 7, the section on the "fixed mindset.") We should stress that the test of a great developer isn't the quality of his or her first-draft code; it's how well the developer codes around the inevitable roadblocks. We should make an effort to praise ingenious solutions to customers' problems.

- *Shape the Path.* **1. Build habits.** Is the customer feedback coming at the most convenient time in the code development cycle? Developers have routines that work for them. Can we make an effort to snap the user-testing onto an existing routine, so we're not complicating the Path? **2. Tweak the environment.** At many companies, programmers are given the best computers. This practice is great for productivity but lousy for customer empathy. One manager says that every time his developers use machines a generation ahead of their customers' equipment, the software they create has usability problems. Why? Because the developers have no intuition about how slowly the software is running for typical end users. Solution: Require developers to program on the same machines customers use. (This is another Path solution that has been pursued by Microsoft.)

4.

When people push for change and it doesn't happen, they often chalk it up to a lack of understanding. A mom grouses, "If my daughter just *understood* that her driving habits are dangerous, she'd change." A scientist says, "If we could just get Congress to *understand* the dangers of global warming, they'd surely take legislative action."

But when people fail to change, it's not usually because of an understanding problem. Smokers understand that cigarettes are unhealthy, but they don't quit. American automakers in the early twenty-first century knew they were too dependent on the sales of SUVs and trucks (and thus on low oil prices), but they didn't innovate.

At some level, we understand this tension. We know there's a difference between knowing how to act and being motivated to act. But when it comes time to change the behavior of other people, our first instinct is to teach them something. *Smoking is really unhealthy! Your chemotherapy medicine is really important!* We speak to the Rider when we should be speaking to the Elephant.

This realization—that we can make an impeccably rational case for change and people still won't change—is pretty frustrating. Why did Robyn Waters need to go through all the trouble of staging demos for her colleagues at Target? Shouldn't the logic of design innovation have been compelling enough on its own?

Why can't we simply think our way into new behavior? The answer is that, in some cases, we really can't trust our own thinking.

5.

As you watch, a stranger walks into a room and sits down behind a table. He picks up a piece of paper and reads aloud a generic-sounding weather report: "Tomorrow, we'll see highs in the upper 80s with an overnight low of 53. . . ." He completes his "report" in about 90 seconds and walks out of the room.

Next, you're asked to guess his IQ.

You're part of a psychology experiment, and you object to the absurdity of the request. *I don't know anything about that guy. He just came into a room and read a report. It wasn't even his report— you gave it to him to read! How am I supposed to know his IQ!?*

Reluctantly, you make a wild guess. Separately, Fake Weatherman is asked to guess his own IQ. Who made a better guess?

Amazingly, you did, even though you know nothing about Fake Weatherman. Two psychologists, Peter Borkenau and Anette Liebler, from Universität Bielefeld in Germany, conducted this experiment, and they found that the strangers' IQ predictions were better than the predictions of those whose IQ was being predicted—about 66 percent more accurate.

To be clear, it's not so much that you're a brilliant predictor; it's that he's a lousy self-evaluator. We're all lousy self-evaluators. College students do a superior job predicting the longevity of their *roommates'* romantic relationships than their own.

Savor, for a moment, the preposterousness of these findings. Fake Weatherman has all the information, and you've got none. He's got decades of data—years' worth of grades, college entrance exam scores, job evaluations, and more. Fake Weatherman should be the world's foremost expert on Fake Weatherman!

If self-evaluation hinged on information alone, the findings of these studies would have been impossible. It'd be like discovering that you could beat randomly selected mothers on a trivia question about how many kids they have.

But self-evaluation involves *interpretation,* and that's where the Elephant intrudes. The Elephant tends to take the rosiest possible interpretation of the facts. ("My 2.1 GPA is a sign of my intelligence—it shows that my intellect simply isn't being challenged enough to keep me engaged.")

We've all heard the studies showing that the vast majority of us consider ourselves above-average drivers. In the psychology literature, this belief is known as a *positive illusion.* Our brains are positive illusion factories: Only 2 percent of high school seniors believe their leadership skills are below average. A full 25 percent of people believe they're in the top 1 percent in their ability to get along with others. Ninety-four percent of college professors report doing above-average work. People think they're at lower risk than their peers for heart attacks, cancer, and even food-related illnesses such as salmonella. Most deliciously self-deceptive of all, people say they are more likely than their peers to provide accurate self-assessments.

Positive illusions pose an enormous problem with regard to change. Before people can change, before they can move in a new direction, they've got to have their bearings. But positive illusions make it hard for us to orient ourselves—to get a clear picture of where we are and how we're doing. How can we dispel people's positive illusions without raining down negativity on them?

6.

One way of cutting through positive illusions is suggested by an example from Massachusetts in a state agency called the Department of Youth Services. DYS dealt with delinquent kids—it was both a corrections agency and a social service organization. In the late 1970s, Massachusetts led a pioneering effort to overhaul its juvenile justice system, scaling back its youth prisons in favor of a network of nonprofits—halfway houses, group homes, outpatient counseling centers, job centers, and more. The goal of these nonprofits was to rehabilitate young offenders and keep them in their home communities.

As Massachusetts embraced this network model, DYS had to change substantially. The agency started working primarily through vendors—such as halfway houses and counseling centers—rather than delivering services to kids directly. As a result, agency staffers had to adapt the way they worked, and most of them handled the transition well.

Except for the accounting department.

The head of accounting was an authoritarian manager who ruled his department with an iron fist. He was known as a yeller; some colleagues called him Attila the Accountant. Attila was meticulous about following the rules, to a fault. If you submitted an expense report to his team and left off a single detail—a date, a subtotal—the accountants would bounce the report right back at you rather than simply filling in the detail themselves. Because of this perceived pettiness, Attila was "pretty much hated throughout the organization," recalled Sim Sitkin, who at that time was the director of planning and research for DYS. Attila's accounting group saw itself more as a watchdog than as an internal service provider.

When DYS shifted to the network model, the focus of the accounting department shifted, too. Now it was outside vendors who were submitting the reimbursement requests, not employees. And we can say one thing for Attila: He was consistent. He treated the new vendors with the same dictatorial style that he had used with his in-house colleagues. If vendors submitted reports that weren't perfect, he rejected them. This created big problems, though. As Sitkin said, "These nonprofits didn't have a lot of slack. They were living on a shoestring, and so delays in payments really jeopardized their ability to serve kids."

Sitkin and Gail Anne Healy, the deputy commissioner of DYS, began to field desperate calls from these nonprofits. In some cases, they couldn't make payroll unless Attila cut their checks quickly. Sitkin and Healy tried to reason with Attila; they tried to explain why it was important to cut the vendors some slack. But, as we've seen repeatedly, the knowledge wasn't enough to trigger a change. Attila stayed Attila.

Frustrated, Sitkin and Healy asked Attila to join them on a road trip. The three of them drove out to visit several of DYS's key service providers. Often, these providers were operating from old houses in run-down neighborhoods. Their offices looked dilapidated and chaotic. And in the midst of this environment, the staffers were earnestly trying to work small miracles. "The typical staffer," said Sitkin, "was like a combination of a beat cop and a social worker. Sometimes they struck you as people who might have once been in the same position as the kids they were trying to reach. They were working hard and obviously not making a lot of money."

During the visits, Attila saw firsthand how busy they were and how distracting the workplace was. They didn't have closed-door offices as he did. It was noisy, thanks to the kids who were living in the homes—they were constantly coming and going, or cooking meals, or just hanging around and talking. Social workers were rushing around, trying to keep tabs on the kids, and shuttling them to doctors' offices or job interviews.

Attila saw and felt the precarious financial situation of these nonprofits. They were hanging by a thread. When he held up one of their checks, it meant that they couldn't pay for something. They might have to delay payroll, or skimp on food, or postpone a doctor's visit for a kid who needed it. For the first time, Attila got a gut-check about the harm he was causing with his nitpicking. He came back to the office a transformed man.

Mind you, he was still Attila. He was still authoritarian, and he still yelled. But he changed what he was yelling about. "Before, he'd yell at his staff, 'Why did you give me this form when it's got something missing?!'" said Sitkin. "Afterwards, he switched to, 'Don't you realize what happens when we don't get this check out on time?! People have to make payroll!'"

Attila's transformation represented a victory over positive illusions. Before the field trip, if Attila had been asked to assess his performance as an accountant, he almost certainly would have put himself in the top 10 percent. In his mind, accounting was about paying attention to details, maintaining rigorous standards, and resisting political pressure.

He would have been right to score himself highly on those measures—but also self-serving. One reason we're able to believe that we're better-than-average leaders and drivers and spouses and team players is that we're defining those terms in ways that flatter us. *(I am really a good team player. I constantly give my coworkers useful tips on how to improve themselves!)* The ambiguity in terms like "leader" or "team player" enables our illusions—that's why it's so much harder for us to fancy ourselves better-than-average pole vaulters.

The ambiguity in being a "good accountant" dissolved when Attila met the social service workers. When he saw how hard they were working, and the raucous conditions they were working in, he couldn't help but empathize with them, and that feeling of empathy gave the lie to his positive illusions. *I thought being a good accountant was about rigor, but now I see that it's also about service.* Having been forced to experience the inadequacy of his old approach, he became a zealot for the new one: *Team, you better get those paychecks out ASAP—people are waiting on us!*

That may not be a heartwarming tale, but it's a big switch. Attila the Accountant was a hard case. Healy and Sitkin managed to break through his prickly exterior and make him feel something. And once he felt something, he changed. That outcome should give all of us hope that we can reach the Attilas in our own life (Attila the Dad, Attila the Boss, or Attila the Teenager).

7.

It's emotion that motivates the Elephant. In fighting for change, we've got to find the feeling. But *which* feeling? Anger, hope, dismay, enthusiasm, fear, happiness, surprise?

HopeLab built a video game for teenagers with cancer that gave them a feeling of control and power. Jon Stegner's Glove Shrine shocked the execs and gave them a determination to fix the matter. The Microsoft usability lab made developers feel empathy for their customers. Will connecting with any old feeling do?

We often hear that people change only when a crisis compels

them to, which implies that we need to create a sense of fear or anxiety or doom. Two professors at Harvard Business School, writing about organizational change, say that change is hard because people are reluctant to alter habits that have been successful in the past. "In the absence of a dire threat, employees will keep doing what they've always done." As a result, the professors emphasize the importance of crisis: "Turnaround leaders must convince people that the organization is truly on its deathbed— or, at the very least, that radical changes are required if the organization is to survive and thrive." In other words, if necessary, we need to *create* a crisis to convince people they're facing a catastrophe and have no choice but to move.

Similar beliefs about the importance of crisis once prevailed among therapists, most of whom believed that alcoholics or drug addicts couldn't be helped until they hit rock bottom. Back in the 1980s, at a professional conference, the therapist Ruth Maxwell gave a presentation suggesting to fellow therapists that the now-familiar technique of family "intervention" could be used to convince addicts to enter a treatment program even if they hadn't yet hit rock bottom. In her book *Breakthrough*, Maxwell wrote she was "nearly booed out of the room. . . . Coming from backgrounds deeply steeped in traditional psychiatric wisdom, they firmly believe that people cannot be treated unless they are motivated for treatment." And being "motivated" required a rock-bottom crisis.

Speaking of the perceived need for crisis, let's talk about the "burning platform," a familiar phrase in the organizational change literature. It refers to a horrific accident that happened in 1988 on the Piper Alpha oil platform in the North Sea. A gas leak triggered an explosion that ripped the rig in two. As a reporter wrote, "Those who survived had a nightmarish choice: to jump as far as 150 ft. down into a fiery sea or face certain death on the disintegrating rig." Andy Mochan, a superintendent on the rig, said, "It was fry or jump, so I jumped." He was eventually saved by a rescue mission involving NATO and the Royal Air Force.

Out of this human tragedy has emerged a rather ridiculous business cliché. When executives talk about the need for a "burning platform," they mean, basically, that they need a way to scare their employees into changing. To create a burning platform is to paint such a gloomy picture of the current state of things that employees can't help but jump into the fiery sea. (And by "jump into the fiery sea," what we mean is that they change their organizational practices. Which suggests that this use of "burning platform" might well be the dictionary definition of *hyperbole*.)

In short, the "burning platform" is a great, uplifting tale for your people: "Team, let's choose a dangerous plunge into the ocean over getting burned to death! Now get back to work!"

Leaving aside the silliness of the burning-platform metaphor, fear can indeed be a powerful motivator. Think of LBJ's famous "Daisy" campaign ad in 1964, in which a young girl holds a flower while a mushroom cloud rises behind her. If you vote for Goldwater, the ad suggested, you might as well nuke your child. Or consider the sleazy real-estate-sales boss in *Glengarry Glen Ross,* David Mamet's Pulitzer Prize–winning play: "First prize is a Cadillac Eldorado. . . . Second price is a set of steak knives. Third prize is you're fired."

Health educators, too, have gotten in on the act. Remember the ads showing photos of smokers' black, gnarled lungs, or the famous "This is your brain on drugs" commercial, which analogized drug users' brains to frying eggs (those visuals, in turn, made pot smokers very hungry).

There's no question that negative emotions are motivating. No one wants to see a kid nuked. But what, exactly, are these emotions motivating?

"If you have a stone in your shoe, it hurts and you'll fix the problem," said Martin Seligman, a psychologist at the University of Pennsylvania. In a sense, removing the stone from your shoe is what negative emotions are designed to do—to motivate specific actions. When you're angry, your eyes narrow and your fists clinch and you get ready for a confrontation. When you're disgusted, your nose wrinkles and you avoid whatever has grossed you out. When you're afraid, your eyes grow wide and your body tenses up and prepares to flee. On a daily basis, then, negative emotions help us avoid risks and confront problems.

Bottom line: If you need quick and specific action, then negative emotions might help. But most of the time when change is needed, it's not a stone-in-the-shoe situation. The quest to reduce greenhouse gases is not a stone-in-the-shoe situation, and neither is Target's mission to become the "upscale retailer," or someone's desire to improve his or her marriage. These situations require creativity and flexibility and ingenuity. And, unfortunately, a burning platform won't get you that.

So what will?

8.

In 1998, after psychologists had spent decades studying negative emotions, the psychologist Barbara Fredrickson wrote a provocative paper called "What Good Are Positive Emotions?" The paper became a classic. It eventually would be cited over a hundred times more often than a typical psychology paper, and it helped to fuel the rise of the discipline of positive psychology, which has yielded many popular books on happiness over the past few years.

As Fredrickson suggested in her title, positive emotions are a bit of a puzzle. Unlike negative emotions, they don't seem engineered to produce particular actions, such as punching or

fleeing or avoiding. They don't even have their own signature fa-
cial expressions. In fact, the emotions of joy, contentment, pride,
love, and interest all tend to produce the same generic "I'm
pleased" expression, which is known as the *Duchenne smile* (lips
curled up at the corners along with a crinkling in the muscles
around the eyes—or the way your spouse looks when you ask,
"Have you lost weight?"). Most of our positive emotions are fun-
neled through this same Duchenne mask, like a symphony
pumped through a tuba. Worse, we can't even distinguish readily
between a genuine Duchenne smile and a fake Duchenne smile,
as generations of beauty pageant winners have illustrated. (Hint:
A genuine Duchenne has the eye-crinkling that is hard to fake.)

Negative emotions tend to have a "narrowing effect" on our
thoughts. If your body is tensing up as you walk through a dark
alley, your mind isn't likely to wander over to tomorrow's to-do
lists. Fear and anger and disgust give us sharp focus—which is
the same thing as putting on blinders. Police detectives, for instance, frequently are frustrated by the testimony of gun-crime
victims, who often can provide a rich description of the gun held
by the perpetrator but can't recall whether the perpetrator had a
beard.

Fredrickson argues that, in contrast with the narrowing effects of the negative emotions, positive emotions are designed to
"*broaden* and *build*" our repertoire of thoughts and actions. Joy,
for example, makes us want to play. Play doesn't have a script, it
broadens the kinds of things we consider doing. We become willing to fool around, to explore or invent new activities. And because joy encourages us to play, we are *building* resources and
skills. For instance, kids learn physical skills through rough-and-
tumble play; they learn to work with objects by playing with toys
and blocks and crayons; they learn to get along with others by
pretending to be animals or superheroes.

The positive emotion of interest broadens what we want to investigate. When we're interested, we want to get involved, to learn new things, to tackle new experiences. We become more open to new ideas. The positive emotion of pride, experienced when we achieve a personal goal, broadens the kinds of tasks we contemplate for the future, encouraging us to pursue even bigger goals.

Most of the big problems we encounter in organizations or society are ambiguous and evolving. They don't look like burning-platform situations, where we need people to buckle down and execute a hard but well-understood game plan. To solve bigger, more ambiguous problems, we need to encourage open minds, creativity, and hope.

This brings us back to Robyn Waters, who was a master of positive emotions. She didn't try to create a burning platform: "Wal-Mart is eating our lunch! Target is on its deathbed! Come with me into the fiery seas!" Instead, she found a way to engage the fresh thinking and enthusiasm of her colleagues. *What if we had colors that "popped" like these iMacs? And look at this Paris boutique's display—what if we could arrange our sweaters like that?*

Waters helped shift an entrenched culture, product by product, because she found a way to instill hope and optimism and excitement in her coworkers. She found the feeling.

6

Shrink the Change

1.

In 2007, two researchers, Alia Crum and Ellen Langer, published a study of hotel maids and their exercise habits. The topic of the study may sound unremarkable, but the results were so surprising that you might find them hard to believe. (In fact, we'll argue that the researchers themselves came to the wrong conclusion in explaining their findings.)

Let's start at the beginning, with the maids.

The average hotel maid cleans fifteen rooms a day, and each room takes 20 to 30 minutes to complete. Take a moment and imagine an hour in the life of one of these maids. If you fast-forward through your brainfilm, you'll see the maids walking, bending, pushing, lifting, carrying, scrubbing, and dusting. What they're doing, in short, is exercising. A lot. In fact, they are dramatically exceeding the daily doses of exercise recommended by even the most exercise-conscious Surgeon General.

But the maids don't seem to recognize what they're doing as exercise. At the beginning of the study, 67 percent of the maids reported to Crum and Langer that they didn't exercise regularly. More than a third said they didn't get any exercise at all. Huh? It's like a third of talk-show hosts complaining that they never get to meet anyone new.

Then again, what is "exercise"? If we accept the cultural definition of exercise as something we do on a treadmill in a fitness club, while surrounded by spandexed women and perspiring men, then the maids were correct. But our bodies don't make style distinctions—a calorie burned is a calorie burned.

The researchers were curious about what would happen if the maids were told, to their surprise, that they were exercise superstars. One group of maids got the good news: They received a document describing the benefits of exercise, and they were told that their daily work was sufficient to get those benefits. Exercise doesn't have to be hard or painful, they were informed—and it certainly doesn't have to be in a gym. It simply requires you to move your muscles in a way that burns calories. The maids in this group were given estimates of the amount of calories they burned doing various activities: 40 calories for changing linens for 15 minutes, 100 calories for a half hour of vacuuming, and so on. Meanwhile, maids in another group received the same information about the benefits of exercise, but they weren't told that their own work was a good form of exercise (nor did they get the calorie-burning stats).

Four weeks later, the researchers checked in again with the maids and found something incredible. The maids who'd been told that they were good exercisers had lost an average of 1.8 pounds. That's almost a half pound a week, which is a pretty substantial rate of loss. The other maids hadn't lost any weight.

Crum and Langer investigated possible explanations. The

weight loss wasn't simply a statistical fluctuation. There were too many maids for a fluke explanation of that kind, and furthermore, the maids who lost weight had a corresponding drop in body fat. Nor had the maids caught the "exercise bug"—they weren't exercising any more outside of work than they had before.

The researchers also ruled out a bunch of other possibilities: The maids weren't working any more hours. They hadn't changed their consumption of alcohol, caffeine, or tobacco. Their dietary habits hadn't changed in any meaningful way—they weren't eating more vegetables or consuming fewer sugary foods. But still they were losing weight.

What was making them slim down?

2.

A local car wash ran a promotion featuring loyalty cards. Every time customers bought a car wash, they got a stamp on their cards, and when they filled up their cards with eight stamps, they got a free wash.

Another set of customers at the same car wash got a slightly different loyalty card. They needed to collect ten stamps (rather than eight) to get a free car wash—but they were given a "head start." When they received their cards, two stamps had already been added.

The "goal" was the same for both sets of customers: Buy eight additional car washes, get a reward. But the psychology was different: In one case, you're 20 percent of the way toward a goal, and in the other case, you're starting from scratch. A few months later, only 19 percent of the eight-stamp customers had earned a free wash, versus 34 percent of the head-start group. (And the head-start group earned the free wash faster.)

People find it more motivating to be partly finished with a longer journey than to be at the starting gate of a shorter one. That's why the conventional wisdom in development circles is that you don't publicly announce a fund-raising campaign for a charity until you've already got 50 percent of the money in the bag. (After all, who wants to give the first $100 to a $1 million fund-raising campaign?)

One way to motivate action, then, is to make people feel as though they're already closer to the finish line than they might have thought.

3.

The researchers Crum and Langer chalked up the maids' weight loss to a placebo effect. In other words, they concluded that awareness of the exercise value of their activities triggered the weight loss, independent of any physical changes in the maids' behavior.

The placebo effect is one of the most reliable phenomena in modern medicine, so at first glance, this explanation seems reasonable. We've all got friends who swear by the healing powers of questionable remedies—stinkweed supplements or goat horn extract. Maybe the maids got a similar mental boost from their new knowledge.

But notice what placebo-effect situations have in common: They apply to conditions that are self-reported. You take a pain pill, and the doctor asks you afterward, "How much pain do you feel now?" You take an antidepressant, and six weeks later, the therapist asks, "How do you feel?" So it's understandable (though still fundamentally weird) that the patients who get placebos, rather than Advil or Prozac, might report feeling a bit better.

But this isn't one of those situations. No one was asking these maids how they felt or whether they perceived themselves to be healthier. The maids simply stepped onto a scale, and the scale reported a lower weight. Scales aren't subject to placebo effects.

OK, but if you've suddenly discovered that you're a good exerciser, might not that trigger some kind of mind-body effect? Couldn't it kick your metabolism into overdrive or something? It's not impossible, we suppose, but let's be honest: If the power of thinking could indeed make you skinnier, that would be a scientific revelation on par with cold fusion (as well as a billion-dollar self-help book—*Think Yourself Thin*).

What's much more likely is that we're seeing a reflection of the car wash study. The maids were given a stamp card with two stamps on it. In other words, they were astonished to discover that, contrary to their own self-assessment, they were *exercisers*. They were 20 percent of the way to the destination, not 0 percent. And that was a tremendously motivating realization. *I'm not a sloth—I'm an Exerciser!*

Think about how you'd feel in their shoes. What if a scientist came to you and said that, unbeknownst to you, your white-collar job is an aerobic wonderland? With every click of the mouse, you burn 8 calories! Every time you check fantasy-baseball stats, you run a mile! Wouldn't you feel a rush of satisfaction? *Hey, look how good I'm doing!*

And here's the main thing—it almost certainly would change the way you behave from that moment forward. Once you realized that exercise could come from little things, maybe you'd be on the lookout for ways to get a smidgen more active.

Similarly, the maids, getting a jolt of enthusiasm from the good news, might have started scrubbing the showers a little more energetically than previously. Maybe they started making multiple trips back to their carts as they changed linens, just to add a bit more walking. Maybe they took the stairs to lunch rather than the elevator. And they exerted that extra effort because someone put two stamps on their exercise cards. Suddenly, they found themselves closer to the goal line than they ever imagined.

That sense of progress is critical, because the Elephant in us is easily demoralized. It's easily spooked, easily derailed, and for that reason, it needs reassurance, even for the very first step of the journey.

If you're leading a change effort, you better start looking for those first two stamps to put on your team's cards. Rather than focusing solely on what's new and different about the change to come, make an effort to remind people what's already been conquered. "Team, I know the reporting structure looks different, but remember that we already had some practice working in these groups on the RayCom account." "Honey, losing forty pounds isn't going to be easy, but you've already given up soda, and I bet that alone will knock off five pounds before the end of the year."

A business cliché commands us to "raise the bar." But that's exactly the wrong instinct if you want to motivate a reluctant Elephant. You need to lower the bar. Picture taking a high-jump bar and lowering it so far that it can be stepped over.

If you want a reluctant Elephant to get moving, you need to *shrink the change.*

4.

If you're like us, you love a clean house but dread housecleaning. And your dread mounts, because with each hour, each day, that passes between episodes of cleaning, the piles of paper in the office grow taller, the loads of laundry pile up, and the dust on the sideboards accumulates. As the problem gets worse, so does the dread, which deters housecleaning, which leads to a dirtier house, which . . . Vicious cycle, anyone?

But what is it, exactly, that we dread? Think about it: Does picking up an undershirt off the floor and tossing it in the hamper inspire *dread*? Nope. Nor does rinsing out a glass and putting it in the dishwasher, or putting a single folder in the filing cabinet, or spraying glass cleaner on the bathroom mirror. So why does dread emerge from a combination of individual actions that seem pretty dread-free? Partly it's because we fear that, in order to "clean house" properly, our work must (by definition) end with a house that's clean. And when we envision our way to that end state, picturing all that we will have to conquer to get there—the closets and dishes and carpets and toilets and floors—we simply can't bear opening that door. It feels like too much.

Yet we don't dread saving for retirement on the grounds that we've got to accomplish it in one mongo-deposit. We understand that retirement savings accumulate one little bit at a time. By the same logic, wouldn't it be easier just to make the house *cleaner* rather than *clean*? Can we free ourselves from dread by scaling down the mission?

That's the insight behind a clever self-help technique called the "5-Minute Room Rescue," proposed by Marla Cilley, a home-organizing guru who calls herself the Fly Lady (think of zooming through your housecleaning with wings). Here's what you do: Get a kitchen timer and set it for 5 minutes. Then go to the worst room in your house—the one you'd never let a guest see—and, as the timer ticks down, start clearing a path, and when the timer buzzes, you can stop with a clear conscience. Doesn't sound so bad, does it?

This is an Elephant trick. The Elephant hates doing things

with no immediate payoff. (If you've ever seen someone strain to pull a mule in a direction it didn't want to go, you've got the right mental image.) To get the Elephant off its duff, you need to reassure it that the task won't be so bad. *Look, it's just 5 minutes. How bad can it be?*

What good is a 5-minute session of cleaning? Not much. It gets you moving, though, and that's the hardest part. Starting an unpleasant task is always worse than continuing it. So once you start cleaning house, chances are you won't stop at 5 minutes. You'll be surprised at how fast things turn around. You'll start to take pride in your accomplishments—starting with the clean sink, then the clean bathroom, then the clean downstairs area—and that pride and confidence will build on itself. A virtuous circle. But you couldn't have enjoyed the virtuous circle without first shrinking the change.

5.

Steven Farrar, a store owner on eBay, and his wife Amanda, a pharmacist, had gotten themselves into a financial pickle. "It all started after we graduated, loaded with $60,000 in student-loan debt; we did what was normal. We bought a house, two new cars, and took on an additional $35,000 in credit card debt. We just didn't bother—we weren't trying to keep up with anyone or buy a lot of miscellaneous stuff over time—we just failed to care." Eventually, panic set in. The Farrars realized they were one accident or one job loss away from bankruptcy. They knew they needed help, so they turned to the work of personal finance guru Dave Ramsey.

Ramsey, in his youth, had a transformative experience. At age 26, he and his wife owned real estate that was worth over $4 million, but then, abruptly, their wealth unraveled. In his book *The*

Total Money Makeover, Ramsey says, "We went through financial hell and lost everything over a three-year period of time. We were sued, foreclosed on, and finally, with a brand-new baby and a toddler, we were bankrupt. *Scared* doesn't begin to cover it. *Crushed* comes close, but we held on to each other and decided we needed a change."

Ramsey emerged from this financial near-death experience with a determination to help others avoid the mistakes he had made. In his books and on his radio show, he provides financial advice to individuals and families who are struggling, and most often, their number-one problem is too much debt.

One of Ramsey's best-known and most controversial debt-fighting techniques is the "Debt Snowball." When the Farrars found themselves with over $100,000 in debt (not including their mortgage), they started working on the Debt Snowball. The first step was to list all their debts—everything from credit cards to overdue electric bills to student loans—and then arrange them in order from smallest to largest. Next, their instructions were to make only the minimum payments on every debt, with one exception: After the minimum payments were made, every available dollar would be put toward the first debt on the list. Because the first debt was the smallest one, it could be paid off relatively quickly, and the Farrars could cross it off the list and then direct every available dollar to paying off the second debt, then the third, then the fourth. As they crossed off each debt, they were able to eliminate a minimum payment, which gave them more cash to attack the next debt. That's why the strategy is called a Debt Snowball. With each debt that is conquered, the "snowball" of money applied to the next debt grows and rolls a little faster.

Notice what's missing here: any mention of interest rates. If the Farrars' smallest debt was a past-due utility bill, with no interest charges whatsoever, Ramsey still advised them to pay it off before tackling any of their credit card bills, which might have interest rates of 20 percent or above.

This advice makes the average financial adviser cringe. After all, simple math tells us that we're financially better-off if we pay down high-interest debt first. But Ramsey knows exactly what he's doing:

> Being a certified nerd, I always used to start with making the math work. I have learned that the math does need to work, but sometimes motivation is more important than math. This is one of those times. . . . Face it, if you go on a diet and lose weight the first week, you will stay on that diet. If you go on a diet and gain weight or go six weeks with no visible progress, you will quit. When training salespeople, I try to get them a sale or two quickly because that fires them up. When you start the Debt Snowball and in the first few days pay off a couple of little debts, trust me, it lights your fire. I don't care if you have a master's degree in psychology; you need quick wins to get fired up. And getting fired up is super-important.

Most financial advisers recommend that their clients pay down high-interest debt first in order to optimize the impact of their money. But Ramsey's not trying to solve an optimization problem; he's trying to solve an Elephant problem. The reason people get themselves into financial trouble, he knows, is that they lose control. They begin to feel powerless in the face of a mountain of debt. And you can't combat powerlessness with math. You combat it by proving to people that they can win. If you pay $185 toward a $20,000 debt on a high-interest credit card, you're still going to feel hopeless. But if you completely pay off a $185 overdue utility bill, you can cross it off your list. You've won a victory over debt.

Ramsey is using the same strategy as the Fly Lady with her 5-Minute Room Rescue—if people are facing a daunting task, and their instinct is to avoid it, you've got to break down the task. Shrink the change. Make the change small enough that they can't help but score a victory. Once people clean a single room, or pay off a single debt, their dread starts to dissipate, and their progress begins to snowball.

CLINIC

How Can You Cut the Budget Without Creating a Political Mess?

SITUATION Mary Carr is the CFO of a university that is experiencing significant drops in enrollment. With fewer students, the university's tuition revenue is declining, leading to a budget shortfall. Carr's job is to oversee meaningful budget cuts across about thirty different departments. [This was a real situation.]

WHAT'S THE SWITCH AND WHAT'S HOLDING IT BACK? Carr needs the heads of the university's departments to cut departmental budgets without lots of resistance or political infighting. She has already made some progress on clarifying the goal: Her analysis reveals that department heads will need to cut budgets by 5 percent. Most of them understand and agree with the need to cut back, but Carr thinks there is a danger of people dragging their heels. She needs to make some quick progress on the budget cuts, and that depends primarily on her ability to motivate the department heads' Elephants.

HOW DO WE MAKE THE SWITCH?

• *Direct the Rider.* **1. Follow the bright spots.** Can Carr find some success stories about department heads who figured out how to save money in creative ways (for example, by installing sensor-controlled lighting/heating or by out-sourcing administrative functions)? If so, she should help to clone the success across departments.

• *Motivate the Elephant.* **1. Shrink the change.** The need to cut 5 percent is clear, but cutting is the kind of task that inspires dread. "People tend to panic a little when you say, 'We have to cut our budget by five percent,'" says Carr. How can she break down the task? Well, as it turns out, Mary Carr is a Fly Lady fan, and she takes inspiration from the 5-Minute Room Rescue. So she picks two or three budget lines every week—say, office supplies, training, and travel—and asks the department heads whether they can cut 5 percent out of those line items. Carr reports, "Picking out tiny chunks of work at a time stays the panic." Carr is shrinking the change, making it less likely to engage the Elephant's resistance. **2. Grow your people.** Once the department heads have tackled the first three budget lines, Carr wants to keep the momentum going. She tells them, "We're already one third of the way there!" She is putting two stamps on their car-wash cards—letting them know that they've already made great progress toward the goal.

• *Shape the Path.* **1. Build habits.** Every Monday, like clockwork, Carr sends out budget updates. She requests updates and gives simple action items, such as, "If you don't think you'll be able to meet the 5 percent cut in travel, call me today." By using a very consistent and predictable process, Carr tries to make the cycle of budget cuts more routine, more automatic. **2. Rally the herd.** At one point in the budget cutting, all the department heads attend their yearly planning retreat. On the first day, everyone sees what cuts all the departments made in the initial round. Then each department head spends some time, overnight, planning a round of deeper cuts. The next morning, they share their proposed cuts with one another. Carr says, "Everyone got to see what each person was already cutting and the implications of future cuts. And knowing that, the whole body made decisions, not just individual department heads. Everyone was looking at the university as a whole." In essence, the department heads are exercising positive peer

pressure on one another. It becomes the social norm to think of cuts from the perspective of the university as a whole (a strong, shared identity), rather than from
the perspective of individual departments.

6.

One way to shrink change, then, is to limit the investment you're
asking for—only 5 minutes of housecleaning, only one small
debt. Another way to shrink change is to think of *small wins*—
milestones that are within reach. (Our dad, Fred Heath, who
worked over thirty years for IBM, would tell his teams that when
"milestones" seemed too distant, they should look for "inch peb-
bles." Nice one, Dad.)

Say that you're trying to motivate your teenager to do some
housecleaning. You might embrace the 5-Minute Room Rescue to
overcome his initial resistance. But what if you also put a bit of
strategic thought into which room he starts with? You might ask
him to start his work in the tiny guest bathroom, because you're
confident that after 5 minutes of work, he'll have it gleaming. The
overall goal—cleaning the whole house—is too distant to be motivating, but if you can engineer a small win in the first 5 minutes,
it might buy you enough enthusiasm to pursue the next milestone.
(Then again, we're talking teenagers, so don't count on it.)

If you've ever faced a really long drive, no doubt you used this
technique on yourself. Maybe you thought about your journey
one town at a time, or an hour at a time, or maybe you promised
yourself a coffee stop after the next 75 miles. It's a lot easier to
think "75 miles to coffee" than to think "8.5 more hours of sitting here until I'm at Grandma's."

You can't count on these milestones to occur naturally. To motivate change, you've got to plan for them.

We've been talking about small wins at an individual level—using them to motivate a road-trip driver or a teenage house-cleaner. But the same concept goes for large organizations. For example, a man named Steven Kelman had to figure out a way to create small wins in the federal government.

Kelman, a professor of public management at Harvard University's Kennedy School of Government, got a call from the Clinton administration in 1993, asking him to lead the Office of Federal Procurement Policy (OFPP). As the head of OFPP, he would be responsible for reforming the government's procurement efforts. Procurement is the process by which people buy things, and the government does a lot of procuring. In 2003, it spent $320 billion on purchases of discretionary goods and services, a figure that includes everything from paper clips to helicopters for the National Park Service. With that kind of money at stake, you can't have people running down to Bell Helicopter and plopping down a credit card for a new helicopter. (On the other hand, think of the airline miles.)

Kelman was reluctant to head up OFPP, knowing there was a pretty good chance that despite his best efforts nothing would change, but in the end he accepted the job. He knew exactly what he was getting into, because three years earlier, he'd written a book about procurement reform.

There were lots of problems with procurement. Over the years, the government had established many protocols and protections to prevent abuses of various kinds. There were good intentions behind these protections, but as they built up, layer upon layer, they began to cause more harm than the abuses they'd been designed to prevent. For instance, when making purchase decisions, procurement officials could not use evidence of vendors' "past performance." As an example, let's say the government gave the company CodeLords a contract to develop software, and the product CodeLords delivered was absurdly behind schedule and inexcusably poor in performance. The government would be barred from using that performance data when evaluating CodeLords for a different job! (Imagine if you had to select a hairdresser without regard to the way he cut your hair in the past.)

Sometimes, too, the sheer quantity of rules was smothering common sense. In one famous example, the Defense Department sought a supplier of chocolate-chip cookies for the troops and published a 20-page set of "milspecs," detailed specifications that dictated, among other things, ingredients, cookie size, and baking process. These requirements led to outrageously high cookie prices because companies that actually understood how to produce lots of cookies efficiently—say, Keebler or Nabisco—would never bid on the job because some part of the milspecs inevitably conflicted with their standard way of doing things. Meanwhile, the contract did not even stipulate that the cookies taste good.

As head of OFPP, Kelman would lead procurement reform, but he didn't have much structural power. He had a staff of about twenty people, none of whom purchased anything significant. The actual purchasing decisions were spread across dozens of large federal agencies. Kelman would have to reform procurement by reforming the *behavior* of purchasing agents scattered across the government.

If ever there was an underdog story, this is it. To put the government's $320 billion in discretionary purchases in perspective, that's about the same amount of money it would take to purchase everything that's produced in a year by the entire computer hardware industry—all the Dell laptops, IBM mainframes, Seagate drives, and others. And then you'd still have enough money left

over to buy every car and every car part produced by the automobile industry.

Thousands of people in the government are involved in procurement, and their desire to please Bill Clinton, the new president in 1993, is tempered by the knowledge that Clinton will be
gone in four years (or, worst case, eight). Into this vast, sprawling
sand trap of inertia walks one guy named Steven. He's a professor,
no less. He wrote a good book about the sand trap. Now he's on
the hook to fix it, yet he doesn't control any of it (except for twenty
grains of sand on the eastern periphery). You might as well hire a
computer-savvy reporter named Phil to overhaul the computer
industry.

Kelman knew he'd have to make some progress quickly or else
he'd be dismissed. "If an example of successful change could
somehow be achieved quickly, it might be possible to use that to
set other changes in motion," he wrote later. He sought a victory
that would be fast, achievable, and visible—a small win that
would work for all of his constituents, whether the Defense Department or the Health and Human Services Department. If he
could get their Elephants moving with an easy mission—the government equivalent of the 5-Minute Room Rescue—he thought
he would be able to keep them moving.

One day, a conversation with a government employee sparked
an idea. The employee told Kelman that when she needed simple, inexpensive items, such as a few computer disks, the procurement rules made it impossible for her to walk to the
computer superstore across the street and buy them. She found
this limitation was infuriating.

Kelman spotted an opportunity. He went to the senior procurement executives and issued a challenge: *I want you to double
your agency's use of government credit cards over the next year.* (Notice the precision of the challenge, à la the 1% milk campaign. By

being specific about the behavioral change, Kelman was directing his constituents' Riders.) In his vision, anytime employees needed something small—computer disks or a replacement hard drive or a carton of office paper—they should be able to march across the street, armed with their credit cards, and purchase what they needed on the spot. Kelman asked the agencies to make a formal "Pledge" to embrace the idea. The agencies were supportive, so Kelman pushed further. Over the next year, he organized four more pledges.

The second pledge was a biggie: Kelman asked the agencies to break with the tradition of ignoring past performance. He knew this would be a tough sell, so he decided to push for it publicly only when he was sure he had at least eight agencies onboard. He hit the phones, and his employees and advisers rallied the people in their networks. Eventually, his team had eight agencies signed up, but he wasn't finished. "After we got to nine agencies, participation started snowballing, and soon we could say to the holdouts, 'Almost everyone but you is participating.'" (This outcome foreshadows a point that we make in Chapter 10 about behavior being contagious. Kelman managed to address all three parts of the framework—directing the Rider, motivating the Elephant, and shaping the Path.)

In the end, twenty different agencies agreed to take the "Past-Performance Pledge." To ensure that the pledge would be taken seriously, Kelman prodded the agencies to identify fifty-eight upcoming contracts in which they would explicitly consider past performance.

With the pledges, Kelman turned an unspeakable level of bureaucratic inertia into demonstrable forward momentum. Five years later, in an internal survey, 70 percent of frontline employees said that they were proponents of procurement reform. The Brookings Institution, a well-respected think tank, published a

study in 1998 that graded the success of various "reinventing government" initiatives attempted over the previous eight years. Kelman's procurement reform was the only initiative that earned an
"A." A single guy had managed to come in and catalyze a big
change in the federal government.

7.

When you engineer early successes, what you're really doing is
engineering hope. Hope is precious to a change effort. It's Elephant fuel.

Once people are on the path and making progress, it's important to make their advances visible. With some kinds of
change, such as weight loss, progress is easy to measure—people
can step on a scale. Unfortunately, there's no off-the-shelf scale for
"new-product innovation" or "reduced carbon impact." Where
do you find a yardstick that can measure the kind of changes
you're leading?

Solutions-focused therapists, whom we mentioned in Chapter 2 in the Rider section, create their own yardsticks. Recall that
they ask their patients the Miracle Question: "Imagine that in
the middle of the night, while you are sleeping, a miracle happens, and all the troubles you brought here are resolved. When
you wake up in the morning, how will you know?"

These therapists know that the miracle can seem distant to
their patients and that they need to keep their patients motivated
and hopeful en route to the destination. To do so, they've devised
a way of quantifying progress toward the miracle. They create a
miracle scale ranging from 0 to 10, where 10 is the miracle. In
fact, in the very first session they often ask their patients where
they'd score themselves. Patients often report back that they're at
2 or 3, which prompts an enthusiastic response from the thera-

pists. *Wow! You're already 20 percent of the way there!* Sound familiar? The therapists are putting two stamps on their patients' car-wash cards.

As the sessions continue, the therapists continue to track patients' self-reported progress. The therapists are trained to celebrate every incremental victory—to react with delight when a patient reports advancing from 3 to 4. This response is counterintuitive for most of us. How many sales managers dance a jig upon hearing that their reps are 40 percent of the way to a quota? But this encouragement is critical, because it's self-reinforcing. When you've celebrated moving from 1 to 2, and then from 2 to 3, you gain confidence that you can make the next advance.

The other advantage of scaling the miracle is that it demystifies the journey. Let's say you're working with your junior-high-age son who is painfully shy. Maybe the miracle for your son would be the ability to ask a girl to the school's homecoming dance. This feat is presently unthinkable to your son, but you and he have been able to talk about his shyness—he acknowledges it and dislikes it—and by virtue of that conversation, he may already be at 2 on the scale.

An SFBT therapist would ask your son, "What would it take to get you to 3? Let's not talk about how we can pole-vault up to the miracle—we're not there yet. Let's talk about 3."

Maybe for your son, reaching 3 would involve something simple like asking a grocery store employee where the toothpaste aisle is. If he did that, he'd prove that he could interact successfully with a total stranger, and in doing so, he'd get to see himself moving toward the miracle. The value of the miracle scale is that it focuses attention on small milestones that are attainable and visible rather than on the eventual destination, which may seem very remote. It's like climbing a tall ladder and focusing on the *next* step rather than gawking up at the top. There may be many more steps to go, but you can take comfort that you're making real progress in the right direction.

Notice, once again, how often Elephant appeals and Rider appeals can overlap. In this case, your son's Rider is getting very clear direction—*Ask the clerk about the toothpaste*—at the same time as his Elephant is getting little boosts of hope—*Maybe I don't have to be so shy forever.*

By using the miracle scale, you always have a clear idea of where you're going next, and you have a clear sense of what the next small victory will be. You're moving forward, and, even better, you're getting more confident in your *ability* to keep moving forward.

8.

NFL coach Bill Parcells, who won two Super Bowls as coach of the New York Giants, supports the notion that "even small successes can be extremely powerful in helping people believe in themselves." In an article published in *Harvard Business Review,* he continued:

> In training camps, therefore, we don't focus on the ultimate goal—getting to the Super Bowl. We establish a clear set of goals that are *within immediate reach:* we're going to be a smart team; we're going to be a well-conditioned team; we're going to be a team that plays hard; we're going to be a team that has pride; we're going to be a team that wants to win collectively; we're going to be a team that doesn't criticize one another.

When we start acting in ways that fulfill these goals, I make sure everybody knows it. I accentuate the positive at every possible opportunity, and at the same time I emphasize the next goal that we need to fulfill. If we have a particularly good practice, then I call the team together and say, "We got something done today; we executed well. I'm very pleased with your work. But here's what I want to do tomorrow: I want to see flawless special teams work. If you accomplish that, we will be ready for the game on Sunday."

When you set small, visible goals, and people achieve them, they start to get it into their heads that they can succeed. They break the habit of losing and begin to get into the habit of winning. [emphasis added]

Former UCLA coach John Wooden, one of the greatest college basketball coaches of all time, once said, "When you improve a little each day, eventually big things occur. . . . Don't look for the quick, big improvement. Seek the small improvement one day at a time. That's the only way it happens—and when it happens, it lasts."

Coaches are masters of shrinking the change. By pushing their teams to attain a sequence of "small, visible goals," they build momentum. Psychologist Karl Weick, in a paper called "Small Wins: Redefining the Scale of Social Problems," said, "A small win reduces importance ('this is no big deal'), reduces demands ('that's all that needs to be done'), and raises perceived skill levels ('I can do at least that')." All three of these factors will tend to make change easier and more self-sustaining.

Let's not get too rosy-eyed here, though. Any important change is not going to feel like a steady, inevitable march toward victory. It won't simply be an unbroken string of small wins.

(Don't forget there are lots of coaches who retired having never won a championship.) More typically, you take one step forward and 1.3 steps back and 2.7 steps forward and then 6 steps to the side, and at that moment, a new CEO will come in and declare a new destination.

No one can *guarantee* a small win. Lots of things are out of our control. But the goal is to be wise about the things that *are* under our control. And one thing we can control is how we define the ultimate victory and the small victories that lead up to it.

You want to select small wins that have two traits: (1) They're meaningful. (2) They're "within immediate reach," as Bill Parcells said. And if you can't achieve both traits, choose the latter! (The 5-Minute Room Rescue wasn't very meaningful by itself, but it made great change possible.)

David Allen, author of *Getting Things Done,* the quintessential personal productivity book, echoes the importance of setting goals that are within reach. He says that most people make a fundamental mistake when they create their to-do lists: They dash off lots of items: "collect expenses," "deal with Helen," "work on slideshow," "tires," and so on. In Allen's judgment, these people are sabotaging the likelihood of action by being too murky. He says it's critical to ask yourself, "What's the next action?" Here's Allen:

> People in my seminars often have things on their lists like "Get a tune-up for the car." Is "Get a tune-up" a next action? Not unless you're walking out with wrench in hand, dressed for grease.
> "So what's the next action?" [said Allen]
> "Uh, I need to take the car to the garage. Oh, yeah, I need to find out if the garage can take it. I guess I need

to call the garage and make the appointment." [said a seminar participant]

"Do you have the number?"

"Darn, no . . . I don't have the number for the garage. Fred recommended that garage to me, and I don't have the number. I knew something was missing in the equation."

And that's often what happens with so many things for so many people. We glance at the project, and some part of us thinks, "I don't quite have all the pieces between here and there." We know something is missing, but we're not sure what it is exactly, so we quit.

When a task feels too big, the Elephant will resist. It is no accident that Alcoholics Anonymous challenges recovering alcoholics to get through "one day at a time." AA is shrinking the change. To an alcoholic, going a lifetime without another drink sounds impossible. But going 24 hours sounds doable.

Here is the way Al-Anon explains the "one day at a time" mantra: "In most cases, we cannot anticipate every possible turn of events, and no matter how diligently we are prepared, we are eventually caught off guard. Meanwhile, we've expended so much time and energy trying to predict future events, soothe future hurts, and prevent future consequences that we have missed out on today's opportunities. And the magnitude of the task we have set for ourselves has left us drained, overwhelmed, and distraught."

9.

Small targets lead to small victories, and small victories can often trigger a positive spiral of behavior. Marriage therapist Michele

Weiner-Davis wrote about her clients Paula and George, who'd been married for eight years but had been fighting consistently for the previous two. Weiner-Davis had been counseling the couple for a while, and they'd made some progress but nothing dramatic. Then came the breakthrough—a kiss.

One morning, George kissed Paula. The kiss surprised her, caught her off guard a little, and made her happy. Being happy prompted her do a little thing she hadn't done in a while: She brewed a pot of coffee. "We used to drink coffee together often, but lately the tradition has fallen by the wayside," she told the therapist.

George smelled the coffee and came down for a cup. He and Paula had a pleasant conversation. Both of them said the morning made them feel more "relaxed and lighthearted." Paula reported that her coworkers noticed the difference in her attitude that day. Even George and Paula's kids seemed affected by the halo of good feelings—they were more relaxed that evening, less argumentative. George's kiss launched a positive spiral.

Why did such a little thing matter so much? Because it generated hope that change was possible.

It's a theme we've seen again and again—big changes come from a succession of small changes. It's OK if the first changes seem almost trivial. The challenge is to get the Elephant moving, even if the movement is slow at first. So don't ask the indebted couple to pay down their high-interest credit card bill; ask them to wipe out their utility bill. Don't ask government employees to embrace a new regime of procurement; ask them to double their spending on government credit cards. Don't ask a couple to stop fighting; ask the husband to give his wife a simple good-morning kiss.

The Elephant has no trouble conquering these micromilestones, and as it does, something else happens. With each step, the Elephant feels less scared and less reluctant, because things are working. With each step, the Elephant starts *feeling* the change. A journey that started with dread is evolving, slowly, toward a feeling of confidence and pride. And at the same time the change is shrinking, the Elephant is *growing*.

7

Grow Your People

1.

The St. Lucia Parrot exists only on the Caribbean island of St. Lucia. It's gorgeous, with a vivid turquoise blue face, lime green wings, and a striking red shield on its chest. In 1977, only one hundred St. Lucia Parrots were left on the island. The population had been decimated by habitat destruction, hunters, and people who trapped them to use as pets. The St. Lucia Parrot seemed doomed; in the words of one biologist, the species "could not escape oblivion by the year 2000."

Enter an unlikely savior: college student Paul Butler. In 1977, Butler was finishing his last year of studies at North-East London Polytechnic. Butler's passion was conservation, and he'd previously spent five weeks completing a field research expedition in St. Lucia, where he'd studied the parrot and submitted recommendations for preserving the species.

Just before graduation—"with unemployment staring me in

the face," said Butler—he received a letter from the head of St. Lucia's forestry department. To Butler's astonishment, he was offered a job. Impressed with Butler's recommendations, the head of forestry asked if Butler was interested in returning for six months as the department's conservation adviser. The job paid $200 a month, and Butler could stay in a government "rest hut." Butler could barely believe his luck. He was 21 years old, and the government of a beautiful Caribbean island was asking for his help in saving an endangered species.

Butler's recommendations to the government had been straightforward: (1) Beef up the punishment for capturing or killing the parrot, from a trivial fine to an enormous fine plus a jail term. (2) Establish within an existing forestry reserve a "parrot sanctuary" that would protect the parrot's habitat. (3) Raise money for the operation of the reserve by licensing "rain-forest tours," which would offer tourists the chance to see the reserve and its star attraction.

A quick time-out: Notice that these recommendations—changing laws, enforcing new penalties—are exactly the sorts of things that we shy away from in this book, because most of us don't have those tools in our kit. But here's the thing: Butler didn't have those tools, either. And neither did the forestry service. For Butler's recommendations to be put into practice, the island's laws would need to change, which meant, in turn, that the public would have to get behind the initiative. So Butler, fresh out of college, working with the forestry department, and armed with a budget in the hundreds of dollars, had to figure out a way to rally the people of St. Lucia behind a parrot that most of them took for granted (and some of them ate).

There was no clear economic case for saving the parrot. It wasn't the linchpin of an ecosystem, and the sad truth was that most St. Lucians probably wouldn't notice if it disappeared completely. Butler knew he couldn't make an analytical case for protecting the bird. He'd have to make an emotional case.

In essence, Butler's goal was to convince St. Lucians that *they were the kind of people who protected their own.* In public events, Butler stressed, "This parrot is ours. Nobody has this but us. We need to cherish it and look after it." He did everything in his power to make the public more familiar with the bird. He hosted St. Lucia Parrot puppet shows, distributed T-shirts, cajoled a local band to record songs about the bird, convinced local hotels to print up bumper stickers, recruited volunteers to dress up in parrot costumes and visit local schools, and asked local ministers to cite relevant Bible verses (for instance, verses that instructed believers to be good stewards of the things that were in their trust). He even talked a telecom company into printing up St. Lucia Parrot calling cards. On one card, the parrot was displayed next to the bald eagle, which was like putting Selma Hayek next to Dick Cheney. It was clear who had the better-looking national bird.

The St. Lucians began to embrace their parrot, as though it had always been a part of their national identity. Polls commissioned by Butler showed a dramatic rise in public support for the bird. The wave of public support made it possible to pass into law the recommendations that Butler and the forestry department, headed up by Gabriel Charles, had proposed.

As the years passed, the species came back from the brink. At last count, there were between six hundred and seven hundred parrots—an astonishing increase for a species that had been written off. Poaching stopped completely. "No St. Lucian has been caught shooting a parrot for fifteen years," said Butler in 2008.

In 1988, the government gave Butler full citizenship and later awarded him the St. Lucia Medal of Merit, one of the country's highest honors. He had shown St. Lucians what it meant to take pride in their identity, and in the process, he'd become a St. Lucian himself.

2.

Other people noticed what Butler accomplished. In the mid-1980s, a board member from Rare, a conservation organization, asked Butler if he would come to St. Vincent and do what he had done in St. Lucia. Intrigued, Butler joined Rare, working alongside St. Vincent's forestry division and its chief forest officer. Within a year, the island passed laws to protect its own native parrot.

Butler and the other leaders of Rare realized they had cracked one of the most pressing problems of conservation. It's very difficult to protect the precious areas of the world without the support of the residents of those areas, but Rare had proved it could inspire those residents to care about their environment. So Rare conservationists resolved to launch similar projects, which they began to call "Pride campaigns," all around the world. By 2009, Rare had successfully launched 120 Pride campaigns in 50 different countries from Panama to Indonesia. (Full disclosure: Inspired by this work, Dan Heath joined Rare's board of trustees in 2009.) Pride campaigns focused on animals ranging from the loggerhead turtle to the Napoleon wrasse, a brilliant blue fish whose habitat is coral reefs.

We've seen that one way to motivate a switch is to shrink the change, which makes people feel "big" relative to the challenge. But here we're seeing something different. Paul Butler didn't shrink the change. Instead, he grew the people. He made the St. Lucians swell with pride over their parrot—a species that exists nowhere else. He inspired them to feel more determined, more ready, more motivated. And when you build people up in this way, they develop the strength to act.

3.

Rare's success in motivating people in fifty countries suggests that something universal is at work here. Confirmation of that comes from the research of James March, a professor of political science at Stanford University. March says that when people make choices, they tend to rely on one of two basic models of decision making: the *consequences* model or the *identity* model. The consequences model is familiar to students of economics. It assumes that when we have a decision to make, we weigh the costs and benefits of our options and make the choice that maximizes our satisfaction. It's a rational, analytical approach. This is the approach that Paul Butler knew would fail with St. Lucians, because there simply wasn't a strong cost/benefit case for the parrot.

In the identity model of decision making, we essentially ask ourselves three questions when we have a decision to make: *Who am I? What kind of situation is this? What would someone like me do in this situation?* Notice what's missing: any calculation of costs and benefits. The identity model explains the way most people vote, which contradicts our notion of the "self-interested voter." It helps to shed light on why an auto mechanic in Oklahoma would vote against a Democrat who'd give him health insurance, and why a Silicon Valley millionaire would vote against a Republican who'd cut her taxes.

Generally, when we use the word *identity,* we're talking about an immutable trait of some kind—such as a racial, ethic, or regional identity. But that's a relatively narrow use of the term. We're not just born with an identity; we *adopt* identities throughout our lives. We aspire to be good mothers or fathers, devout Catholics or Muslims, patriotic citizens, and so on.

Or consider a professional identity, such as being a "scientist." Clearly, you're not born a scientist. It's an identity you seek out and one that others, such as your professors and mentors, consciously cultivate in you. As you develop and grow in that identity, it becomes an increasingly important part of your self-image and triggers the kind of decision making that March describes. For instance, imagine that as a science professor teaching chemistry, you had a lucrative opportunity to consult on the toxicity study of a new drug for a big pharmaceutical company. From a consequences point of view, the decision to accept the job would be a no-brainer—the work might pay far more than your university salary. But from an identity point of view, the decision to accept the job would seem less clear-cut. You'd wonder what strings were attached, what subtle compromises you'd have to make to please the client. You'd wonder, "What would a scientist like me do in this situation?"

Because identities are central to the way people make decisions, any change effort that violates someone's identity is likely doomed to failure. (That's why it's so clumsy when people instinctively reach for "incentives" to change other people's behavior.) So the question is this: How can you make your change a matter of identity rather than a matter of consequences?

4.

Lovelace Hospital Systems in Albuquerque, New Mexico, was concerned about the rapid turnover among its nurses. Its turnover rate wasn't any worse than the national average (between 18 and 30 percent per year), but that was small comfort. When nurses left, replacing them cost a lot of money, morale suffered, and patient care was put at risk during the transition period.

Kathleen Davis, a registered nurse and vice president of hospital operations, decided to try an unconventional approach to analyzing the turnover problem. She hired Susan Wood, a consultant who specialized in Appreciative Inquiry, a process for changing organizations by studying what's working rather than what's not (this is another example of the bright-spots focus that we discussed in Chapter 2).

Wood and Davis decided not to investigate why so many nurses were leaving. Instead, they began to explore why other nurses were *staying*. In a hospital with three hundred nurses, the team interviewed more than one hundred. Wood asked nurses what made their jobs satisfying. She recalled, "These nurses were beaten down and overworked, but as soon as we started them in a conversation about what they were good at, the tone changed."

Davis and Wood found that the nurses who stayed at the hospital were fiercely loyal to the profession of nursing. In other words, their satisfaction was an identity thing—the nobility of the nursing profession gave meaning to their work. Once the hospital administrators realized this, they knew they'd have to do more to help the nurses cultivate their identity. For instance, they began to find ways to recognize people for extraordinary nursing performance. They developed a new orientation program that stressed the inherently admirable nature of nursing work. They created mentorship programs to help nurses improve their knowledge and skills.

The first hint that something had changed was evident on the annual employee satisfaction survey. Nursing satisfaction scores increased markedly in multiple categories, particularly "communication"—all those interviews and conversations about identity had an impact. But the impact went beyond the survey:

Over the following year, turnover decreased by 30 percent. And then the success made an unexpected leap: On regional surveys, Davis and Wood started seeing improved ratings on *patient* satisfaction with Lovelace Hospital.

It's critical to realize that these identity stories aren't just special case situations, confined to scientists or nurses or St. Lucians. Identity is going to play a role in nearly every change situation. Even yours. When you think about the people whose behavior needs to change, ask yourself whether they would agree with this statement: "I aspire to be the kind of person who would make this change." If their answer is yes, that's an enormous factor in your favor. If their answer is no, then you'll have to work hard to show them that they should aspire to a different self-image. And that's exactly what Paul Butler did in St. Lucia. He convinced the island's citizens to think, "This is our bird—if we want to be good St. Lucians, we'd better protect it."

To see what this means in a business context, consider a firm that *invented* an identity that subsequently became the engine of its success. The firm is Brasilata—it's a US$170 million manufacturing firm in Brazil that produces various kinds of steel cans. As you'd imagine, the can manufacturing industry is relatively mature—not much growth, not much excitement. But Brasilata defies the stereotype of a boring, stuck-in-its ways manufacturer. In fact, it has one of the best reputations for innovation of any company in Latin America.

How does a manufacturer of cans become known as an innovator? Brasilata's founders were inspired by the philosophy of Japanese car manufacturers like Honda and Toyota, which empowered their frontline employees to take ownership of their work. For instance, at Toyota, any employee who spotted a defect could stop the assembly line (this would have been unthinkable in Detroit at the time). Toyota and Honda also actively solicited ideas for innovation from their employees. In 1987, the founders of Brasilata launched an employee-innovation program modeled on the Japanese forerunners.

A new identity was the core of the program. Employees of Brasilata became known as "inventors," and when new employees joined the firm, they were asked to sign an "innovation contract." This wasn't simply feel-good language. Top management challenged employees to be on the lookout for potential innovations— ideas for how to create better products, improve production processes, and squeeze costs out of the system. Procedures developed within the factory made it easy for inventors to submit their ideas. The program succeeded beyond any reasonable expectations. In 2008, employees submitted 134,846 ideas—an average of 145.2 ideas per inventor! This figure puts Brasilata on par with the Japanese trendsetters that had inspired the program.

Many of the suggestions led to the development of new products. For instance, in late 2008, Brasilata came up with a new approach for steel cans designed to carry dangerous or flammable liquids. To meet United Nations standards, such cans must be able to withstand a drop from 1.2 meters (roughly 4 feet). Traditionally, most manufacturers had reached this standard by thickening the metal layers, which used up more raw material and required new production processes. And the reinforced designs weren't foolproof—the metal seams were prone to split if a can landed on an edge.

Brasilata's inventors suggested a new design, inspired by car bumpers that collapse on impact. Their new steel can deformed slightly on impact, reducing stress on the critical seam. The new design resisted impact better while also reducing the amount of steel in the can.

The inventors have led Brasilata through emergencies. In 2001, a severe energy crisis—the "blackout syndrome"—forced the government of Brazil to ration energy. Businesses received a strict quota of electricity. The inventors went to work dreaming up power-saving ideas—hundreds of them. Within a few weeks, Brasilata's energy consumption was reduced by 35 percent, falling below the company's quota and allowing the company to resell its extra energy.

Another unexpected idea was jointly suggested by two employees: *Eliminate our jobs; they're not necessary anymore.* The idea was accepted, but the company found a new place for the employees. Brasilata has a no-dismissal policy and also distributes 15 percent of its net profits to employees. It's no surprise that Brasilata consistently appears on "best places to work" lists in Brazil.

Let's remember something: This "inventor" identity, which has fueled business success and employee satisfaction, was made up. None of Brasilata's employees were born "inventors." The identity was introduced to them, and they liked the sound of it. It seemed to be a mantle worth wearing. Being an inventor has become a source of pride and strength.

5.

If cultivating an identity sounds daunting, take heart. A classic study in psychology shows that you can start with small steps. In the 1960s, two psychologists from Stanford University, Jonathan Freedman and Scott Fraser, asked a researcher to go door-to-door in an upscale neighborhood in Palo Alto, California. When home owners answered the door, the researcher announced himself as a volunteer for "Citizens for Safe Driving" and asked whether they would allow a billboard reading "Drive Carefully" to be installed on their lawns. They were shown a photo of the billboard on the lawn of a different house, and it was a real eyesore—crudely constructed and so enormous that it obscured much of the front of the house. The home owners were assured that the sign would make "just a small hole in your lawn."

No doubt if this volunteer knocked on your door, you'd have a colorful response. And, indeed, 83 percent of the home owners passed on the "opportunity." But here's the twist: In a different neighborhood, the researchers used a simple technique that more than quadrupled the number of yesses!

The technique was remarkably subtle: Two weeks earlier, the same home owners had been approached by a volunteer claiming to represent a different driver-safety organization. They were asked to put a tiny "Be a Safe Driver" sign—less than half the size of a postcard—in the window of their car or home. The volunteer said the sign was intended to make citizens more aware of the need to drive carefully. This seemed such a trivial commitment that almost all of the home owners said yes. Their little-yes seemed to pave the way for the big-yes. When the researchers came back two weeks later and asked the home owners to install the eyesore billboard, 76 percent accepted it. Freedman and Fraser called this strategy a "foot in the door" technique. Accepting the tiny driver-safety sign greatly increased the likelihood that the home owners would accept the gigantic driver-safety sign.

Then the results got even stranger. Volunteers approached a third group of home owners with a different request. Rather than being presented with the tiny sign about driving safety, home owners in the third group were asked to sign a petition to "Keep California beautiful." Hard to oppose that, so again almost everyone complied. Then two weeks later, those petition-signers were approached about hosting the eyesore billboard, and half of them said yes! That's *three times* the acceptance rate of the home owners who hadn't signed the petition.

This result confused even Freedman and Fraser. They hadn't

expected the "Keep California beautiful" petition to be a "foot in the door" for a commitment to driver's safety. The two domains were completely unrelated. After some reflection, they speculated that the petition signing might have sparked a shift in the home owners' own sense of identity. Freedman and Fraser wrote, "Once [the home owner] has agreed to the request, his attitude may change, he may become, in his own eyes, the kind of person who does this sort of thing, who agrees to requests made by strangers, who takes action on things he believes in, who cooperates with good causes."

In a sense, signing the petition became evidence to the home owners that they were "concerned citizens," and this subtle shift in identity led to a shift in their behavior. Two weeks later, when they were approached with the option to put a billboard on their lawns, they subconsciously asked themselves James March's three identity questions: *Who am I? What kind of situation is this? What would someone like me do in this situation?* If you consider yourself to be a "fit in with the neighbors person," you'll deny the request. If you consider yourself to be an "immaculate lawn person," you might assault the researcher. But if you're a newly hatched "concerned citizen," you'll find it honorable to host the sign.

6.

Now, let's be clear: The Freedman-Fraser study is kind of sleazy. We'll try to separate the sleazy part from the science part.

The sleazy part is the deception. The home owners are being tricked into doing something stupid. None of the other examples we've provided of building identity hinges on this kind of deception. Is it deceptive to persuade people to rally behind a national bird? To cultivate professional pride in nurses? To encourage employees to act like inventors? Of course not. No one at Brasilata would have been disturbed to hear the CEO say, "We're trying to get you to think and act more like an 'inventor' because that will make our company more competitive and innovative." The yard-sign study is different: Home owners would indeed have been offended if Freedman and Fraser had come clean and said, "We're asking you to sign this petition so that, two weeks from now, we can dupe you into putting a giant billboard on your lawn."

Leaving aside the sleaze factor, the science of the billboard study says something pretty remarkable. It shows us that people are receptive to developing new identities, that identities "grow" from small beginnings. Once you start seeing yourself as a "concerned citizen," you'll want to keep acting like one. That's tremendously good news for someone leading a change effort. It means, for example, that if you can show people why the environment is worth caring about, it won't take years for them to think of themselves as "environmentalists." It took only a few days for the home owners to think of themselves as "concerned citizens."

7.

There is a problem, though. A new identity can take root quickly, but living up to it is awfully hard. For instance, it probably took a while before Brasilata's employees were any good at inventing. At first, they probably struggled to come up with *any* suggestions for the company, and they might have felt like impostors calling themselves "inventors."

We can empathize. At different times in our lives, both of us (Chip and Dan) were urged by our significant others to take salsa-dancing lessons. This was not our first choice of weekend activities, but we agreed to give it a shot. The fantasy was an attractive one—we could picture ourselves with our partners, full of passion and artistic flair, drawing envious glances from passersby. No question: This "dancer identity" had appeal.

It did not take us long to realize how deeply misguided our fantasies were. All too quickly, we discovered that salsa is a sadistic style of dancing created for the purpose of making middle-aged men feel ridiculous. Salsa requires an array of sensual hip movements that we found structurally implausible. We managed to perform this beautiful dance with all the seductive force of Al Gore giving a lap dance.

We did not continue with our salsa lessons.

Here's the thing: When you fight to make your switch, especially one that involves a new identity, you and your audience are going to have Salsa Moments. (Don't worry, we're not going to adopt that as a buzz phrase.) Any new quest, even one that is ultimately successful, is going to involve failure. You can't learn to salsa-dance without failing. You can't learn to be an inventor, or a nurse, or a scientist, without failing. Nor can you learn to transform the way products are developed in your firm, or change minds about urban poverty, or restore loving communication with your spouse, without failing. And the Elephant really, really hates to fail.

This presents a difficulty for you when you are trying to change or when you're trying to lead change. You know that you or your audience will fail, and you know that the failure will trigger the "flight" instinct, just as the two of us fled our salsa lessons. How do you keep the Elephant motivated when it faces a long, treacherous road?

The answer may sound strange: You need to create the *expectation* of failure—not the failure of the mission itself, but failure en route. This notion takes us into a fascinating area of research that is likely to change the way you view the world.

8.

Read the following four sentences, and write down whether you agree or disagree with each of them:

1. You are a certain kind of person, and there is not much that can be done to really change that.
2. No matter what kind of person you are, you can always change substantially.
3. You can do things differently, but the important parts of who you are can't really be changed.
4. You can always change basic things about the kind of person you are.

If you agreed with items 1 and 3, you're someone who has a "fixed mindset." And if you agreed with items 2 and 4, you tend to have a "growth mindset." (If you agreed with both 1 and 2, you're confused.) As we'll see, which mindset you have can help determine how easy it will be for you to handle failure, and how dogged you'll be in pursuing change. It might even determine how successful you are in your career.

People who have a fixed mindset believe that their abilities are basically static. Maybe you believe you're a pretty good public speaker, an average manager, and a wonderful organizer. With a fixed mindset, you believe that you may get a little bit better or worse at those skills, but basically your abilities reflect the way you're wired. Your behavior, then, is a good representation of your natural ability, just as the swirled-and-sniffed first taste of wine is a good representation of the bottle you've bought.

If you are someone with a fixed mindset, you tend to avoid challenges, because if you fail, you fear that others will see your failure as an indication of your true ability and see you as a loser (just as a bad first taste of wine leads you to reject the bottle). You feel threatened by negative feedback, because it seems as if the critics are saying they're better than you, positioning themselves at a level of natural ability higher than yours. You try not to be seen exerting too much effort. (People who are really good don't need to try that hard, right?) Think about tennis player John McEnroe as a young star—he had great natural talent but was not keen on rigorous practice or self-improvement.

In contrast, people who have a growth mindset believe that abilities are like muscles—they can be built up with practice. That is, with concerted effort, you can make yourself better at writing or managing or listening to your spouse. With a growth mindset, you tend to accept more challenges despite the risk of failure. (After all, when you try and fail to lift more weight at the gym, you don't worry that everybody will mock you as a "born weakling.") You seek out "stretch" assignments at work. And you're more inclined to accept criticism, because ultimately it makes you better. You may not be as good as others right now, but you're thinking long-term, in a tortoise-versus-hare kind of way. Think Tiger Woods, who won eight major championships faster than anyone in history and *then decided his swing needed an overhaul.*

Fixed versus growth: Which are you? This isn't one of those Cosmo Personality Quizzes in which there are no wrong answers ("Are you a Labrador retriever or a poodle?"). Carol Dweck, a professor of psychology at Stanford University, has spent her career studying these two mindsets—she is the source of the terms. And her research results are clear: If you want to reach your full potential, you need a growth mindset.

Dweck has studied how these two mindsets influence the performance of Olympic athletes and virtuoso musicians and everyday businesspeople. In her must-read book *Mindset: The New Psychology of Success,* she makes an airtight case that a growth mindset will make you more successful at almost anything. That's because people with a growth mindset—those who stretch them-selves, take risks, accept feedback, and take the long-term view—can't help but progress in their lives and careers.

Once you become aware of these concepts, you start to spot the fixed mindset everywhere. Look at the way we praise our chil-dren: "You're so smart!" "You are so good at basketball!" That's fuel for the fixed mindset. A growth mindset compliment praises *effort* rather than natural skill: "I'm proud of how hard you worked on that project!" "I could tell you listened to your coach's com-ments—you really had your elbow under those jump shots today."

Our salsa-dancing experience was a classic example of a fixed mindset failure. After trying an unfamiliar movement for a while, we concluded, definitively, that we were Terrible Salsa Dancers and were born that way. And we quit because letting other people see that natural lack of ability made us uncomfortable. Someone with a growth mindset never would have jumped to this conclu-sion. In fact, they never would have expected to be any good at salsa early on. The mindset would make all the difference.

Which, of course, prompts an obvious question: Can people with a fixed mindset learn to adopt a growth mindset?

9.

In 2007, Dweck and two colleagues, Kali Trzesniewsi of Stanford and Lisa Blackwell of Columbia, decided to run an experiment on junior-high-school students: If they trained the students on the growth mindset, would the kids get better at math?

Junior high is, as you know, a tough transition time for kids. Most people have decidedly mixed memories of junior high, and 40 percent of people actually rank adolescence as the *worst* time in their lives. (Presumably the other 60 percent didn't have acne.) Just as puberty begins to kick in, students move to new schools with harder work and a new crop of teachers who don't give them the warm individual attention they got used to in elementary school. Junior high is a turning point for fixed mindset kids: Dweck found that in elementary school, fixed-mindset students do about as well as growth-mindset students but in junior high suffer an immediate drop in grades and then continue to slide in the next few years.

The students in Dweck's study often came up with fixed-mindset explanations for their decline: "I am the stupidest." "I suck in math." Notice how they're talking about their abilities as permanent traits, as if they were saying, "My eyes are brown." (Other students tended to place the blame elsewhere, saying things like "I didn't do well because the teacher is on crack" or "My math teacher is a fat male slut.")

Dweck and her colleagues set up a study for seventh-grade math students in a school where 79 percent of students were eligible for the federal free lunch program—exactly the kind of low socioeconomic environment in which students are at risk for starting a pattern of academic failure. The control group was taught generic study skills, and the experimental group was taught the growth mindset.

The growth-mindset students were taught that the brain is like a muscle that can be developed with exercise—that with work, they could get smarter. After all, Dweck told them, "nobody laughs at babies and says how dumb they are because they can't talk."

Classroom mentors asked the students to think about skills they already had learned—Remember when you first stepped onto a skateboard or played *Guitar Hero?*—and to recall how practice had been the key to mastering those skills. Students were reminded that "Everything is hard before it is easy," and that they should never give up because they didn't master something immediately. In total, the students in the growth-mindset group received two hours of "brain is like a muscle" training over eight weeks. And the results? Astonishing.

Students in the control group who were taught generic study skills started out their seventh-grade year with math grades at about a C+ level. Over the course of the year, their grades slipped to a C and then toward C–. The "brain is like a muscle" training, however, stopped this slide and reversed it. The students who received it significantly outperformed their peers.

Some students made dramatic transformations. In *Mindset*, Dweck reported, "One day, we were introducing the growth mindset to a new group of students. All at once Jimmy—the most hard-core, turned-off, low-effort kid in the group—looked up with tears in his eyes and said, 'You mean I don't have to be dumb?' From that day on, he worked. He started staying up late to do his homework, which he never used to bother with at all. He started handing in assignments early so he could get feedback and revise them. These kids now believe that working hard was not something that made you vulnerable, but something that made you smarter."

The teachers, unaware of the experimental conditions their students were assigned to, were asked to identify the students who they thought had experienced a positive change during the spring term. Seventy-six percent of the students they identified were in the "brain is like a muscle" training group.

Those results were dramatically out of proportion with the intervention itself. Math is a cumulative topic, after all, and the students in this experiment were already a third of the way into the spring term. Two hours of instruction, in the junior-high sandstorm of hormones and popularity and YouTube, should have had all the transformative effect of an after-school lecture on the Food Pyramid. Instead, two hours of training in how to think about intelligence made students demonstrably better at math. Dweck proved that the growth mindset can be taught and that it can change lives.

10.

In the business world, we implicitly reject the growth mindset. Businesspeople think in terms of two stages: You plan, and then you execute. There's no "learning stage" or "practice stage" in the middle. From the business perspective, practice looks like poor execution. Results are the thing: *We don't care how ya do it, just get it done!*

But to create and sustain change, you've got to act more like a coach and less like a scorekeeper. You've got to embrace a growth mindset and instill it in your team. Why is that so critical? Because, as Harvard Business School professor Rosabeth Moss Kanter observes in studying large organizations, "Everything can look like a failure in the middle." A similar sentiment is expressed by marriage therapist Michele Weiner-Davis, who says that "real change, the kind that sticks, is often three steps forward and two steps back."

If failure is a necessary part of change, then the way people understand failure is critical. The leaders at IDEO, the world's preeminent product design firm, have designed products and experiences ranging from the first Apple mouse to a new Red Cross blood donation procedure. They understand the need to prepare their employees—and, more important, their clients—for failure.

Tim Brown, the CEO of IDEO, says that every design process goes through "foggy periods." One of IDEO's designers even sketched out a "project mood chart" that predicts how people will feel at different phases of a project. It's a U-shaped curve with a peak of positive emotion, labeled "hope," at the beginning, and a second peak of positive emotion, labeled "confidence," at the end. In between the two peaks is a negative emotional valley labeled "insight."

Brown says that design is "rarely a graceful leap from height to height." When a team embarks on a new project, team members are filled with hope and optimism. As they start to collect data and observe real people struggling with existing products, they find that new ideas spring forth effortlessly. Then comes the difficult task of integrating all those fresh ideas into a coherent new design. At this "insight" stage, it's easy to get depressed, because insight doesn't always strike immediately.

The project often feels like a failure in the middle. But if the team persists through this valley of angst and doubt, it eventually emerges with a growing sense of momentum. Team members begin to test out their new designs, and they realize the improvements they've made, and they keep tweaking the design to make it better. And they come to realize, *we've cracked this problem*. That's when the team reaches the peak of confidence.

Notice what team leaders at IDEO are doing with the peaks-and-valley visual: They are creating the expectation of failure. They are telling team members not to trust that initial flush of good feeling at the beginning of the project, because what comes next is hardship and toil and frustration. Yet, strangely enough, when they deliver this warning, it comes across as *optimistic*.

That's the paradox of the growth mindset. Although it seems to draw attention to failure, and in fact encourages us to *seek out failure*, it is unflaggingly optimistic. *We will struggle, we will fail, we will be knocked down—but throughout, we'll get better, and we'll succeed in the end.*

The growth mindset, then, is a buffer against defeatism. It reframes failure as a natural part of the change process. And that's critical, because people will persevere only if they perceive falling down as *learning* rather than as *failing*.

This lesson was learned the hard way by several hospitals that were trying to embrace a new kind of heart surgery called "minimally invasive cardiac surgery" (MICS). Amy Edmondson, a professor at Harvard Business School, studied the way that sixteen hospitals implemented MICS.

Traditional open-heart surgery is very invasive: A patient's breastbone is split open, his or her blood is circulated through a heart-lung bypass machine, and the heart is stopped. MICS is much less invasive because it allows the heart to be fixed without the chest being opened. Surgeons sneak up to the heart through a small, 3-inch incision between two ribs. Meanwhile, a tiny catheter with a deflated balloon is threaded through the groin, guided into the aorta, and then inflated, blocking blood flow from the inside. The surgeon proceeds to operate using the small, cramped horizontal space between the ribs.

That cramped operating space changes everything about the surgery. With open-heart surgery, the surgeon blocks off the aorta with external clamps, like putting a Chip Clip on a really precious bag of Doritos. No input is needed from the surgical team. With MICS, the balloon gizmo must act as an internal clamp, inflating to block the flow of blood. The surgeon can't see it or feel it yet has to inflate it in exactly the right place at exactly the right pressure. To accomplish this, the surgeon must rely heavily on the anesthesiologist to monitor the path of the balloon as it moves toward the heart. Once the balloon is finally in place and inflated, the work still isn't done. The balloon's position has to be monitored continuously to make sure blood isn't flowing past it. As one nurse said, "When I read the training manual, I couldn't believe it. It was *so* different from standard cases."

The procedure requires precarious maneuvers, in a life-or-death situation, by a team mostly blinded. Kind of like landing a jet on an aircraft carrier at night. (Not that we know what either of these things feels like. We just picture both being substantially more dangerous than writing a nonfiction book.) But there's a big payoff for these precarious maneuvers: a lot less suffering for the patients. MICS heart patients go home from the hospital in four days instead of eight, and they recover fully in three weeks instead of two months.

The promise of MICS, then, is that it offers big benefits to the patients of teams that adopt it, but only if the surgery teams are willing to endure the initial learning period. Lots of new technologies require this trade-off: Think of architects who stopped creating drawings by hand and started using computer-aided design or distributors who learned to use PDAs in the field to track their shipments and deliveries. Pain now for a payoff later.

Edmondson studied sixteen hospitals as they adopted the new MICS technology. She found that some hospitals successfully learned and embraced the new technique, but several failed and retreated back to open-heart surgery. What she learned about the successful and unsuccessful teams is powerful testimony to the power of the growth mindset.

11.

The most effective teams tended to adopt what Edmondson called a "learning frame." Members of these teams pictured MICS as something that would be difficult at first but would get easier over time if they were open to changing how they behaved and communicated.

At Mountain Medical Center, Dr. M adopted a learning frame. He often wore a head camera, which allowed the team to see what was going on, and he encouraged questions about what he was doing and why. He also made sure his team practiced diligently: He deliberately scheduled the first six MICS cases in the same week, so team members could practice repeatedly, with no chance of forgetting what they were learning in the lag times between cases. He also ensured that the same team would be together on the first fifteen cases. After that, he added new members one at a time, so each new person could learn without introducing much risk to the procedure. Mountain Medical Center had great success using MICS, and this success can be attributed to the growth mindset. Dr. M put the focus on practice, he acted as a coach, and he set up the routines to allow the maximum chances to learn and improve.

Other hospitals abandoned their adoption of MICS. At Decorum Hospital, the chief cardiac surgeon, Dr. D, was motivated to adopt MICS for competitive reasons. "We'd like everyone to know we can do it. It's a marketing thing. Patients want to know we can do it." His team members talked about adopting the procedure to "keep up with the Joneses" (the other large hospitals in the area). MICS, then, was seen almost like a desirable new toy to be acquired—especially since all the cool kids had one.

Dr. D ended up implementing the procedure in a unique way: He continued to split the breastbone of his patients, albeit with a smaller incision. One of his nurses remarked, "Dr. D is a creature of habit." And the old habits eventually won out. The use of the new procedure gradually dwindled, and eventually it was abandoned.

Across the hospitals she studied, Edmondson found that the teams who failed made the mistake of trying to "get it right on the first try" and were motivated by the chance to "perform, to shine, or to execute perfectly." But of course no one "shines" on the first few tries—this mindset set the teams up for failure. By contrast, the successful teams focused on learning. They didn't assume that mastery would come quickly, and they anticipated that they'd face challenges. In the end, they were the ones who were more likely to get it right.

Failing is often the best way to learn, and because of that, early failure is a kind of necessary investment. A famous story about IBM makes that point well. In the 1960s, an executive at IBM made a decision that ended up losing the company $10 million (about $70 million in 2009 dollars). The CEO of IBM, Tom Watson, summoned the offending executive to his office at corporate headquarters. The journalist Paul B. Carroll described what happened next:

> As the executive cowered, Watson asked, "Do you know why I've asked you here?"
>
> The man replied, "I assume I'm here so you can fire me."
>
> Watson looked surprised.
>
> "Fire you?" he asked. "Of course not. I just spent $10 million educating you."

12.

In 1995, Molly Howard, a longtime special education teacher in Louisville, Georgia, watched as the new Jefferson County High School building was being built.

"Every day I'd drive by the building, and I'd wonder, 'Who's gonna run that school?' And it kept tugging at me, 'Why don't *you* apply?'" Howard said.

She applied and got the job, but with the promotion came a very tough challenge. Eighty percent of the school's students lived in poverty. Only 15 percent of students in the previous high school had continued on to college. "The kids you'd expect to be successful were successful," said Howard. "But what about the other 85 percent?"

Many teachers had a nearly defeatist attitude. "There was this belief that some children *can* and some children *can't*. That we're here for the ones that can get it, and we've got to accept that we're going to lose some. I knew I'd have to challenge that," said Howard.

Howard acted quickly. First, she had to sell a new identity. Howard believed that every student could aspire to go to college, so she abolished the school's two-track system that had separated "college-bound" students from "vocational" students. In her school, everyone would share the college-bound identity.

She beefed up assessments and tutorial programs. She matched students with teachers who'd be their "on-campus advisers" through all four years. Perhaps her most distinctive change, though, was to the grading system. Under her new system the only grades offered at Jefferson County High School were: A, B, C, and NY.

Not Yet.

In Howard's view, the students at Jefferson had accepted a "culture of failure." In a fixed-mindset way, they acted as though they were failures to the bone. Students often didn't do their homework, or they turned in shoddy work. Getting a D or an F was an easy way out in a way. They might get a poor grade, but at least they would be done.

In the new system, the students couldn't stop until they'd cleared the bar. "We define up front to the kids what's an A, B, and C," said Howard. "If they do substandard work, the teacher will say, 'Not Yet.' . . . That gives them the mindset: *My teacher thinks I can do better*. It changes their expectations."

The school was reborn. Students and teachers became more

engaged, the school's graduation rate increased dramatically, and student test scores went up so much that remedial courses were eliminated. In 2008, the National Association of Secondary School Principals declared Howard the U.S. Principal of the Year, out of 48,000 candidates.

Howard transformed her students. She cultivated a new identity in them. *You're all college-bound students.* Then she flipped Jefferson from a fixed-mindset school to a growth-mindset school. She believed that every student was capable of doing acceptable work, that no student was doomed to failure. There's no "never" at Jefferson anymore, only a "Not Yet."

13.

In times of change, we need to remind ourselves and others, again and again, of certain basic truths: Our brains and our abilities are like muscles. They can be strengthened with practice. We're not born skateboarders or scientists or nurses; we must learn how to skateboard, do science, or care for sick people. And our inspiration to change ourselves comes from our desire to live up to those identities.

In the story of Molly Howard, we see that amazing things can happen when you combine the aspiration of a new identity with the persistence of the growth mindset. That's how you grow your people.

Over the past few chapters, we've seen that the central challenge of change is keeping the Elephant moving forward. Whereas the Rider needs direction, the Elephant needs motivation. And we've seen that motivation comes from feeling— knowledge isn't enough to motivate change. But motivation also comes from confidence. The Elephant has to believe that it's *capable* of conquering the change. And there are two routes to building people's confidence so that they feel "big" relative to their challenge. You can shrink the change or grow your people (or, preferably, both).

Our picture of change is still incomplete, though, because it's clear that in some situations even a reluctant Elephant and a confused Rider will manage to change their behavior. For instance, consider the fact that even a lost, angry driver who is hopelessly late for an appointment will stop dutifully for a red light.

That's why, to make changes stick, we've got to think about shaping the Path.

SHAPE
THE
PATH

8

Tweak the Environment

1.

When some guy cuts you off in traffic, you probably think, instinctively: *What a jerk.* (Or perhaps your inner voice is more vulgar.) What you almost certainly don't think to yourself is, *Gosh, I wonder what's wrong that he is in such a hurry.*

It's not hard to see why we don't think that—it seems kind of naive, as if we're making an excuse for a bad person. But think about your own behavior. Think of a time when you were driving so crazily that others would have been justified to curse you. Was your crazy driving on that day a manifestation of your true character (i.e., you're a jerk to the core)? Or was it sparked by the situation you were in?

In the very first story in Chapter 1—about moviegoers who ate more popcorn when given bigger buckets—we saw how easy it can be to jump to conclusions about people. If we hadn't known about the effect of bucket size, it would have been easy to conclude that the big-bucket people were Popcorn-Gorging Gluttons. But of course the surprising part of the study is that, when you give people a giant bucket, they *become* Popcorn-Gorging Gluttons. And when someone behind the wheel of a car is twenty minutes late for a crucial appointment, that person *becomes* a terrible driver. What looks like a person problem is often a situation problem.

The same phenomenon holds true in the business world. W. Edwards Deming, the chief instigator of the Total Quality Management movement that revolutionized manufacturing, told a story about a company that used a variety of flammable products in its production process. Unsurprisingly, fires frequently broke out in its plants. But the president of the company didn't think he had a situation problem; he thought he had a person problem. He sent a letter to every one of the company's 10,500 employees, *pleading with them to set fewer fires.* Ahem. (What looks like a pyromania problem is often a flammable chemical problem.)

We are frequently blind to the power of situations. In a famous article, Stanford psychologist Lee Ross surveyed dozens of studies in psychology and noted that people have a systematic tendency to ignore the situational forces that shape other people's behavior. He called this deep-rooted tendency the "Fundamental Attribution Error." The error lies in our inclination to attribute people's behavior to *the way they are* rather than to *the situation they are in.*

The Fundamental Attribution Error complicates human relationships. Marriage therapist Michele Weiner-Davis said, "Most people attribute their marital problems to some deeply engrained personality characteristics of their spouse." A wife might say, "My husband is a stubborn person." But Weiner-Davis might respond: "You've got to admit that your husband isn't *always* stubborn. He doesn't resist when his coworkers suggest a new client approach at work. And he doesn't drag his feet when you propose new ways to handle the family's finances. The stubbornness emerges mainly when you suggest a new approach with the kids at home—and when you do that, he is stubborn almost every time. It's the situation, not an immutable stubbornness built into his character, that produces the behavior." (This doesn't excuse his stubbornness, of course, but it should provide hope for a solution, since situations should be easier to tweak than people's core character.)

The Fundamental Attribution Error is the reason why we love TV shows like *The Dog Whisperer* or *Supernanny,* in which seemingly irredeemable dogs and kids are tamed by outsiders who come in with a new system of discipline. At the beginning of the episodes, we're presented with a dog that bites everything in sight, or a child who won't obey the simplest of commands, and we simply can't avoid jumping to conclusions about their character: That dog is vicious. That boy is a terror. And when they're reformed, in the course of a short intervention, it blows our minds.

If we could cure ourselves of the Fundamental Attribution Error, these shows would seem obvious to the point of absurdity. (It would be like watching a show whose premise was that if you take scalding-hot liquids—dangerous and slippery—and stick them in the freezer for a long time, they renounce their fiery former selves and *turn to ice*!)

Now you can see why the third element of our framework, the Path, is so critical. If you want people to change, you can provide clear direction (Rider) or boost their motivation and determination (Elephant). Alternatively, you can simply make the journey easier. Create a steep downhill slope and give them a push. Remove some friction from the trail. Scatter around lots of signs to tell them they're getting close.

In short, you can shape the Path.

2.

To see how a smoother Path can change behavior, consider some research that studied why college students did (or didn't) donate food to a canned-food drive for charity. The researchers knew some students would be more charitable and generous than others and would be more inclined to donate food. The researchers wondered: *Can we alter the situation so that jerks give, too?*

First, to distinguish "saints" from "jerks," they polled all the students in a particular dorm, asking them to assess which of their dorm-mates (out of roughly one hundred) were *most likely* and *least likely* to make a donation. Once they compiled those rankings, they had a pretty good idea of which students were charitable or uncharitable types.

Then they altered the Path. Some students received a basic letter announcing the launch of a food drive the following week and asking them to bring canned food to a booth on Tressider Plaza (a well-known spot on campus). Other students received a more detailed letter, which included a map to the precise spot, a request for a can of beans, and a suggestion that they think about a time when they'd ordinarily be near Tressider Plaza so they wouldn't have to go out of their way to get there.

The two letters were randomly sent to the saints and the jerks. A week later, after the food drive was over, the researchers had a precise list of who had given food and who hadn't.

Students who received the basic letter were not very generous. Only 8 percent of the saints donated and not a single one of the jerks. So far, the jerks were living up to their reputation (but the saints weren't exactly outperforming).

Then came the shock. Students who received the more detailed letter were substantially more charitable: 42 percent of the saints donated, and so did 25 percent of the jerks! This is an inspiring result. These researchers got 25 percent of the *worst individuals in the dorm* to donate simply by smoothing the Path a bit. (Bottom line: If you're hungry and need a can of food, you're three times better-off relying on a jerk with a map than on a budding young saint without one.)

What's more, the Path wasn't changed in any dramatic way— the letter just gave moderately more concrete instructions. Imagine what would have happened with a more aggressive intervention: What if volunteers had gone door-to-door collecting the canned food?

What looks like a people problem is often a situation problem. And no matter what your role is, you've got some control over the situation.

3.

Today, as you go through your day, notice how many times people have tweaked the environment to shape your behavior. Traffic engineers wanted you to drive in a predictable, orderly way, so they painted lane markers on the roads and installed stoplights and road signs. Grocery store managers wanted you to spend more time in their store, so they positioned the milk coolers all the way at the back. Your boss's boss wanted to encourage more collaboration among employees, so she approved an "open floor plan" layout with no cubicles or dividers. The bank was tired of your leaving your ATM card in the machine, so now the machine forces you to remove it before you can claim your cash.

Tweaking the environment is about making the right behaviors a little bit easier and the wrong behaviors a little bit harder. It's that simple. As an inspiration, think about Amazon's 1-Click ordering. With one-tenth the effort of dialing a phone number, you can buy a new book or DVD. Talk about instant gratification.

Amazon's site designers have simply made a desired behavior—you spending money on their site—a little bit easier. They've lowered the bar to a purchase as far as humanly possible (at least until they launch "1-Blink Ordering"). By doing this, they've generated untold millions of dollars in incremental revenue.

The opportunities are endless for simple, 1-Click-style tweaks. A few years ago, a consultant named Peter Bregman was asked to help a management consulting firm with an administrative problem. Employees weren't submitting their time sheets on time, which slowed the firm's billing because charges to clients were based on hours worked. Traditionally, the consultants had submitted their time sheets on paper, and they'd done so pretty reliably. Then the firm developed an online time-sheet tool. Consultants weren't using it. The executives held education classes to explain the new tool, but people kept on submitting their time sheets on paper.

Frustrated, the executives tried using fiat power, announcing that the new online tool was mandatory. "That worked for about half of the employees," said Bregman. "The rest simply ignored it." The executives were ready to escalate the battle: They prepared a memo saying that people wouldn't get their paychecks unless they used the online tool. (Side note: In our experience, people who are trying to change things often reach instinctively for carrots and sticks. But this strategy indicates a pretty crude view of human behavior—that people act only in response to bribes and punishments. And it quickly becomes absurd. Are you going to break out the "no paycheck" stick for every change you want to make in your workplace?)

Bregman put the brakes on. "Wait," he said. "Do we know *why* people aren't doing the online time sheet?" The executives assumed that the consultants were Luddites or simply obstinate—classic labels inspired by the Fundamental Attribution Error. Bregman persuaded the executives to do a bit more investigation.

The employees who turned in paper time sheets were asked why they weren't using the online tool. Paper was easier, they said. Skeptical, the interviewers asked if they could observe the employees while they filled out the online time sheet. The results were telling.

Lots of employees started grousing as soon as they encountered the "wizard" that was built into the online tool. Ironically, the wizard was intended to help people fill out the form. Think of the annoying paper clip guy in Microsoft Office who wants to help you write a letter. Now imagine that you have no choice but to accept his "help." When the executives killed the wizard, allowing people to skip directly to the form itself, compliance rates rose immediately, and within a few weeks everyone was using the online tool.

"People weren't being defiant," said Bregman. They were just proceeding on the easiest Path.

What's sadly typical about this story is that the executives didn't initially look for a Path solution. Instead, they wanted to spook the Elephant by threatening to withhold a paycheck. Bregman says they were mentally stuck: " 'Well, I already *asked* them to do it. I *taught them* how to do it. I *told them* they had to do it. I don't know what else to do!' " At that point, the executives felt they'd tried every tool in their toolbox, so they jumped to punishments.

"We're taught to focus on incentives by our business background," says Bregman. "Or even our parents: 'Do this or you won't get your allowance!' " But executives—and parents—often have more tools than they think they have. If you change the path, you'll change the behavior.

--- **CLINIC** ---

Can You Get Problem Students to Come to
Class on Time?

SITUATION Bart Millar, an American history teacher at Lincoln High School in Portland, Oregon, is frustrated by a few of his students, like Robby and Kent, who frequently arrive late and then sit in the back of the room, talking to each other and laughing and disrupting the class. Millar has tried getting tough with them— being strict and even sending them to the principal a few times. Nothing seems to work. What can he do to get these students under control? [Bart Millar and the situation are real, but the kids' names are disguised.]

WHAT'S THE SWITCH AND WHAT'S HOLDING IT BACK? If Millar tries to get Robby and Kent to "act like model students," he'll be doomed to fail. Let's focus on the critical move: Millar wants Robby and Kent to be in their seats before the class starts. If he manages to succeed with that (no small feat), he can keep snowballing the change.

What's holding back the switch? Let's face it, this probably isn't a Rider problem. Robby and Kent know exactly when they're supposed to be in their seats, so we won't even think about the Rider. It's an Elephant problem. The kids aren't enthused about showing up on time, especially if doing so means less time hanging out with their friends in the hallways. The Path might also play a role: Are there aspects of the environment or culture that make it easier for the kids to get away with their tardiness?

HOW DO WE MAKE THE SWITCH?

• *Direct the Rider.* **N/A.** The teens know what is expected of them.

• *Motivate the Elephant.* **1. Find the feeling.** Maybe the kids see Millar as an abstract authority figure rather than as a human being. Imagine a one-on-one conversation with each kid in which Millar says, "I feel stressed out because

I'm expected to cover so much material in so little time. And that's how I'm judged. And I know you don't think it's a big deal when you're a few minutes late, but it makes my chances of doing a good job harder and harder. Can you do me a favor and just get here a second or two early?" Depending on the kids' empathy level, this might work. Or, more likely, fail utterly.

• *Shape the Path.* **1. Tweak the environment.** Lock the door when the bell rings so latecomers are stuck in the hallway. **2. Build habits.** Start having a daily quiz with one or two quick questions at the beginning of every class. If Robby and Kent aren't present to take the quiz, they'll fail. **3. Rally the herd.** Post a class "on-time" record on the wall. Maybe when Robby and Kent see that they're the only students violating the social norm to be on time, they'll change their ways. **4. Build habits.** Set a policy that the last student in his or her seat every day will be asked to answer the first question. **5. Rally the herd.** Find a way to let Robby and Kent know that the *other students* dislike what they're doing (as they almost certainly do). Often troublemakers have the illusion that their defiant behavior makes them folk heroes. They can be deflated quickly by frank peer feedback. **6. Tweak the environment.** Do what Bart Millar actually did: He bought a used couch and put it right at the front of the classroom. It was immediately obvious that this couch was the cool place to sit—students could slouch and relax instead of sitting at a dorky desk. Suddenly Robby and Kent started getting to class *early* every day so they could "get a good seat." *They were volunteering to sit at the front of the classroom.* Genius.

4.

Becky Richards worked at Kaiser South San Francisco Hospital, where nurses administer about eight hundred medications a day. "Medication administration" is what happens between the time a doctor prescribes a certain medication (such as 100 mg of ibuprofen) and the patient receives it. Nurses take the doctor's chicken-scratch prescription, transcribe it so it's legible, then fax the order to the pharmacy. When the medication arrives from the pharmacy, they deliver it in the right dosage by the right method (IV drip, injection, orally) to the right patient at the right time.

Nurses have an impressive accuracy record: On average, they commit approximately 1 error per 1,000 medications administered. Still, given the huge volume of medications delivered at Kaiser South, that error rate led to about 250 errors annually, and a single error can be harmful or even deadly. For instance, if a patient receives too much heparin, a blood thinner, the patient's blood will no longer clot and the patient could hemorrhage. If a patient gets too little heparin, the patient could develop a blood clot that could lead to a stroke.

Richards, who was director of adult clinical services at Kaiser South, and her nursing staff wanted to drive down medication errors. Richards believed that most errors happened when nurses were distracted. It was easy to become distracted, because in most traditional hospitals, the medication administration areas are right in the middle of the nursing units, which tend to be the noisiest places on the floor. From memory, Richards quoted Tess Pape, a professor at the University of Texas who has studied medication errors, saying, "Today we *admire* people for multitasking, we celebrate people who can accomplish many things at once. But when you're giving out medications it is the *last* time you should be multitasking."

Put yourself in Richards's shoes for a moment. Your goal is clear: Change your nurses' behavior so they can focus better, so they're less likely to get distracted. How can you accomplish that? First, you need to identify the core problem.

The nurses understand what's expected of them—the critical moves are clear—so this isn't a Rider problem. Nor do the nurses have any emotional resistance to better focus. In fact, it annoys them when they're distracted by others, which means that, in this case, we have the luxury of a supportive Elephant. The problem, it seems, is the distractions themselves. No one thinks twice before calling out to a nurse who's walking the halls delivering medication. Worse, nurses feel an obligation to respond when others distract them. No one wants to tell a surgeon, "Sorry, bub, can't help right now. I'm dealing with medication." Yet that's exactly what needs to happen if errors are to be reduced.

What Richards needed to do was make other people aware that they were interrupting the nurses. She needed to make the bad behavior visible. Ideally, when the nurses were administering medication, they would work inside a soundproof bubble, like the "Cone of Silence" from *Get Smart.* With that solution being architecturally infeasible, Richards came up with the idea of using a visual symbol, something that could be worn by nurses, that would signal to other people, *Hey, don't bother me right now. I'm passing out medication.*

After considering armbands and aprons, Richards settled on vests and decided to call them "medication vests." Where do you buy a medication vest? Richards had to make do with what she could find: "The first vest we ordered was off the internet. It was really cheesy. Cheap plastic. *Bright* orange. Be careful what you order off the internet."

Later, with vests in hand, Richards unveiled the idea to her staff: *When you're administering medication, you'll put on a medication vest. It's bright enough that people can see it from down the hall. And all of us, including the doctors, will know that when someone is wearing one of these vests, we should leave that person alone.*

She selected two units at Kaiser South for a six-month pilot study of the medication vests, and in July 2006 it began.

Richards quickly encountered a problem. The nurses hated

the vests. So did the doctors. "Nurses thought the vest was de-meaning, and they couldn't find it when they needed it," said Richards. "They didn't like the color. They'd ask, 'How do you clean it?' And physicians hated not being able to talk to their nurses when they passed them in the hall."

The nurses' written feedback was scathing: "Oh, so you want to draw *attention* to the fact we can make a mistake." "You want people to think I have a dunce cap on, that I'm so stupid I can't think on my feet." "Give me a hard hat and a cone and I can go work for Caltrans [the state highway department]."

"They were pretty brutal," said Richards. The reception was so universally poor that Richards was ready to write off the idea and try something else.

Then the data came back.

During the six-month trial period, errors dropped 47 percent from the six months prior to the study. "It took our breath away," said Richards.

Once the data were in, the hatred faded. Impressed by the re-sults, the entire hospital adopted the medication vests, except for one unit that insisted they weren't needed. Errors dropped by 20 percent in the first month of the hospitalwide adoption, except in one unit, which actually saw an increase in errors. (Guess which one.)

You know you've got a smart solution when everyone hates it and it still works—and in fact works so well that people's hate turns to enthusiasm. Becky Richards had found a way to change the Path.

5.

The airline industry has long used a consistent practice. Because most aircraft accidents happen during takeoffs and landings—the most hectic and coordination-intensive parts of any flight—the industry adopted the "sterile cockpit" rule. Anytime a plane is below 10,000 feet—whether on the way up or the way down— no conversation is permitted in the cockpit, except what's directly relevant for flying. At 11,000 feet, members of the cockpit crew can talk about football, their kids, or the loathsome passengers. But not at 9,500 feet.

One IT group adopted the "sterile cockpit" concept to advance an important software project. The group had embraced a substantial goal—to reduce new-product development time from three years to nine months. In previous projects with tight deadlines, the work environment had become increasingly stressful. When workers fell behind schedule, they tended to interrupt their colleagues for quick help, and their managers would wander by regularly and ask to be "statused" on the project. As a result, the software engineers were interrupted more and more, and workweeks expanded to sixty and seventy hours as people started showing up on weekends, hoping to get some work done without interruption.

The leaders of the IT group decided to try an experiment. They established "quiet hours" on Tuesday, Thursday, and Friday mornings before noon. The goal was to give coders a sterile cockpit, allowing them to concentrate on complex bits of coding without being derailed by periodic interruptions. Even the socially insensitive responded well to this change in the Path. One engineer, previously among the worst interrupters, said, "I always used to worry about my own quiet time and how to get more of it, but this experiment made me think about how I'm impacting others."

In the end, the group managed to meet its stringent nine-month development goal. The division vice president attributed this accomplishment to the sterile cockpit quiet hours: "I do not think we could've made the deadline without it," he said. "This is a new benchmark."

In these disparate environments—airplane cockpits and hospitals and IT work groups—the right behaviors did not evolve naturally. Nurses weren't "naturally" given enough space to work without distraction, and programmers weren't "naturally" left alone to focus on coding. Instead, leaders had to reshape the Path consciously. With some simple tweaks to the environment, suddenly the right behaviors emerged. It wasn't the people who changed; it was the situation. What looks like a people problem is often a situation problem.

6.

We've seen lots of environment tweaking in organizations—offices and airlines and hospitals—but, make no mistake, we can turn these tools on ourselves, too. Many people have discovered that, when it comes to changing their own behavior, environmental tweaks beat self-control every time.

For instance, Brian Wansink, the author of the popcorn-bucket study described in Chapter 1, has a devoted following of dieters who swear by his prime directive: Shrink your dinnerware. Use smaller plates, bowls, and cups.

Wansink knows that if we use big plates, we feel obligated to cover them with food—a half-full plate feels morally wrong somehow. And because we're wired to finish what's on our plate, that's a big problem. Big plates = big portions = overeating. To achieve eating control, according to Wansink, you must start with plate control. Store your dinner plates in a box in your closet, and start eating dinner every night off your salad plates. Use small wineglasses, not huge goblets. Never, ever eat snack food directly out of the bag or box; instead, pour a reasonable portion onto a small appetizer plate. These very simple environmental tweaks—swapping out the plates and bowls and glasses in your cabinet—have *huge* effects on eating behavior.

We all play these games with ourselves, trying to nudge ourselves to do the right thing. We know a guy who religiously lays out his jogging clothes and shoes before he goes to sleep. That way, when he wakes up, it's just a tiny bit easier to get going. Another friend never goes to bed without setting the coffeepot to auto-brew at wake-up time. The aroma of fresh-brewed coffee helps to fight the oversleeping urge. And there's a woman who actually freezes her credit card in a block of ice, so that when she feels the urge to spend, she forces herself to have a cooling-off (or, rather, a warming-up) period.

Self-manipulation works. Amanda Tucker used these same environment-tweaking principles to improve her management style at work. Tucker was the country manager for Nike in Vietnam. She traveled frequently to visit factories in outlying regions, and while she was out of the office, work piled up. When she returned home, she was often overwhelmed. "I had more plates spinning than I felt I could handle," she said. It was tempting to shut her office door and plow through the accumulated work, but she knew it was important to stay accessible to her team. In fact, she established an open-door policy, allowing the individuals who reported to her directly to see her at any time she was in town.

Nine months into the job, Tucker solicited feedback from her team members about her performance as a manager. She was astonished when they complained that she didn't seem to have time to talk to them. "Some of them were offended that when they walked into my office, I would often continue to look at my computer screen and type while they were talking. This of course gave them the strong signal that what I was doing was more important to me than they were," Tucker said.

She knew they were right. It was a bad habit. And she also knew that the layout of her office was encouraging the habit. When people came to see her, they sat in chairs across from her desk. When she faced them, she still had the computer monitor in her field of view. So it was easy—too easy—for Tucker to glance back and forth from their faces to the screen.

Tucker simply rearranged her office. She moved the desk so it no longer separated her from her guests, and she added a meeting area with two small couches and a table. Now, when she was facing the people who came to see her, the computer was completely out of sight. No more temptation.

"Just by rearranging the furniture, I was able to connect much better with people who came to see me," she said. Six months later, she solicited more feedback and was pleased that her communication scores had soared.

If you'd seen Tucker's initial performance appraisals, you might have concluded that, despite her stated open-door policy, she was one of those insensitive managers who never listen to their subordinates. And you would have been committing the Fundamental Attribution Error. Simply by rearranging the furniture in her office, Tucker made herself into a different "kind of person." That's the power of shaping the Path.

7.

There is something satisfying about outsmarting ourselves. (By now, you realize what "outsmarting ourselves" means—that our Riders are outsmarting our Elephants.) Tucker's solution was appealing in its elegance—a seemingly messy management problem solved by an afternoon office makeover. Tucker shaped her environment to *disallow* her own bad behavior.

This is a topic that hits home for the two of us (your co-authors). While we were writing this book, we got annoyed by our tendency to get distracted by e-mail. We were aware of the irony of our giving advice to readers about reining in their Elephants while our own Elephants habitually prompted us to check Outlook. So we decided to take some of our own medicine.

If you use Microsoft Outlook, you know that when you get new e-mail, an alert sound plays through your computer's speakers. That sound is like digital catnip. How can you not check your mail when you hear it? What if a rich Nigerian politician went down in a plane crash and you had a limited time to capture part of his fortune?

Chip decided to tweak his environment: He rummaged through the control panel until he found the place that allowed him to delete the e-mail sound at the system level. Later, he noticed that new e-mail also triggered an alert icon on the taskbar—more irresistible bait for the Elephant. He covered it with a Post-it note blackened with one of his daughter's felt-tip markers. Now it can't torment him. Ignorance is bliss.

Meanwhile, Dan went nuclear. He bought an old laptop, deleted all its browsers, and, for good measure, deleted its wireless network drivers. Now when he needs to focus, he takes the "way-back machine" with him to a coffee shop or library. There's no hope of getting online. He's been liberated by this restriction.

Our struggles with e-mail are a bit pathetic, but the larger topic is worth considering: Is it possible to design an environment in which undesired behaviors—whether yours or your colleagues'—are made not only harder but *impossible*? As it turns out, lots of people actually make their living contemplating how to wipe out the wrong kinds of behaviors.

Consider industrial safety. Many factories use dangerous machines that have a bad habit of lopping off fingers or hands that are in the wrong place at the wrong time. Suppose you're a factory foreman and one of your workers loses an index finger in an industrial accident. You want to make sure this never happens again. How might you accomplish that?

You could give your workers' Riders clear direction by means of clear signage—KEEP HANDS CLEAR OF THE MACHINE or DANGER: RISK OF INJURY—accompanied by an illustration identifying the machine's trouble spot.

You could appeal to your workers' Elephants, using fear. Here we can take inspiration from driver's-education courses in which teenagers watch films full of bloody, gruesome car crashes, so that when they finish driver's ed they will avoid driving like teenagers. In homage to these films, you could call together your workers and show them a video of the guy who lost his finger. Show them what the gory wound looked like. Have him urge his colleagues to take safety seriously. "I wish I'd paid more attention," he'd say.

Or you could focus on the Path, in which case you would disregard hearts and minds entirely. In fact, suppose you stipulated outright that your workers are hopeless, that they're irredeemable daredevils who are determined to waggle their fingers in the machine's danger zone for the sheer sport of it. Could you still keep them from dismembering themselves?

Absolutely. Many factories have done exactly that. For instance, one machine is designed so that it can be activated only if two buttons are pressed at the same time. The buttons are positioned so that to press both of them you must place your arms high and wide (like the "Y" in the "YMCA" dance). The beauty of this arrangement is that, if your hands are pressing those buttons, they are (by design) nowhere near the danger zone. And if they're not pressing the buttons, the machine is off. Either way, your fingers win.

Poof—you have made a dangerous behavior impossible.

8.

With that example in mind, think about all the innovations that have made "bad behavior" impossible or nearly impossible: child-proof caps on medicine bottles, cars that won't shift out of park unless the brake pedal is pressed, anything that's fireproof. Notice that these are product-design innovations created to prevent injuries. "Injury prevention" is, in fact, a thriving field. Every state government has a few people on staff—usually heinously under-funded—whose job is to think about how to reduce injuries or deaths caused by small children falling into swimming pools, the elderly falling in their homes, car crashes, and other misfortunes. Rarely can such incidents be made impossible, but injuries resulting from them can be reduced.

In trying to minimize the risk of bad outcomes, injury-prevention experts often turn to the Haddon Matrix, a simple framework that provides a way to think systematically about accidents by highlighting three key periods of time: pre-event, event, and post-event.

Let's say our goal is to reduce serious injuries from car wrecks. *Pre-event* interventions would include anything that would tend to prevent wrecks from happening: installing bright lighting on highways, painting clear lane markers on the roads, popularizing antilock brakes, launching advertising campaigns against drunk driving.

With *event* interventions, we accept that crashes will happen and ask ourselves how we can reduce the chances of injury. Seat belts and air bags are classic event interventions, but also think about breakaway light poles and those big orange barrels that line exit ramps (which are intended to soften collisions).

With *post-event* interventions, we acknowledge both that crashes will occur and that people will be injured. The goal of post-event interventions is to minimize the severity of the injuries and optimize the health outcomes. A speedy, effective emergency medical team will be important.

The Haddon Matrix is also useful for thinking about matters that aren't so life-and-death. Let's say you are the IT person in a small business and one of your many duties is to prevent the loss of important data that occurs frequently when computers crash. Some IT support people in this situation embrace not the Haddon Matrix but the "Hectoring Manifesto" and berate their colleagues for not backing up their work (all the while committing the Fundamental Attribution Error: *My colleagues are reckless and lazy people!*). But if you think in Haddon Matrix terms, you begin to see a more holistic picture.

Think about pre-event interventions: If computers don't crash, then you can't lose data. So maybe you schedule monthly computer check-ups, buy extra-padded laptop bags for everyone, and budget for complete replacements every three years.

Event interventions would call for ways of preventing a crash from leading to data loss. For instance, some computers have an extra hard drive where all data are mirrored in real time. A crash would be less likely to take out both drives.

Post-event interventions would accept the reality of data loss but focus on ways to minimize the damage. The most obvious strategy here would be to create an automated nightly network backup, so that if a crash happens and data are lost, you can restore the previous night's data. Another post-event strategy would be to find ways to prevent mission-critical data from ever ending up on a laptop. For instance, you might use an online application such as SalesForce.com to host customer contact information, so that precious data would never depend on the health of a local hard drive.

Note that we've managed to create a robust plan against data loss without worrying about what our employees were thinking or feeling. We didn't mention their Elephants or their Riders. We simply tweaked the environment to make bad behavior impossible.

9.

In 1999, some bad behavior was abruptly made impossible at a company called Rackspace. At one particular moment, company employees stopped doing one thing and starting doing another thing, and that behavior shift became the most important inflection point in the company's history. But before we get to that moment, a bit of backstory is necessary.

Rackspace is a company that hosts internet sites for other companies. It prides itself on customer service, as suggested by its slogan, "Fanatical Support." The firm's focus on customer service has paid off. Over the years, Rackspace has won an armload of trade awards for its service, and its "Net Promoter" score—a commonly used benchmark of customer word-of-mouth—has consistently been the envy of the industry.

But Rackspace wasn't always so customer-friendly. In 1999, Rackspace didn't think much about customer service. Company founder Graham Weston said that in the early days, Rackspace had a "denial of service" business model. Customer-service interactions were viewed as costs to be minimized—the more roadblocks that could be erected to keep the phone from ringing, the better the profits would be. (Notice the uncomfortable echoes of the Haddon Matrix: If you view customer calls as bad behavior to be prevented, you will do all you can to deter them. Recall that for many years, Amazon.com's policy was not to publish a customer-service phone number.)

Then in the fall of 1999, Rackspace received The Call. It started normally enough. A customer tried to call for support. He pressed 5 to get help, but instead he got voice mail, which in effect said, "Feel free to leave a voice mail here, but we don't check it very often, so you're better-off sending us an e-mail." The customer grudgingly sent an e-mail message to the suggested address. And the team at Rackspace never answered it.

After a few more of these irritating cycles, the customer was furious, and with a bit of legwork he managed to track down Graham Weston at the office of a real estate business he owned. Surprised, Weston asked the customer to forward the e-mails he'd sent and promised to look into the matter.

Weston reviewed the long chain of e-mails, which had become increasingly angry as past inquiries were ignored. "Something hit me about what the customer was asking for," said Weston. "It was something that we could do very easily that he couldn't do. So the question in my mind was, why are we not serving the customer happily?"

Weston knew that his team couldn't sustain a business based on dodging its customers. "We made a 180-degree turn," he said.

Weston hired David Bryce to be the head of customer support. At his first meeting with the team, Bryce announced that Rackspace was going to transform itself from a company that dreaded customer support to a company that was passionate about support. He posted an aspirational banner on the wall: RACKSPACE GIVES FANATICAL SUPPORT. The phrase stuck immediately.

This was just talk, of course, but there was action to back it up. Weston started by overhauling the company's business model. Providing great service would cost more, and if Rackspace offered both premium service and cutting-edge technological expertise, it would be forced to set its prices so high that no one would buy. So, remarkably, Weston began pushing for the company to become technologically dull: "We don't want to be on the bleeding edge of technology. We believe in standardization. We want a narrow focus—these are the things we do, and these are things we don't do. If you're E*Trade or Amazon, you should host your own site, we can't help," he said. (Notice that this is clear direction for the Rider.)

Perhaps the most dramatic change made by Weston and Bryce was also the simplest. Rackspace, like all hosting companies, had a call-queuing system. ("Your call is important to us. Please press 1 for recorded tips that don't address your problem. Press 5 to leave us a message we won't return. Press 8 to repeat these options.") The call queue is perhaps the most basic tool of customer support.

Weston threw it out.

"When a customer calls, that means they need our help, and we've got to answer the telephone," he said. Without the queuing system, there was no safety net. The phone would keep ringing until somebody picked it up. To Weston, this was a critical symbol of the service ethic. "When a customer has a problem, we shouldn't deal with it when it's convenient for us. We should deal with it when it's convenient for the customer." When Weston threw out the queuing system, it became *impossible* to dodge the customer. By 2007, the company was talking to an average customer three times per week.

Subsequently, the company launched the "Straightjacket Awards," including actual Rackspace-branded straightjackets as trophies, which were presented to employees who'd been so fanatical about service that they'd become downright insane. (That's an identity appeal for the Elephant: *We are zealots—that's what makes us special.*) Not coincidentally, in 2008, Rackspace was one of the companies in *Fortune*'s list of Best Places to Work.

The focus on service paid off. In 2001, Rackspace was the

first internet hosting firm to turn a profit, and over the next six years, it *averaged* 58 percent annual growth. By 2008, Rackspace had passed AT&T as the highest-grossing firm in the industry.

10.

What transformed the character of Rackspace's customer-service people? Nothing. They had the same core character before and after the change. They were just people operating in a new environment. The old behavior (ignoring customers) had become harder, and the new behavior (serving customers) had become easier.

In this chapter, we've seen that what looks like a "character problem" is often correctible when you change the environment. The transformations are stunning. Take a bunch of customer-service slackers and rip out their call-queuing system, and they start helping customers. Take a boss whose employees say she "won't listen" and rejigger her furniture, and suddenly the employees' frustrations fade. Take the biggest jerks in the Stanford dorms and give them a page of instructions, and they'll donate more food to the needy than the saints.

Simple tweaks of the Path can lead to dramatic changes in behavior.

9

Build Habits

1.

Mike Romano was born in 1950 and raised in Milwaukee, the youngest of four brothers. His dad was a handyman who fixed plumbing and heating fixtures. His mom had a commercial art degree; she stayed at home to raise the boys, taking jobs from time to time to pay the bills.

Romano had a temper. In high school, when he was 18, he got into a fight and threw a guy through a window. Afraid of what would happen in court, he enlisted in the army. He figured he was going to be drafted anyway. The court let him go.

Romano eventually ended up being assigned to the 173rd Airborne Brigade in Vietnam, an elite and well-respected unit of paratroopers. The soldiers of the 173rd had an open secret, however: rampant drug use. Others nicknamed them "jumping junkies." Coming into the military, Romano had no real drug experience. He tried to keep his nose clean with the jumping junkies.

A few months after he arrived in Vietnam, a Claymore land mine detonated near him, and he was struck in his right hand, forearm, and foot. He was taken to a hospital in Camron Bay for recovery. That was where he first tried opium.

He quickly became hooked, like so many others around him. Even when he transferred to other hospitals, his supply wasn't interrupted. He mostly smoked opium-laced joints, but it was also easy to find liquid opium and even opium chewing gum (not to mention other drugs, such as LSD and marijuana). His addiction continued to torment him throughout his thirteen-month tour of duty.

Romano's fall into drug use was a typical story during the Vietnam War. The White House was so troubled by reports of drug use among soldiers that it commissioned a study to investigate the scope of the problem. The results were disturbing. Before the war, the typical soldier had only casual experience with hard drugs, and less than 1 percent had ever been addicted to narcotics. But once in Vietnam, almost half of the soldiers tried narcotics, and 20 percent became addicted. Demographics did not predict who would become drug users in Vietnam—race and class were irrelevant.

The drug use started early. Twenty percent of all users started in their first week in Vietnam, 60 percent within the first three months. Oddly, drug use did not seem to be triggered by trauma. The researchers found no statistical relationship between drug use and the difficulty of soldiers' assignments, or the danger they faced, or the death of friends. Unlike most soldiers, Romano started using opium because he was injured. For most soldiers in Vietnam, drugs were simply a fact of life, a part of the culture.

Government officials were terrified by what would happen when thousands of drug addicts began to return to America. Military and civilian leaders worried that the country's drug-treatment programs would be flooded, stretched far beyond capacity. They worried that vets might not be able to hold down jobs, that they might turn to crime.

Mike Romano was one of the people the officials were worried about. When he finally boarded his flight back to the United States in 1969, headed home to Milwaukee, he smuggled back with him a stash of opium-laced joints.

Then his life began to change. A week or two after his return home, he was driving with friends in town when he saw a girl he'd known in grade school. "Stop the car!" he said. He chased her down. She was working as a countergirl at a nearby drugstore. "I thought she was very beautiful," said Romano.

The two started dating. She caught on fairly quickly that Romano was an addict, and she put pressure on him to stop. He tried to quit a few times, but each time he started to feel sick as withdrawal pains kicked in, and then he'd begin using again. Meanwhile, he started work—construction and house painting and other temporary jobs—and he started taking art classes at the University of Wisconsin at Milwaukee. He got a job there designing promotional posters for bands who played at the student union.

After a few quit-and-relapse cycles, he began to wean himself off opium, and within about a month he was clean. He hasn't touched opium since. What we see in Mike Romano's life seems like an almost impossible change story: an opium addict who recovered. Mike Romano was one of the lucky ones.

2.

Or was he? White House researchers continued to investigate the drug problem among returning soldiers, and a puzzle started to emerge. Following up with the troops who returned home, the

investigators called them eight to twelve months after their return to ask about their ongoing drug use. During the war, 50 percent of soldiers had been casual users, and 20 percent had become
seriously addicted, meaning that they used drugs more than once
a week for an extended period of time and experienced withdrawal symptoms (chills, cramps, pain) if they tried to stop. But
when the investigators conducted the follow-up, what they found
blew their minds. Only 1 percent of the vets were still addicted
to drugs. That was essentially the same rate as existed before the
war. The feared, drug-fueled social catastrophe had not occurred.
What had happened?

3.

People are incredibly sensitive to the environment and the
culture—to the norms and expectations of the communities they
are in. We all want to wear the right clothes, to say the right
things, to frequent the right places. Because we instinctively try
to fit in with our peer group, behavior is contagious, sometimes
in surprising ways.

Imagine that your job was to design an environment that
would extinguish drug addiction. You could take drug-addicted
U.S. soldiers, drop them into this environment, and feel confident that the forces within it would act powerfully to help them
beat their habits. Think of this environment as an antidrug theme
park, and assume that you can spend as much as you want to
construct it. What would your theme park look like?

It might look a whole lot like Romano's neighborhood in
Milwaukee.

You'd want to surround the former soldiers with people who
love them and care about them—and who treat them as the drug-
free persons they once were. You'd give them interesting work to

do—perhaps designing posters for rock bands—so that their minds would be distracted from the joys of opium. You'd create well-publicized sanctions against drug use. You'd keep the drug economy underground, making the former soldiers sneak around to obtain and use drugs. You'd make sure their girlfriends gave them a hard time about their drug use. You'd set up social taboos so that the soldiers would feel derelict, even pathetic, if they kept using. You'd remove the contagious drug-using behavior from the environment—no more addicted soldiers around—and replace it with contagious drug-free behavior. And you would provide rich environmental cues—sights, songs, food, clothes, and homes—that remind the former soldiers of their prewar, drug-free identities.

The Milwaukee Theme Park: That's exactly why Mike Romano became a *former* addict. When Romano relocated to Milwaukee, his environment changed, and the new environment changed him.

4.

As the Romano story shows, one of the subtle ways in which our environment acts on us is by reinforcing (or deterring) our habits.

When we think about habits, most of the time we're thinking about bad ones: biting our fingernails, procrastinating, eating sweets when we're anxious, and so on. But of course we also have plenty of good habits: jogging, praying, brushing our teeth. Why are habits so important? They are, in essence, behavioral autopilot. They allow lots of good behaviors to happen without the Rider taking charge. Remember that the Rider's self-control is exhaustible, so it's a huge plus if some positive things can happen "free" on autopilot.

To change yourself or other people, you've got to change

habits, and what we see with Romano is that his habits shifted
when his environment shifted. This makes sense—our habits are
essentially stitched into our environment. Research bears this out.
According to one study of people making changes in their lives,
36 percent of the successful changes were associated with a move
to a new location, and only 13 percent of unsuccessful changes
involved a move.

Many smokers, for example, find it easier to quit when they're
on vacation, because at home, every part of their environment is
loaded with smoking associations. It's like trying to quit smoking
inside a Camel advertisement—everywhere you look are re-
minders of the habit. There's that drawer in the kitchen where
the lighters are stashed, the clay pot on the porch that's become
an archive of ashes, the ever-present scent of smoke in the car and
the closet. When a smoker goes on vacation, the environment re-
cedes toward neutrality. That doesn't mean it's easy to quit, but it's
easier.

It's unrealistic, however, to think that most of us can shift our
environment so dramatically. If you're trying to change your
team's habits at work, then yes, relocating your office would be a
big help. Good luck selling that idea. What are some more practical ways to create a habit?

The first thing to realize is that even small environmental
tweaks can make a difference—that's what we saw in Chapter 8.
Remember how Amanda Tucker rearranged her office to make it
easier for her to listen to her employees? That was the first step in
establishing a new habit. (Environmental tweaks can even *force*
a habit, as we saw in the Rackspace example. When the call-
queuing system was thrown out, the customer-service staffers
quickly developed the habit of answering the phone.)

But forming a habit isn't all environmental—it's also mental.
It would be very difficult, for instance, to tweak the environment

in a way that would *compel* you to learn how to play the piano. So how do you lay the mental groundwork for a new habit?

5.

Say that you've been putting off going to the gym. So you resolve to yourself: Tomorrow morning, right after I drop off Anna at school, I'll head straight to the gym. Let's call this mental plan an "action trigger." You've made the decision to execute a certain action (working out) when you encounter a certain situational trigger (the school circle, tomorrow morning).

Peter Gollwitzer, a psychologist at New York University, is the pioneer of work in this area. He and colleague Veronika Brandstatter found that action triggers are quite effective in motivating action. In one study, they tracked college students who had the option to earn extra credit in a class by writing a paper about how they spent Christmas Eve. But there was a catch: To earn the credit, they had to submit the paper by December 26. Most students had good intentions of writing the paper, but only 33 percent of them got around to writing and submitting it. Other students in the study were required to set action triggers—to note, in advance, exactly when and where they intended to write the report (for example, "I'll write this report in my dad's office on Christmas morning before everyone gets up"). A whopping 75 percent of those students wrote the report.

That's a pretty astonishing result for such a small mental investment.

Does this mean that simply by *imagining* a time and place where you'll do something, you increase the likelihood that you'll actually do it? Yes and no. Action triggers won't get you (or anyone else) to do something you truly don't want to do. An action trigger never would have convinced college students to participate in an online calculus camp on Christmas Day. But, as the extra-credit study demonstrates, action triggers can have a profound power to motivate people to *do the things they know they need to do.*

Peter Gollwitzer argues that the value of action triggers resides in the fact that we are *preloading* a decision. Dropping off Anna at school triggers the next action, going to the gym. There's no cycle of conscious deliberation. By preloading the decision, we conserve the Rider's self-control.

The concept of preloading is easier to see with an example. Imagine that you are one of the college students in Gollwitzer's study. It's Christmastime, and you're at home. Your parents are doting on you, and your siblings are having an interesting conversation. The TV is on, the Christmas tree is lit up, and your elderly Chihuahua Fredo is staring at you adoringly. Let's not forget the food—turkey and dressing, pecan pie, chocolate truffles—and *Guitar Hero,* and naps, and the calls you're getting from old high school friends. Distractions are everywhere. So if you walk into this buffet line of stimuli and you haven't preloaded a decision about your extra-credit report—if you haven't told yourself, "I'll do this report in my dad's office on Christmas morning before everyone gets up"—you are sunk.

That's why action triggers have unexpected value. Gollwitzer says that when people predecide, they "pass the control of their behavior on to the environment." Gollwitzer says that action triggers "protect goals from tempting distractions, bad habits, or competing goals."

There are countless ways to use action triggers at work. If your salespeople are more motivated to close new business than to cultivate existing relationships, give them a "coffee and call" trigger. Tell them that whenever they pour their first cup of coffee, they are to place a check-in call to one of their most important customers. Or think about your employees who will be attending an industry conference. By the time they get back to the office, their e-mail will be so backed up that they won't be in the mood to share their learnings. So give them an action trigger—suggest that during the flight home, whenever the "OK to use electronics" announcement is made, they type up some reflections for everyone on the team. Action triggers simply have to be specific enough and visible enough to interrupt people's normal stream of consciousness. A trigger to "praise your employees when they do something great" is too vague to be useful.

Gollwitzer has shown that action triggers are most useful in the most difficult situations—the ones that are most draining to the Rider's self-control. One study analyzed people's success in accomplishing "easy" goals or "hard" goals. With easy goals, the use of action triggers increased success only slightly, from 78 to 84 percent. But with hard goals, action triggers almost *tripled* the chance of success—goal completion skyrocketed from 22 to 62 percent.

To see how action triggers can aid people in difficult times, consider a study of patients recovering from hip- or knee-replacement surgery. On average, the patients were 68 years old, and they had been in pain for about a year and a half before the surgery. The surgeries initially make things even worse; they take such a toll on the body that the patients require assistance with the basic tasks of daily life, such as bathing, getting into bed, and even standing up. The road to recovery can be long and painful.

All patients aspired to get back on their feet as soon as possible, of course. But patients in one group were asked to set action triggers—for instance, "If you are going to go for a walk this week, please write down when and where you plan to walk."

The results of the study were dramatic. On average, action-trigger patients were bathing themselves without assistance in 3 weeks. Other patients took 7 weeks. Action-trigger patients were standing up in 3.5 weeks. The others took 7.7 weeks. In just over 1 month, the action-trigger patients were getting in and out of a car on their own. The others took 2.5 months.

Gollwitzer says that, in essence, what action triggers do is create an "instant habit." Habits are behavioral autopilot, and that's exactly what action triggers are setting up. Here's the proof of the "instant habit" concept: One study showed that the single biggest predictor of whether women gave themselves a monthly breast examination was if they had a habit of doing so. When another group of women who didn't have such a habit were asked to set action triggers, they ended up doing just as well as the women with longtime habits. By preloading a decision, they created an instant habit.

Action triggers are not foolproof, of course. Teens with a serious smoking habit, for example, did not reap any benefit from setting action triggers to quit smoking. Their nicotine-enhanced habit was simply too strong.

But even though action triggers aren't perfect, it's hard to imagine an easier way to make an immediate change more likely. A recent meta-study that analyzed 8,155 participants across 85 studies found that the typical person who set an action trigger did better than 74 percent of people on the same task who didn't set one.

Instant habits. This is a rare point of intersection between the aspirations of self-help and the reality of science. And you can't get much more practical. The next time your team resolves to act in a new way, challenge team members to take it further. Have them specify when and where they're going to put the plan in motion. Get them to set an action trigger. (Then set another one for yourself.)

How Can You Get Workers
to Respect a New Safety Policy?

SITUATION Patti Poppe is a department manager in the General Motors automotive plant in Lordstown, Ohio, and she is struggling with how to roll out a new safety policy. Her department, composed of 950 people, is responsible for welding big pieces of metal onto the skeletal car frames. The work can be dangerous. The edges of the metal are sharp when they come off the presses. If a worker puts his hand on an edge and leans against it, the metal will slice his hand. For that reason, gloves and protective clothing are essential. Also, welders wear goggles, but they are sometimes hurt when sparks fly into their eyes from the side. So the new policy prescribes goggles with protective side shields. The old safety policy was complex and filled with exceptions—for instance, a worker driving a forklift didn't have to wear safety equipment. Poppe says, "Everyone thinks they fall under the 'this doesn't apply to me' clause." She is determined to get everyone to take the new policy seriously. (This was a real situation.)

WHAT'S THE SWITCH AND WHAT'S HOLDING IT BACK? Poppe wants the workers to protect themselves from lacerations and sparks. There are three potential barriers. First, the complexity of the old policy may have deterred some workers from embracing it. Remember that what looks like resistance is often a lack of clarity. Poppe needs to script the critical moves. Second, in any safety situation, a "macho" vibe often comes into play. That's an identity problem. If it seems manlier to ditch the goggles than to wear them, then the Elephant will resist. Third, social pressure is working *against* safety, because of the "this doesn't apply to me" sentiment. Poppe needs to flip that social norm. Also, might there be ways to use the environment to cue the right behaviors?

HOW DO WE MAKE THE SWITCH?
• *Direct the Rider.* **1. Script the critical moves.** Poppe threw out the old complicated policy and boiled down the new safety policy to two specific be-

haviors: (1) Everyone is required to wear hard side shields and safety glasses. (2) No one can expose any bare skin (no shorts or short-sleeve shirts). That's it. Then Poppe found a way to make these rules very concrete. At an all-hands meeting, she hosted a safety "game show." A worker was called onstage to be the contestant; he was asked to assess whether a series of models was in compliance with the new safety rules. Some of the models violated the code in subtle ways, such as wearing safety glasses with one eyepiece missing. She invited audience members to help the contestant, and they shouted out answers, thereby rehearsing and absorbing the new behaviors expected of them. **2. Point to the destination.** Poppe worried about rationalization, the excuse that "this doesn't apply to me." So she created a B&W goal to eliminate the wiggle room. If you were in the plant, you were required to follow the two rules, regardless of what you were doing. The rules applied to everyone at all times.

• *Motivate the Elephant.* **1. Grow your people.** Macho men don't like to wear dorky safety glasses. Maybe Poppe could find glasses that look more like Bono's and less like a junior-high-school shop teacher's. That might make the change less of an identity threat.

• *Shape the Path.* **1. Rally the herd.** By requiring everyone in the plant to wear the safety gear at all times, Poppe is flipping the social norm in favor of compliance. When you look around and everyone is wearing safety glasses, you are more likely to wear them yourself. **2. Build habits.** Poppe added one final, inspired touch: She painted a large blue line around the plant and made the new safety policy effective anywhere inside the line. Also, at the entry points, she posted blue wooden men who are wearing the appropriate gear. By installing the blue line and the blue men, Poppe was basically introducing an action trigger. She was training the workers to think, *When I cross this line, that's my cue to put on my gear.* The action trigger helped make the behavior habitual.

[What happened: As a result of Poppe's innovations, injuries at the plant dropped 21 percent from previous levels (which were already among the best of manufacturers doing similar work).]

6.

Habits are behavioral autopilot, and that's why they're such a critical tool for leaders. Leaders who can instill habits that reinforce their teams' goals are essentially making progress for free. They've changed behavior in a way that doesn't draw down the Rider's reserves of self-control.

Habits will form inevitably, whether they're formed intentionally or not. You've probably created lots of team habits unwittingly. If your staff meetings always start out with genial small talk, then you've created a habit. You've designed your meeting autopilot to yield a few minutes of warm-up small talk. The hard question for a leader is not how to form habits but which habits to encourage.

General William "Gus" Pagonis led the logistics operation for the Gulf War under President George H. W. Bush. Pagonis was responsible for moving 550,000 troops halfway around the world, along with all of their equipment. His team made the arrangements to serve 122 million meals, pump 1.3 billion gallons of fuel, and deliver 32,000 tons of mail. Even a Wal-Mart executive would get spooked thinking about this.

Needless to say, clear and efficient communication was essential. Every morning, General Pagonis held a meeting that started at 8 a.m. and ended at 8:30. No great innovation there, but Pagonis made two changes to the routine. First, he allowed anyone to attend (and he required that at least one representative from each functional group be present). That way, he could ensure a free and open exchange of information across the organization. Second, he required everyone to *stand up* during the whole meeting.

Here's Pagonis on the benefits of the stand-up meeting:

> Early on, I discovered that making people stand up keeps the ball moving at a quicker pace. People speak their piece and then quickly yield the floor to the next

person. On the rare occasion that someone starts to get long-winded or wax philosophic, an unmistakable kind of body language begins to sweep through the crowd. People shift from foot to foot, fidget, look at their watches—and pretty quickly, the conversation comes back into focus. . . . I can't recall the last time I had to crack the whip. The peer group has great power.

Pagonis was consciously creating a habit. *Any* meeting format he chose would have quickly become habitual. It would have been just as easy for him to enshrine a two-hour, seated blabfest. What's exciting here is not the existence of the habit, but rather the insight that *the habit should serve the mission.* When you've got 550,000 troops to relocate, you need focus and clarity and efficiency. A stand-up meeting won't guarantee any of that, but it will help, and it's "free"—it's not any harder to create than the blabfest would have been. (Similar stand-up meetings are used in Agile programming projects in Silicon Valley, which place a premium on quick collaboration.)

How can you create a habit that supports the change you're trying to make? There are only two things to think about: (1) The habit needs to advance the mission, as did Pagonis's stand-up meetings. (2) The habit needs to be relatively easy to embrace. If it's too hard, then it creates its own independent change problem. For instance, if you're trying to exercise more and you decide to "create a habit" of going to the gym, you're really only renaming the core problem. It might be more productive to try to start by building an easier habit, like laying out your gym clothes before you go to bed or asking a friend who already works out to pick you up on his way to the gym.

Consider a one-year study of dieters conducted at Penn State University. A baseline diet condition led to weight loss of

17.8 pounds over the course of the year. That's an impressive re-sult, but the drawback of many diet programs is that once the program ends, the dieters' old habits start to reemerge and their weight begins to creep up again. In this study, one warning flag was that only 36 percent of the people in the baseline condition rated themselves as "very full" or "extremely full" on the diet. How sustainable is a diet that doesn't make you really full?

Other dieters in the same study were asked to eat two cups of soup each day, in addition to their regularly scheduled meals. The two cups of soup were bonus food. These dieters lost 15.4 pounds over the year, and 55 percent of them rated themselves as "very full" or "extremely full." They didn't lose quite as much weight, but their odds of feeling full went up substantially. Eating two cups of soup is a classic supporting habit. It was an easy habit to implement—the researchers were simply asking the dieters to *eat more*. And it helped the broader mission—it helped the dieters feel full, which made it easier for them to control their portions at mealtime.

7.

This focus on creating habits was used masterfully, in a totally different context, by Natalie Elder, an elementary school princi-pal in Chattanooga, Tennessee. When Elder was first consider-ing the job as principal of Hardy Elementary School, she asked to see a copy of the school's results on statewide tests. As it turned out, she didn't get to see the data until after she'd already accepted the job. Looking back, she joked that the school board tricked her into taking the job first.

When Elder finally saw the scores, she could not believe what she was reading. Hardy Elementary didn't just have low test scores; it had *the lowest* scores in the state of Tennessee. She wondered, "What have I gotten myself into?"

It was a brutal beginning, but things got even worse. On the first day of school, she had to expel a student. Every week, it seemed, Elder encountered a new form of bad behavior. In the classrooms, students were cussing at their teachers. (Remember, we're talking about 6-to-8-year-old kids.) Parents sometimes barged into classrooms in the middle of a lesson to talk to their kids. One parent was escorted out of the building in handcuffs after he verbally abused the cafeteria manager.

Elder's attempts to restore discipline in the school were met with resistance. "Parents were coming in and cussing at me, hollering at me. One parent tried to run me over with a car," she said. Elder wasn't facing a teaching problem or a learning problem. She was facing something much more fundamental. She said, "I knew I had to get control of the building before I could teach."

She forbade parents from entering the building during school hours without permission from her office. She suspended the chronic misbehavers in the classroom. She got the police involved, when necessary, to enforce the new rules.

But those actions were just a way of eliminating the really egregious behavior. Her real goal was to transform chaos into calm. In her judgment, the trouble began the moment students arrived at school. If students were rowdy by 8:30 a.m., Elder reasoned, there wasn't much hope for the rest of the day. She resolved to conquer the morning by creating a series of consistent routines that would settle the students and prepare them to learn.

The problems began in the driveway where parents dropped off their kids each day. Elder said that often "the mom would already be yelling at the child, and sometimes the music was going BOOM-ta-ta-BOOM, and by the time the kid comes into the building, they're already upset or angry." So Elder and her staff did something amazing: They turned themselves into valets.

They resolved to greet every student before he or she entered the school building. They waited at the curb outside, opened car doors for the kids, smiled and said good morning to the parents, and then walked each child inside to the cafeteria. Their valet service helped smooth the transition to the school day from what for many kids was a raucous home environment.

Once the kids were gathered inside the cafeteria, Elder started every day with a disciplined group assembly. "Continuity is good for any child," she said. "What these kids don't get in their lives is stability. They have to know that here they'll get structure and order."

At the assembly, Elder began with announcements and a brief call-and-response with the kids. "We're a school of what?" a teacher would call out. The kids would respond by shouting, "Excellence!" At 7:50, Elder taught a brief lesson in character education, typically focusing on a single word, such as *perseverance*. She'd have volunteers spell the word and define it. At 7:55, everyone stood and said the Pledge of Allegiance, then sang a patriotic song (for instance, the Whitney Houston version of "America"). Sometimes kids read aloud, or Elder gave them a quick spelling or math quiz. (Often the prize was a coveted "out of uniform" pass for Friday, allowing them to wear what they wanted.)

At 8:00, the kids stood and silently walked to class with "traveling arms," meaning that the kids' arms were folded behind them, reducing the nearly irresistible urge to mess with their friends. By the time the kids sat down at their desks, they were ready to learn.

Elder shows us how new habits can clear the Path. She inherited chaos at Hardy Elementary School, and she asked herself, "Which parts of this chaos can I tame? What kind of morning routine can I set up that will improve the chances that the kids are ready to learn?"

She had to fight the forces that stirred up kids before they'd even set foot in the classroom: the tense drop-offs, the cafeteria pandemonium, the erratic transition to the classroom. By bringing order and continuity to the environment, she was able to create forward movement for a group of children who'd grown used to a destructive cycle of behavior.

Notice, too, that because of the calm environment that Elder managed to create, "bad" kids started acting like good kids. A good change leader never thinks, "Why are these people acting so badly? They must be bad people." A change leader thinks, "How can I set up a situation that brings out the good in these people?"

8.

So far, as we've discussed how to shape the Path, we've encountered two strategies: (1) tweaking the environment and (2) building habits. There's a tool that perfectly combines these two strategies. It's something that can be added to the environment in order to make behavior more consistent and habitual.

That tool is the humble checklist. We discuss it with some trepidation, because we know the associations buzzing in most readers' heads: mundane, routine, bureaucratic. "Use a checklist," we admit, sounds like advice a dad would give a college student, along with some tips on tire-pressure gauges and not charging beer to his Exxon card.

But bear with us, because your perceptions are about to change. What if we asserted that checklists can be game-changing, that checklists can save lives?

The Holy Grail of checklists may be one reported by Atul Gawande in *The New Yorker*. Patients in intensive care units

(ICUs) often have intravenous lines put in to deliver medication. If those lines become infected, nasty health complications can result. Frustrated by these "line infections," which are preventable, Dr. Peter Pronovost of Johns Hopkins compiled a five-part checklist.

The checklist contained straightforward advice: Doctors should wash their hands before inserting a line, a patient's skin should be cleaned with antiseptic at the point of insertion, and so on. There was no new science in the checklist, nothing controversial. Only the results were surprising: When the checklist was put into practice by Michigan ICUs over a period of eighteen months, it nearly eliminated line infections, saving the hospitals an estimated $175 million because they no longer had to treat the associated complications. It also saved about fifteen hundred lives.

How can something so simple be so powerful? Checklists educate people about what's best, showing them the ironclad right way to do something. (That means that checklists are effective at directing the Rider.) As Dr. Pronovost said, his five steps were black and white, backed by solid medical research. You could ignore the checklist, but you couldn't dispute it.

Even when there is no ironclad right way to do things, checklists can help people avoid blind spots in a complex environment. Has your business ever made a big mistake because it failed to consider all the right information? A checklist might have helped. Cisco Systems, one of the largest internet hardware companies, uses a checklist to analyze potential acquisitions: Will the company's key engineers be willing to relocate? Will we be able to sell additional services to its customer base? What's the plan for continuing to support the company's existing customers? As a smart business development person, you'd probably remember to investigate 80 percent of these critical issues before any deal is struck. But it would be inadvisable to recall the other 20 percent after the close of a $100 million acquisition. (*Whoops! Those hot-shot engineers refuse to leave the snow in Boulder.*) Checklists provide insurance against overconfidence.

And overconfidence is worth insuring against because we all have a knack for it. In one classic study, people were asked to come up with solutions for their university's chronic parking problem. Ideas ranged from raising parking fees to creating more "Compact Only" parking spaces. After the ideas were collected, a panel of experts assessed them—eliminating wacky or impractical options—and identified a set of "best solutions."

The average individual brainstormer came up with 30 percent of the best solutions, which is pretty good for a solo effort. Here's what's not so good: The brainstormers confidently predicted that they'd identified 75 percent of the best ideas. (We all know people who believe that the world's accumulated wisdom only adds an incremental 25 percent to their own contribution. You may have married one of them.)

A checklist could have helped these people. Imagine if you'd provided them with a list of "solution categories" to guide their thinking, reminding them to think about "solutions that raise the cost of parking" and "solutions that help more cars park in the same amount of space" and so on. That list would have served the same role as Cisco's acquisition categories; it would have sparked their thinking and kept them from forgetting key areas of consideration.

People fear checklists because they see them as dehumanizing—maybe because they associate them with the exhaustive checklists that allow inexperienced teenagers to operate fast-food chains successfully. They think if something is simple enough to be put in a checklist, a monkey can do it. Well, if that's true, grab a pilot's checklist and try your luck with a 747.

Checklists simply make big screwups less likely. As Dr. Pronovost said, "We wanted people to standardize on the mission-critical elements—the areas where we have the strongest evidence. And these things that are mission-critical, we've got to do them every time."

What does your organization need to do in every product cycle? What do you need to check for in every contract or negotiation? What does your family need to do to prepare for each new school year? Put these things in a checklist. You may not save a life, but you'll sure avoid a painful blind spot.

You'll also avoid making the Fundamental Attribution Error. Dr. Pronovost's research showed that line infections—life-threatening problems that are preventable—were rampant. Yet he didn't conclude, "We've got a health care system full of sloppy, negligent doctors." Instead, he asked himself, "How can I change these doctors' situations so that they're more likely to avoid line infections?" (So before you conclude that your husband is hopelessly absentminded, always forgetting to pick up the dry cleaning and the milk, maybe you should try shaping his Path. How about taping a checklist to his steering wheel?)

As you try to make a switch, the hardest struggle will be to maintain your motivation, to keep your Elephant on the road. This puts a huge burden on your Rider, who has to rein in the Elephant when it strays. In this chapter, and the last one, we've been searching for ways to use the environment to relieve the Rider's burden. We started with the story of Mike Romano, the soldier who came back from Vietnam with an addiction to opium. If Romano's fate had hinged solely on the one-on-one battle between his Rider and his Elephant, he couldn't have kicked his addiction. It was the environment that tipped the forces in his favor. When Romano came back to his hometown of Milwaukee, he found it a lot easier to change.

How can you create an environment that would make it easier for you, or your team, to change? We've seen that supportive habits—like holding stand-up meetings or eating two daily bowls of soup—can help, and so can action triggers that allow you to preload difficult decisions. Even a simple checklist can make a difference. In the next chapter, we'll get the final piece of the puzzle: the influence of other people. It's easier to persevere on a long journey when you're traveling with a herd.

10

Rally the Herd

1.

Think of the last time you were in a situation where you weren't totally sure how to behave. Maybe it was your first time in a new church, or your first time in another country, or maybe it was a dinner party where you didn't know many of the guests. What did you do to try to fit in?

You watched other people, of course.

In ambiguous situations, we all look to others for cues about how to behave. Maybe you've had the experience of scanning the table frantically at a fancy dinner, trying to figure out which fork is for dessert. (If you haven't had that experience, we hope you know your forks, because the rest of us copied you.) When the environment is unfamiliar, we sprout social antennae that are exquisitely sensitive.

In the fancy dinner situation, our antennae work great, because *someone* at the table knows what to do, and we can just copy that person. But sometimes in times of change, *nobody* knows how to behave, and that can lead to problems. For instance, if you ever find yourself in an emergency situation, we pray that there's only one person in the vicinity who can help you, rather than a crowd. To see why, consider some research conducted by Bibb Latané and John M. Darley.

Columbia University students, having volunteered for a research study, were asked to sit in a room and fill out a survey. Some were left alone; others were put in rooms with two other students. As they filled out their surveys, a "crisis" emerged. Smoke began to pour into the room through a wall vent. The smoke continued to flow, in irregular puffs, until eventually the room was filled with haze. Of the students sitting in a room by themselves, 75 percent got up and found someone to alert about the smoke. But when three students were placed in the room at the same time, only 38 percent of the groups of three ever reported the smoke. They just sat there, inhaling the smoke, each individual's inaction signaling to the other two people in the room that *this smoke cloud isn't such a big deal.*

In a similar study, individuals or pairs who were completing a survey heard what sounded like a woman falling down loudly on the other side of a room divider. Of the lone bystanders, 70 percent went to help her, but only 40 percent of the pairs helped. Even when the pairs helped, they acted more slowly than the individuals.

Why do groups fail to respond as well as individuals?

In ambiguous situations—smoke pouring into a room, the apparent sound of a fall—people look to others for cues about how to interpret the event. If you see a man suddenly collapse at the mall, your brain races through possible interpretations: It's a heart attack! Or, wait, maybe he tripped and fell down. Or what if he's playing a gag on someone? You're reluctant to rush over immediately, because if he simply tripped, your alarm-bell behavior will leave you both embarrassed.

If you're the only person around to react, you'll probably make your best guess—*heart attack*—and rush over. But if there's a crowd, you've got two stimuli to process: the collapse itself and the crowd's reaction to the collapse. You might pause briefly to study the crowd. *Are other people acting like he's had a heart attack?* You stand there, idling, ready to spring into action at the first sign of crisis. But as you wait, other people are looking back at you, and when they see you idling, your behavior becomes data for their theory that it's not an emergency. And that's why three people can sit in a room filling with smoke and not make a peep.

We all talk about the power of peer *pressure,* but "pressure" may be overstating the case. Peer *perception* is plenty. In this entire book, you might not find a single statement that is so rigorously supported by empirical research as this one: You are doing things because you see your peers do them. It's not only your body-pierced teen who follows the crowd. It's *you,* too. Behavior is contagious. Let's take a quick epidemiological tour of behavior.

We start with a mind-blowing finding: Obesity is contagious. A groundbreaking study led by Dr. Nicholas Christakis of Harvard Medical School, which followed 12,067 people for thirty-two years, found that when someone became obese, the odds of that person's close mutual friends becoming obese tripled! Remarkably, proximity didn't seem to matter. Obesity seemed to "spread" between friends even when they were in different parts of the country. In explaining these findings, Dr. Christakis said, "You change your idea of what is an acceptable body type by looking at the people around you."

Drinking is contagious. A study showed that when college males were paired with a dormitory roommate who drank frequently in high school, they saw their GPAs go down by a quarter point on average. There's an endless list of other behaviors that are contagious, as well: marriage; shaking hands to greet someone; wearing fashionably fluffy boots; and investing in Google. And you might want to avoid hanging around with baseball players, lest you start compulsively spitting.

It's clear that we imitate the behaviors of others, whether consciously or not. We are especially keen to see what they're doing when the situation is unfamiliar or ambiguous. And change situations are, by definition, unfamiliar! So if you want to change things, you have to pay close attention to social signals, because they can either guarantee a change effort or doom it.

When you're leading an Elephant on an unfamiliar path, chances are it's going to follow the herd. So how do you create a herd?

2.

The Elephant constantly looks to the herd for cues about how to behave. This is why baristas and bartenders seed their tip jars— they're trying to send signals about the "norm" of the herd. It's a time-honored tactic. In fact, opera companies used to plant stooges in the audience to laugh and applaud at the appropriate times. (If that seems quaint, remember that the "stooges" are alive and well on the laugh tracks of your favorite sitcom.)

But sometimes social cues are hidden. For instance, hotel bathrooms often display little cards asking guests to use their towels more than once, usually appealing to a pro-environmental objective such as the conservation of water. (Also conserved, coincidentally, are labor costs in the hotel laundry room.) So should you reuse your towel? It's not a clear-cut situation. At home, you probably use your towel more than once, but in a hotel, you might expect a bit more pampering, including a clean towel every time you need one. There's no obvious social norm to consult, because you can't peek into the other guests' bathrooms.

Well aware of the power of contagious behavior, a group of social psychologists persuaded a hotel manager to test out a new sign in the hotel bathrooms. The sign didn't mention the environment at all; it simply said that the "the majority of guests at the hotel" reuse their towels at least once during their stay. It worked—guests who got this sign were 26 percent more likely to reuse their towels. They took cues from the herd.

Note the downside, though. If the sign had said, "About 8% of our guests decide to reuse their towels," new guests would have been *less* likely to reuse theirs. (The same effect explains why you don't tip the person who bags your groceries, even though that person is doing as much valuable work as your barista. The herd told you not to.) In situations where your herd has embraced the right behavior, publicize it. For instance, if 80 percent of your team submits time sheets on time, make sure the other 20 percent knows the group norm. Those individuals almost certainly will correct themselves. But if only 10 percent of your team submits time sheets on time, publicizing those results will hurt, not help.

When the norms are against you, what can you do to rally the herd? That, in essence, was the problem facing Gerard Cachon, a Wharton School operations professor. In 2006, Cachon became the editor of the journal *Manufacturing and Service Operations Management (MSOM)*. Here are the titles of some of the articles featured in *MSOM*:

- "Requirements Planning with Substitutions: Exploiting Bill-of-Materials Flexibility in Production Planning"
- "A General Framework for the Study of Decentralized Distribution Systems"

- "Stock Positioning and Performance Estimation in Serial Productions-Transportation Systems"
- "Contract Assembly: Dealing with Combined Supply Lead Time and Demand Quantity Uncertainty"

If you just felt your pulse quicken, you are definitely an operations person.

Needless to say, *MSOM* isn't the kind of mass-appeal periodical that will be shelved between *Maxim* and *People* at the local newsstand. Its role is to showcase the latest thinking in the field of operations. Professors compete strenuously to get their articles published in journals like *MSOM*, because in order to get promoted within their university departments, they need a solid track record of publication. (You've probably heard the expression "Publish or perish.")

Getting articles published is a long process. First, you do a lot of research—often several years' worth. Then you write an article describing the research and submit it to a journal. The journal editor farms out your article to "peer reviewers"—other professors who agree to critique your piece (anonymously). The editor then summarizes the opinions of these reviews and delivers a verdict—yes, no, or revise and resubmit. If you get the R&R verdict, you'll often have to launch some new research to plug the holes in your work, and if you do that, you can eventually resubmit your paper for a new cycle of reviews. It's an exhausting process—it routinely takes years to get a paper published.

A key bottleneck is the peer review stage. If it takes a long time for other professors to read the article and give feedback, the whole process grinds to a halt. The standard review times for many academic journals range from three to six months. A frontline scientific journal like *Science* or *Nature* might get reviews done in a few weeks.

When Gerard Cachon took over *MSOM*, most peer reviews were taking from seven to eight *months,* and many were taking over a year. Early in his tenure, Cachon got e-mails from professors who were hesitantly checking in with him about a paper. A typical note might say, "I submitted this paper two years ago and I just wanted to check into progress." In several cases, when Cachon checked on the paper in question, he learned that the journal had no record of its ever being submitted. Imagine writing that e-mail response. (And take a second to contemplate an environment in which professors feel bad about checking in after two years! Talk about learned helplessness.)

Ironically, operations people are supposed to be the folks who make the trains run on time—they deal with logistics and bottlenecks and supply chains and cycle times. For a psychology journal to outperform an operations journal—that's as disgraceful as Michael Phelps being trounced in the 100m freestyle by Dr. Phil.

Cachon's goal was obvious—make things move faster. But what could he do? He had no power over any of the reviewers. They didn't report to him. Reviewers are volunteer labor who perform a difficult task for free. How would you like to verify the logic of someone's mathematical derivations in a paper on optimal serial transport systems?

Cachon's game plan provides a great review of the *Switch* framework. First, he spoke to his constituents' Riders by pointing to the destination. "I knew there was a collective goal that I could appeal to," he said. "Every author wants fast cycle time and is willing to provide it if everyone else does. But no one wants to be the one sucker who provides the fast lead time, and then when they submit their papers it takes forever." Cachon announced that *MSOM* would review papers within sixty-five days—that was 72 percent faster than its previous average!

Second, he appealed to identity. *We're operations people, for*

Pete's sake. We should be leading the way on efficiency and turn-around time! Third, he defined a clear behavior: Every reviewer had to submit feedback within five weeks. Cachon got the reviewers to commit up front that they could meet the deadline.

Finally, Cachon found a way to rally the herd. Every Friday, he posted an Excel spreadsheet on the internet that showed the status of every paper submitted to the journal. Every reviewer could see what the other reviewers had done (and when). If they violated their five-week commitment, the tracking sheet created powerful pressure, especially when Cachon called them and said, "Look, other people are doing this on time, and, by the way, here's the data." When people saw the data, they realized, *Whoops, I'm the bottleneck.*

With the online tracking sheet, Cachon was using the hotel-towel strategy. He was publicizing the group norm. *Other people are getting their work done on time. Why won't you?*

Cachon set out to make good behavior contagious, and he succeeded. As a result of Cachon's brilliant plan, *MSOM* now has the fastest turnaround time of any journal in the field of management science. And, because of his work, Cachon was asked to take over the flagship journal of the whole field, *Management Science.*

Cachon said, "Now, when people get their reviews in fifty days, they come back and say, 'Wow! I can still remember the paper!'"

3.

We've seen that behavior is contagious at the individual level (obesity and tip jars) and at the group level (Cachon's on-time reviewers). It probably will not surprise you that behavior also is contagious at the societal level (see bell-bottoms and organic food and the phrase "at the end of the day"). But what may interest you is that there's a particular behavior, now ubiquitous in America, that we can trace back to its origin. What follows is the story of a guy who, at the end of the day, changed the way a society behaved.

In the 1980s, Jay Winsten, a public health professor at Harvard, got interested in the idea of a "designated driver." He'd picked up this concept from Scandinavian countries, where it was already a norm. At the time, the concept did not exist in the United States. No one here knew what a "designated driver" was.

Winsten and his team at Harvard made it their goal to create a social norm in the United States: If you were going out drinking, you would pick a designated driver who would commit *not* to drink for the evening. How do you create a social norm out of thin air? Winsten's inspiration was that you could make the behavior contagious by repeatedly exposing people to it, in many different contexts, even if those contexts were fictional.

Winsten and his team collaborated with producers, writers, and actors from more than 160 prime-time TV programs, sprinkling designated-driver moments naturally into the plots. Segments featuring designated drivers appeared on *Hunter, The Cosby Show, Mr. Belvedere,* and *Who's the Boss?* On an episode of the smash-hit 1980s legal drama *L.A. Law,* the heartthrob lawyer played by Harry Hamlin asked a bartender to call his designated driver. A designated-driver poster appeared in the bar on *Cheers.*

"Jay's crusade was one that we could do something about fairly easily, unlike a lot of other worthwhile causes," said Grant Tinker, then a vice president of NBC, who introduced Winsten to dozens of writers at all the major networks. Winsten always requested just "five seconds" of dialogue featuring the designated-driver idea, not a whole episode or even a whole scene. "Considering the simplicity of it all," said Tinker, "it was very hard for us to feel our independence was being challenged."

Notice how smart Winsten was: He used the power of the Path to change the public's behavior, but he used the power of the Rider and the Elephant to change the network executives' behavior. With his five-second requests, he was directing the Rider by describing a simple action that could help on a complex problem, and he was motivating the Elephant by shrinking the change.

In 1991, three years after the campaign launched, nine out of ten people were familiar with the term *designated driver*. And they were behaving differently as a result. Thirty-seven percent of all Americans reported having acted as designated drivers, and 54 percent of frequent drinkers had been driven home by one. The behavior change saved lives. Alcohol-related traffic fatalities declined from 23,626 in 1988 to 17,858 in 1992.

Winsten used the power of television to simulate a social norm. But you don't need Hollywood to create a herd. When Steven Kelman, whom we discussed in the "Shrink the Change" chapter, took over the government's procurement reform efforts, he realized that one of his best strategies was to "unleash" change. By that, he meant that he needed to send signals to the people who already supported procurement reform. Kelman knew he needed to tell the supporters, "It's safe to get vocal now." In the beginning, he didn't need to create new believers so much as he needed to unleash the believers he already had.

In the fall of 2007, a group of public-health and AIDS experts had a chance to get involved in a situation where change needed to be unleashed. The setting was Tanzania, and the subject was sugar daddies.

4.

In Tanzania, "sugar-daddy" relationships are common. You know the drill: An older man pursues a younger woman; they start having sex; and as part of the "deal," the young woman receives gifts or favors—a cell phone, money for school tuition, clothes, and so on. This is hardly a unique feature of Tanzanian culture, as evidenced by Hugh Hefner and his sextuplet blond housemates.

But the sugar-daddy relationships in Tanzania are more troubling. First, the women are often underage girls—15, 16, 17 years old. Second, the power dynamics in the Tanzanian sugar-daddy relationships often lead women to engage in unsafe sex. (It's not easy to insist that your partner put on a condom when he's your elder and your benefactor.) This power dynamic is universal, of course. American teens who date men who are six or more years older are almost four times more likely to get pregnant than teens who date within two years of their own age.

The reality is that when older men want unsafe sex, they tend to get their way. In America, that means the girls get pregnant. In Tanzania, it means they get AIDS and die. And that's why sugar daddies in Tanzania are a serious public-health problem.

Health experts call these sugar-daddy relationships "cross-generational." In the age group 15 to 24, women in sub-Saharan Africa are three times more likely to be HIV-positive than men in the same age range. It's the relationships that these younger women have with older men that explain the disparity. The cross-generational relationship opens up a bridge for HIV to travel between populations that ordinarily wouldn't intersect.

The other thing that's different about sugar-daddy relationships in Tanzania is that, despite the health risks, there's no strong social taboo against the behavior. In the United States, 50-year-old lechers who chase college girls are punished for it socially. Can't you just hear the man's sister telling him, "You're pathetic"? Can't you just see the eyes rolling at his office? But there's no real equivalent of this social stigma in Tanzania. It's accepted that high-status men will display their status in this way.

Yet the great majority of Tanzanians—89 percent in one poll—believe that cross-generational relationships are wrong. Unfortunately, their opposition tends to be quiet and private; it's an uncomfortable issue to discuss.

In August 2007, Pamela White and Mike Gehron of USAID, a relief organization that's part of the U.S. State Department, called together a diverse team of experts (including the two of us) in a hotel in Dar es Salaam. The mission: to develop a campaign to fight cross-generational sex. Leading the team was a group from Johns Hopkins University's Bloomberg School of Public Health. Others included AIDS experts and about a dozen local artists and creatives (producers, actors, writers, and at least one Tanzanian soap-opera star, who was interrupted at one point for an autograph).

The discussions were difficult. The issue was complicated, and it wasn't even clear where to start. For example, no one believed that scolding the sugar daddies would be effective in stopping their behavior. And the public-health experts thought that we were unlikely to convince young women to refuse the advances of these men, because the social and financial pressures on them were too intense to be countered by a campaign. So we started thinking: If we can't change the main characters in this story, can we change their environment?

Recall from Chapter 8 that Rackspace changed individuals by changing their environment, their culture. But that was one company. Was it possible to change the social atmosphere *in an entire country*? The team knew that Tanzanians objected to cross-generational relationships but, for whatever reason, remained quiet about them. Could the team give a voice to that resentment?

We needed to find a way to make Tanzanians feel comfortable discussing something uncomfortable, a way to disarm the conversation. And someone blurted out: "We need people to be able to laugh at this! We need *humor!*"

Inspired, the team hatched the idea for a villain. He'd be a villain people would love to hate, like J.R. Ewing, the eternally scheming oilman of the old TV show *Dallas*. As the group kicked around the idea, a portrait of the villain began to emerge: He'd be an older man who encapsulated the sugar daddy—someone who hit on young girls constantly, relentlessly, shamelessly. He'd approach them anywhere he could find them, and he'd offer favors—free meals, free drinks, clothes, or time on his cell phone.

Someone suggested that the villain be called "Fataki," and everyone's eyes lit up. *Fataki* is a Swahili word that translates loosely as "explosion" or "fireworks"—something dangerous and a bit unstable. In other words, Fataki is someone you want to stay away from.

The plan was to start telling Fataki's story in radio commercials, because radio comes closest to being a universal medium in Tanzania. The team started dreaming up dozens of situations to put Fataki in, and across these situations there would be a common element: Despite his status and wealth advantages, and despite his smooth talk, Fataki never succeeds. He fails again and again because an outsider intervenes to disrupt his seductive efforts. Like Wile E. Coyote stalking the Road Runner, Fataki chases and chases and chases but never gets his prey. He's pathetic. He's someone you can laugh at.

Here's the translation of a Fataki spot called "Chicken and Chips":

> (*Noisy sounds of a restaurant*)
> GIRL: Oh so many choices . . .
> FATAKI: Please pick one . . .
> GIRL: Ah, waitress, is this chicken or . . . ?

WAITRESS: I would recommend this one . . .

FATAKI: That's too expensive! Listen. Give her chicken and chips with some sauce. That's good, right, my love?

GIRL: Hmmmm . . . OK.

(*Waitress acknowledges their order and walks away.*)

FATAKI (*to Girl*): Oh, please go and tell her it is a take-away!

GIRL: Okay . . .

(*Background voices of waiters ordering food*)

WAITRESS (*whispering*): I'm glad that I have a chance to talk to you alone. Don't you feel ashamed to have a relationship with such an old man? Here, take your chips and leave quickly through this back door . . .

(*Sound of door opening*)

FATAKI: Waiter, what is going on there?

WAITRESS: Sir, the girl just went away. Would you like something?

FATAKI: What?! I came with her. She went through which door?

WAITRESS: But you have not paid for the chips, sir . . .

FATAKI: Ehhh???

WAITRESS: Sir, this kid is not your age . . .

FATAKI: Ah, take the money and leave me alone!!

WAITRESS: Hee hee hee! Got him!

ANNOUNCER: Protect your loved ones from a Fataki!

Radio spots like that one became part of a unified campaign that was piloted in a rural region called Morogoro. The campaign consisted of 10 different radio spots that were played on 3 stations, and 170 banners that were hung on stores and public buildings. The typical person heard about one radio spot a day. The campaign had two goals. The first was to create a mocking label for sugar-daddy behavior. The creative team's objective was to someday walk into a Tanzanian nightclub and overhear one patron telling another, "That guy is such a Fataki." By making it OK to mock the Fatakis, the team would help to counteract the natural status advantages of older and wealthier men. The second goal of the campaign was to encourage "interventions" by outsiders—friends, relatives, teachers, even waitresses—by modeling the behavior in the radio spots. The message was: "It's *your* responsibility to look out for these young women. Protect your loved ones from a Fataki!"

The results from the pilot campaign were unexpectedly strong. By the end of the four-month campaign, 44 percent of people who were asked "What would you call a 50-year-old man who is always trying to seduce younger women?" spontaneously replied "Fataki." Seventy-five percent of Morogorans reported discussing Fataki with others. And the percentage of people who said "I can do something about cross-generational sex" increased from 64 percent before the pilot to 88 percent afterward.

Having succeeded in Morogoro, the campaign was rolled out nationally in Tanzania, and the word began to spread nationwide. A health care worker setting up HIV clinics in the outer reaches of Tanzania reported that even in remote villages, Fataki had managed to bring a conversation out of the closet. Within weeks of the national launch of the campaign, the banner front-page headline of a Tanzanian tabloid accused Kanumba, a popular actor, of being a Fataki. (He'd been spotted checking into the Lambada Hotel with a young girl.) The Tanzanian public had taken ownership of a name and a character who symbolized the bad behavior they'd resented, quietly, all along.

CLINIC
How Can You Stop John's
BlackBerry Addiction?

SITUATION John has a BlackBerry addiction. His body twitches every time his BlackBerry goes off. He can't stop himself from checking every message that comes in. It's become a serious distraction. In meetings at work, he finds himself sneaking the device under the table to read messages covertly. (It annoys John's colleagues that he thinks he's fooling them.) John's wife becomes increasingly irritated that he can't focus on their dinner conversation, and one day he almost has a fender-bender because he is trying to e-mail someone while driving. John knows that he needs to cut it out, but every time he resolves to stop, the Black-Berry buzzes. [John is fictitious, but we all know a John.]

WHAT'S THE SWITCH AND WHAT'S HOLDING IT BACK? This is the last Clinic in the book, and by now, we hope you'll make easy work of this situation. The behavior change is clear enough: John needs to stop using his Black-Berry all the time (and especially while driving). What's holding him back? His Elephant, of course. In any addiction situation, the Elephant is the culprit. To rein in John's Elephant, we'll use all three parts of the framework. Take a moment to generate an action plan for John, and then compare your notes with ours.

HOW DO WE MAKE THE SWITCH?
• *Direct the Rider.* **1. Find the bright spots.** Are there times when John doesn't feel the BlackBerry compulsion? What's different about those times, and can we find a way to replicate those conditions? **2. Point to the destination.** John needs a B&W goal, like BP's "No dry holes." Recall that B&W goals are particularly useful in situations where people are prone to rationalize. (John is constantly telling himself, "I just need to check and see if this one specific e-mail has come in.") John could experiment with different B&W goals: *No BlackBerry during dinner*, or *No BlackBerry after 6 p.m.*, or *The BlackBerry comes out only when I'm traveling.* He needs to eliminate his own wiggle room.

• *Motivate the Elephant.* **1. Find the feeling.** Have John's wife force him to read aloud the last ten e-mails that he received and then ask whether any of them is really worth getting twitchy over. A little embarrassment might do him good. **2. Find the feeling.** Car accidents are happening more and more because of people like John. Confronting John with a particularly sobering news story— for example, "Cute Puppy Run Over by E-Mailing Driver"—might be a good idea. **3. Build identity.** John's wife (or his colleagues) could highlight how his Black-Berry habit doesn't fit with his character: "John, you're usually such an 'in control' guy. It's weird to see you so flaky." **4. Build the growth mindset.** Some smokers quit successfully on the seventeenth try. If John truly wants to curb his habit, his friends shouldn't let him give up if he "relapses" a few times.

• *Shape the Path.* **1. Break the environment.** John's wife can simply smash his BlackBerry with a hammer. Problem solved. **1a. Tweak the environment.** If smashing it isn't possible, John could lock his BlackBerry in the trunk of his car every time he drives. That way, he wouldn't have to fight the Elephant when it buzzes. **2. Tweak the environment.** The siren song of the BlackBerry is its buzz (or ring or flashing red light). Can you turn off the sound? Cover up the light? (Paint over the light with Wite-Out if necessary.) **3. Rally the herd.** John's colleagues should make sure he knows he's not fooling anybody in meetings. They should make a pact that, each time John sneaks a look at his BlackBerry under the table, they will all stare at him until he meets their (disapproving) eyes.

5.

The Fataki case study may have felt foreign to you. It probably doesn't bear many superficial similarities to the changes you're contemplating. But look at the underlying dynamics: You want certain people to act differently, but they are resistant to the change. So you rally the support of others who in turn could influence those you hope to sway. In essence, it's an attempt to change the culture, and culture often is the linchpin of successful organizational change. As former IBM CEO Lou Gerstner said, "I came to see, in my time at IBM, that culture isn't just one aspect of the game—it *is* the game." But organizational culture is a slippery, abstract concept. How do you change it? Where do you start?

In 1984, Libby Zion, an 18-year-old freshman at Bennington College, at home visiting her parents in Manhattan, died in a New York teaching hospital. She'd been given the wrong medication by a medical resident who'd been working for over 19 hours. Her death sparked an outcry over the excessive hours worked by medical interns. (Interns are first-year residents. They've completed three years of medical school and are beginning full-time work in hospitals.) Traditionally, interns have worked an astonishing 120 hours per week.

The story of Libby Zion became the centerpiece of a campaign to limit the workweeks of medical residents. Almost two decades later, in 2003, Congress finally seemed ready to move. Then the American Council for Graduate Medical Education—which accredits medical schools—made an effort to preempt congressional legislation by requiring 80-hour workweeks for residents starting in July 2003. That might seem to be the end of the story. A switch happened in medical schools because someone with fiat power mandated the change.

In this case, though, fiat power failed. A subsequent study by the *Journal of the American Medical Association* found that only a third of general surgery residency programs complied with the new workweek limits. Why would hospitals fail to change their ways in spite of the fact they were putting patients at risk (as well as their own accreditation)?

Katherine Kellogg, an ethnographer at MIT's Sloan School of Management, wanted to understand why some organizations complied with such regulations and others didn't. She decided to study two northeastern teaching hospitals, nicknamed Alpha and

Beta, that were well matched in size, sector, structure, and other factors. She was given full access to the staffers of the two hospitals, and she observed the two hospitals for an average of twenty hours a week, each, for fifteen months. Kellogg was the perfect eyewitness to a real-world cultural change effort.

6.

In the quest to reform, the fiercest battle would be fought over a surprisingly mundane practice called the "daily signout." The daily signout is the point, usually about 9 or 10 p.m., when surgical interns hand off their patients to the on-call night resident. During the signout, the intern briefs the resident on each patient's status, so that the resident is prepared to take care of any emergencies that happen overnight.

But interns weren't really handing off their work, and that's one reason why they were working 120 hours a week. On every third night, there was no handoff at all—the interns were on duty all through the night. And on the other nights, they stayed late to finish the paperwork they should have handed off. Worse, night residents usually refused to do any paperwork overnight, so the interns had to show up early the next morning—at, say, 4 a.m.—to complete it before beginning their normally scheduled rounds at 6 a.m.

To enforce an 80-hour workweek, the hospitals needed to start taking the daily signouts seriously, but that wasn't quite as easy as it sounds. Emotional resistance to reform was entrenched in both Alpha and Beta and, indeed, in most hospitals across the country. Signing out conflicted with long-standing cultural practices. For instance, one opponent said, "You learn by being here. There is a huge amount of information passed on in an ad hoc fashion at 2 o'clock in the morning when the senior resident and you are trying to get a patient's blood pressure up or an IV in. You need to be the one managing it, doing it, in order to learn." (In other words, interns would be putting their medical education at risk by, er, sleeping.)

Other opponents stressed the importance of "continuity of care"—minimizing the number of times that patients were passed among doctors. As one resident said, "The problem with hand-offs is that things fall through the cracks and things get missed." A final objection, in essence, was that if the interns didn't pay their dues, it would be unfair to everyone who'd already put in time as the paperwork lackeys: "These guys have been there and done that. . . . You can see how it would be tough as a fourth-year resident to be told to do the intern job all over again."

Fortunately, at both Alpha and Beta, there was substantial support for signout change among the interns' superiors, such as senior residents and chief residents. At Alpha, 13 out of 31 superiors were "reformers" who supported the change; at Beta, 12 out of 18 were reformers. Because of this support, circumstances looked ripe for real change. All signs were "Go." At long last, the 120-hour workweek would be abolished.

There was just one problem: The interns wouldn't sign out. As one intern said, "Being considered a good intern has nothing to do with what you know or how well you manage your patients. It is totally based on working hard and not handing stuff off. It's your attitude, not your ability. . . . This is where I live. I only go home to sleep. It sounds sick, but these people are like my family. The worst thing would be not to be respected by these guys."

For the interns, social status was at stake. The interns felt they wouldn't be respected if they embraced the signout. Change was coming into conflict with culture, and let's face it, a new rule is no match for a culture.

Could the hospitals change their culture? Here's where their paths diverge: Fifteen months into Katherine Kellogg's research, Alpha had managed to win the culture battle, and Beta had lost it. Anyone who wants to create organizational change needs to understand why.

7.

Kellogg discovered that the change hinged on the smallest work teams at the hospital, which met each day for "afternoon rounds." Each team was composed of three or four residents (both interns and more senior people), and during afternoon rounds, they discussed the patients under their care and other important issues.

The afternoon rounds at the two hospitals differed a great deal:

- At Alpha, the rounds were lengthy (around an hour) and had a high attendance rate. The teams tended to meet in quiet corners, moving from patient to patient around the hospital floor.
- At Beta, the rounds were more casual. They were shorter (twenty or thirty minutes), and team members often called in or sent a message instead of showing up in person. The teams at Beta didn't meet at patients' bedsides; they met in the computer lounge, where all the residents hung out between shifts. (Take a moment to contemplate the different behaviors that might be encouraged by the differing formats of these rounds.)

Teams were shuffled about once a month, and every so often, by the luck of the draw, all the people on a team would be reformers who supported the shorter workweeks. At Alpha, the reform-minded teams found great strength in their rounds. They were spending an hour in private discussions with a group of their fellow believers. But at Beta, the format of the afternoon rounds blocked any momentum for reform. The teams met for only a short time, and members often were missing. Worse, teams were meeting in the computer lounge, where lots of people who opposed reform could overhear their conversation, which led reform-minded members to self-censor.

Bottom line: At Beta, the afternoon rounds were irrelevant to the change. At Alpha, they became the spark, and the rounds became, in essence, underground resistance meetings.

8.

Researchers who study social movements call situations like these "free spaces"—small-scale meetings where reformers can gather and ready themselves for collective action without being observed by members of the dominant group. Free spaces often play a critical role in facilitating social change. Civil rights leaders, for instance, were able to use southern black churches as free spaces to prepare themselves for action.

Kellogg was present, every day, at Alpha and Beta as one reform movement blossomed and the other wilted. She attended thirty-one free-space meetings at Alpha and twenty-two meetings at Beta. The meetings at Beta had a comparable number of reformers but weren't conducted in a free space.

At Alpha, 77 percent of the meetings included discussion about the legitimacy of the signout process, and 81 percent of the meetings drew boundaries between "us" and "them"—reformers versus resisters. At Beta, none of the meetings featured either kind of discussion.

During the Alpha free-space meetings, the reformers began to develop a language for talking about the advantages of the reform. For instance, during one meeting, the chief resident deconstructed the "continuity of care" argument made by change resisters:

> It is important to take personal responsibility. But I think you can preserve this personal commitment without having one person there all the time. Some people are *old school* and say, "I'm going to do it myself." For me, it is *the team* that is going to take care of everything. Each of us takes personal responsibility to make sure that patient care is the best it can be, but *that doesn't mean doing it all yourself* as long as all of the pieces fit together. [emphasis added]

This resident was developing what Kellogg calls an "oppositional identity." Every culture, whether national or organizational, is shaped powerfully by its language. Across the reform-minded Alpha teams, a new language was being incubated that reflected a new set of values. Old school versus new school. Trusting your team versus doing it all yourself. Being efficient versus living in the hospital.

At Alpha, the reformers had the space and the language needed to brew a new identity. At Beta, they didn't. The lessons are clear. If you want to change the culture of your organization, you've got to get the reformers together. They need a free space. They need time to coordinate outside the gaze of the resisters.

Counterintuitively, you've got to let your organization have an identity conflict. For a time, at least, you've got to permit an "us versus them" struggle to take place. We know this violates our "we're all on the same team," Kumbaya-ish instincts. It's not desirable, but it's necessary. Think of it as organizational molting.

To encourage this molting in your culture, think of all the tools we've built up in the Path section. First, you need to tweak the environment to provide a free space for discussion. At Alpha, the rotational teams had a private place to meet, and that created a free space where the new identity could grow. Do your own "reformers" have a private place where they can meet and coordinate?

Second, you should build good habits. Recall the idea of action triggers—visualizing when and where you are going to do something important. The interns at Alpha were essentially setting action triggers. They thought about what they would say, and how they would act, when 9 p.m. came and the signout process was triggered. They mentally rehearsed how they would respond if an argument flared up with the night resident. Have members of your team rehearsed how they'll react when they meet resistance from your organization's "old guard"?

Finally, you should rally the herd. At Alpha, the leaders helped the reformers find one another, and the reformers began to create a language—as we saw in the examples of the designated driver and Fataki—that allowed them to talk about their values with others. As a leader, you can help prod them to create this language, to find ways to articulate what is different and better about the change you seek.

9.

We started the Path section by discussing the Fundamental Attribution Error—the tendency to attribute behavior to people's character rather than to their environments. Look again at the teaching-hospital example. At Alpha, 42 percent of superiors supported the change; at Beta, 66 percent supported it. Almost all of us would have put our money on Beta. Not many of us, when confronted with that data, would have immediately thought, *Yes, but what about the situational forces?*

At the two hospitals, individual character competed with situational forces, and situational forces won. This brings us back full circle to the food drive study, where a jerk with clear instructions was more charitable than a saint with generic instructions. The line between saints and jerks wasn't as clear as we might have thought. Neither was the line between supporters and resisters of hospital reform.

If the right Path can turn a jerk into a saint, then the right Path can also turn a change enemy into an ally.

11

Keep the Switch Going

1.

"A long journey starts with a single step." As clichés go, that's pretty wise.

But you know what else starts with a single step? An ill-conceived amble that you abandon after a few minutes.

So, yes, a long journey starts with a single step, but a single step doesn't guarantee the long journey. How do you keep those steps coming?

The first thing to do is recognize and celebrate that first step. Something you've done has worked. You've directed the Rider, you've motivated the Elephant, you've shaped the Path—and now your team is moving, or you're moving. When you spot movement, you've got to reinforce it. On this front, we can take inspiration from a rather unlikely source: trainers of exotic animals.

The writer Amy Sutherland studied animal trainers who teach dolphins to jump through hoops and monkeys to ride skateboards. These are very, very long journeys indeed. What do you do, in the first hour of the first day, to teach a monkey how to ride a skateboard?

The answer doesn't involve punishment. Animal trainers rarely use punishment these days. You can punish an elephant only so many times before you wind up as a splinter. Instead, trainers set a behavioral destination and then use "approximations," meaning that they reward each tiny step toward the destination. For example, in the first hour of the first day of training, the future skateboarding monkey gets a chunk of mango for not freaking out when the trainer puts the board in his cage. Later, he gets mango for touching the board, then for sitting on it, then for letting the trainer push him back and forth on it. Mango, mango, mango. Hundreds of sessions later, you've got a mango-bloated monkey ready to skate a half-pipe.

As Amy Sutherland studied the exotic-animal trainers, she had an epiphany: She wondered what would happen if she used these techniques on that "stubborn but lovable species, the American husband." Inspired by the idea, she wrote a hilarious *New York Times* article on her attempts to train her husband. The article, "What Shamu Taught Me About a Happy Marriage," became the most e-mailed article on the *Times* website in 2006, and it led to a book on the same topic.

Frustrated by her husband's various pecadilloes, Sutherland began to use approximations with him: "You can't expect a baboon to learn to flip on command in one session, just as you can't expect an American husband to begin regularly picking up his dirty socks by praising him once for picking up a single sock. With the baboon you first reward a hop, then a bigger hop, then an even bigger hop. With Scott the husband, I began to praise every small act every time: if he drove just a mile an hour slower, tossed one pair of shorts into the hamper, or was on time for anything." And Scott, basking in the appreciation, began to change.

This approach contrasts with much of the thinking on improving relationships at work. For instance, you probably have been asked to take a personality test or a "work style" test for a job. The idea is that if you understand your colleagues' "types," you'll all get along better. And some people may find the knowledge of types useful. But notice that this sounds like Fundamental Attribution Error thinking. To develop better relationships, you don't need to know whether your colleague is a Navigator or a Pleaser or a Passive-Aggressive Chieftain. You just need to notice and reinforce your colleague's positive behaviors—as Sutherland did with her husband—and trust that your colleague will do the same with you. After all, advice about aligning styles and expectations can't be the answer to everything. A trainer in California taught six elephants to stand in a line and urinate on command, and they hadn't even completed a Myers-Briggs.

Reinforcement is the secret to getting past the first step of your long journey and on to the second, third, and hundredth steps. And that's a problem, because most of us are terrible reinforcers. We are quicker to grouse than to praise. At work, we love to bond with our colleagues through communal complaining. (Sutherland calls this behavior "verbal grooming.") But this is all wrong: We need to be looking for bright spots—however tiny!—and rewarding them. If you want your boss or your team to change, you better get a little less stingy with the mango.

Learning to spot and celebrate approximations requires us to scan the environment constantly, looking for little rays of sunshine, and it isn't easy. Our Riders, by nature, focus on the negative. Problems are easy to spot; progress, much harder. But the progress is precious. Shamu didn't learn to jump through a hoop because her trainer was bitching at her. She learned because she had a trainer who was patient and focused and reinforced every step of the journey.

Psychologist Alan Kazdin prescribes an almost identical set of techniques for parents. Kazdin urges parents to "catch their children being good." He said, "If you want your child to do two hours of homework on her own every night, you don't withhold praise and rewards until she does two hours of homework without being asked to." Instead, you set small goals and gradually build her up. And when a child doesn't get something right, Kazdin advised: "Ask yourself, 'Was there anything about it that's a component of what I'd like her to do?' If the answer's yes, and it almost always is, then jump on that component: *It was great that you did X.*"

Kazdin points out that in certain situations, parents do this kind of reinforcement instinctively—for instance, when a child first starts trying to walk: "You praised him wildly when he pulled himself up from a crawling to a standing posture. You held his hands and helped him to take a few steps, encouraging him by exclaiming, *Look at you! You're walking! What a big boy!* He was not walking, of course . . . but you were shaping that behavior by reinforcing the stages on the way to it."

Let's be clear, we're not advising that you treat your colleagues or fellow citizens like monkeys or children—*Roger, you cut back your expenses last month! What a big boy you are!* Reinforcement doesn't have to be condescending, and it doesn't have to come with a power dynamic. Think of the way a friend urges you on at the gym ("Good work—now do one more rep!"). But reinforcement does require you to have a clear view of the destination, and it requires you to be savvy enough to reinforce the bright-spot behaviors when they happen.

The most important lesson we can learn from Kazdin and the animal trainers is this: Change isn't an event; it's a process. There is no moment when a monkey learns to skateboard; there's a process. There is no moment when a child learns to walk; there's a process. And there won't be a moment when your community starts to invest more in its school system, or starts recycling more, or starts to beautify its public spaces; there will be a process. To lead a process requires persistence.

A long journey requires lots of mango.

2.

In the Elephant section, we told the story of Steven Kelman, the man who accepted the daunting task of reforming the federal government's procurement processes. In his book *Unleashing Change,* he observed an encouraging dynamic in his change efforts: Once the change started, it seemed to feed on itself.

We've seen this snowballing effect many times. The citizens of Miner County, eager to revitalize their community, began their efforts by simply digging up tree stumps. Within a few years, they managed to build up the tax base of the entire county. At Rackspace, the customer-service team had the call-queuing system unplugged. It was a simple change, but it didn't take long before the customer-service ethic took root and led the company to a spectacular period of growth.

Kelman, the procurement guru, attributed the snowballing effect to several phenomena. Psychologists call one of them the *mere exposure effect,* which means that the more you're exposed to something, the more you like it. For instance, when the Eiffel Tower was first erected, Parisians hated it. They thought it was a half-finished skeletal blight on their fair city, and they responded with a frenzy of protest. But as time went by, public opinion evolved from hatred to acceptance to adoration. The mere exposure principle assures us that a change effort that initially feels unwelcome and foreign will gradually be perceived more favorably as people grow accustomed to it.

Also, *cognitive dissonance* works in your favor. People don't like to act in one way and think in another. So once a small step has been taken, and people have begun to act in a new way, it will be increasingly difficult for them to dislike the way they're acting. Similarly, as people begin to act differently, they'll start to think of themselves differently, and as their identity evolves, it will reinforce the new way of doing things. (Think of Brasilata's "inventors.")

Kelman points out that these forces aren't contingent on change efforts being successful in the early going; these aren't the reinforcing spoils of achieving "small wins." Rather, they kick in automatically as time goes by. So, although inertia may be a formidable opponent in the early goings of your switch, at some point inertia will shift from resisting change to supporting it. Small changes can snowball to big changes.

3.

These are encouraging realizations: Big changes can start with very small steps. Small changes tend to snowball. But this is not the same as saying that change is easy. If it were, we wouldn't see around us so many struggling alcoholics and troubled marriages and lagging companies and thwarted social change efforts. Change isn't always easy and it isn't always hard. In some ways change is ubiquitous; in others it's unlikely.

We can say this much with confidence: When change works, it tends to follow a pattern. The people who change have clear direction, ample motivation, and a supportive environment. In other words, when change works, it's because the Rider, the Elephant, and the Path are all aligned in support of the switch.

Take becoming a parent. If you think the organizational change you're contemplating is wrenching, forget about it—it can't hold a candle to the amount of change required by having kids. Whatever acts of will may be required to execute your new idea at work, no one will be called upon to send the controller to college (or to burp the CFO).

Raising children is an absolutely massive change that works pretty darn well, and it's no great mystery why. For one thing, it's a clear and vivid destination. We've all been kids, and we've all seen parents (our own and others) in action. We've received decades of vicarious training in parenting. So the Rider knows what direction to go and what kinds of behaviors lead to success. (Mind you, there's still a lot of winging it en route to the destination.)

People have kids because of feelings, not knowledge. A rosy-eyed couple looks forward to raising a child. They think about what it'll be like to have their own little bundle of joy. So the Elephant is excited to begin a long and arduous journey that, in other circumstances, might induce panic. Furthermore, parenthood is an identity that appeals—you start making your decisions based on what's good for the kids rather than on what's most comfortable for you. The identity is so powerful, in fact, that your Elephant starts embracing short-term *sacrifices* for the good of the kids.

Once we become parents, our friends and families find ways to shrink the change, especially in the first few months: Your mom comes to help in the first few weeks; your friends bring you food; your employer gives you leave from work; and your relatives keep tabs on you.

And think of all the other ways that society has shaped the Path for raising kids: from little things, like high chairs at Olive Garden, to big things, like maternity leave and school systems and neighborhoods built explicitly to be good places for raising children.

Maybe this sounds like common sense to you. But if it's common sense, then it's common sense that stays confined to the "parenting area" of our brains. Because if we really did understand why an extreme change like having kids works while minor changes routinely fail—if we really did understand that change rarely happens unless it's motivated by feeling, or that the environment can act as a powerful brake or accelerant on our behavior—then, let's face it, the Food Pyramid would not exist, managers would never kick off change initiatives with PowerPoint presentations, and global warming activists would never talk about the number of carbon parts per million in the atmosphere. If it's common sense, it hasn't quite made the leap to action.

When change happens, it tends to follow a pattern. We've got to stop ignoring that pattern and start embracing it.

4.

When Mike Romano went to Vietnam, surrounded by drugs, he started doing opium, and when he came home, surrounded by friends and family, he stopped. When the employees at Rackspace had a call-queuing system, they didn't answer customers' calls, and when the system was thrown out, they started answering. Change follows a pattern.

When the two of us started jury-rigging our computers to fight e-mail distractions, we were fighting the same battle as the people who purchased a Clocky, determined to keep themselves from oversleeping. Change follows a pattern.

When some hotel maids were given an identity of themselves as serious exercisers, they turned up their activity level a notch. When the "inventors" at Brasilata faced an electricity shortage, they came up with so many energy-saving ideas that the firm ended up with a surplus. Change follows a pattern.

When Jerry Sternin went to Vietnam, the government gave him six months to make a dent in malnutrition. He didn't speak a word of Vietnamese, but he knew how to look for the bright spots, and soon mothers had learned cooking techniques that foiled malnutrition. When the conservationists at Rare saw how St. Lucians had rallied behind their parrot, they realized they had a bright spot on their hands, and since then, they've spread "Pride campaigns" to over fifty countries. Change follows a pattern.

What's *not* part of the pattern is the type of person who's doing the changing. We mentioned a few CEOs in this book, but we mentioned vastly more people who had less impressive titles and who didn't have much money in their budgets: professors and nurses and middle managers and government bureaucrats and principals and parents. Their quests ranged from eccentric to epic. We saw a professor who shrank moviegoers' popcorn containers, and two people who reined in Attila the Accountant, and a woman who reformed child abusers, and a man with a staff of 75 who saved 100,000 lives.

Their situations were different, and the scale of their changes was different, but the pattern was the same. They directed the Rider, they motivated the Elephant, and they shaped the Path. And now it's your pattern.

What will you switch?

HOW TO MAKE A **SWITCH**

For things to change, somebody somewhere has to start acting differently. Maybe it's you, maybe it's your team. Picture that person (or people).

Each has an emotional Elephant side and a rational Rider side. You've got to reach both. And you've also got to clear the way for them to succeed. In short, you must do three things:

➤ **DIRECT** the Rider

FOLLOW THE BRIGHT SPOTS. Investigate what's working and clone it. [Jerry Sternin in Vietnam, solutions-focused therapy]

SCRIPT THE CRITICAL MOVES. Don't think big picture, think in terms of specific behaviors. [1% milk, four rules at the Brazilian railroad]

POINT TO THE DESTINATION. Change is easier when you know where you're going and why it's worth it. ["You'll be third graders soon," "No dry holes" at BP]

➤ **MOTIVATE** the Elephant

FIND THE FEELING. Knowing something isn't enough to cause change. Make people feel something. [Piling gloves on the table, the chemotherapy video game, Robyn Waters's demos at Target]

SHRINK THE CHANGE. Break down the change until it no longer spooks the Elephant. [The 5-Minute Room Rescue, procurement reform]

GROW YOUR PEOPLE. Cultivate a sense of identity and instill the growth mindset. [Brasilata's "inventors," junior-high math kids' turnaround]

➤ **SHAPE** the Path

TWEAK THE ENVIRONMENT. When the situation changes, the behavior changes. So change the situation. [Throwing out the phone system at Rackspace, 1-Click ordering, simplifying the online time sheet]

BUILD HABITS. When behavior is habitual, it's "free"—it doesn't tax the Rider. Look for ways to encourage habits. [Setting "action triggers," eating two bowls of soup while dieting, using checklists]

RALLY THE HERD. Behavior is contagious. Help it spread. ["Fataki" in Tanzania, "free spaces" in hospitals, seeding the tip jar]

Here we list twelve common problems that people encounter as they fight for change, along with some advice about overcoming them. (Note that we're speaking in shorthand here—this advice won't make sense to anybody who hasn't read the book.)

Problem: People don't see the need to change.
Advice: **1.** You are not going to overcome this by talking to the Rider. Instead, find the feeling. Can you do a dramatic demonstration like the Glove Shrine, or like Robyn Waters's demos at Target? **2.** Create empathy. Show people the problems with *not* changing (think Attila the Accountant). **3.** Tweak the environment so that whether people *see* the need to change is irrelevant. Remember, Rackspace employees didn't necessarily see the need to improve customer service, but after the call-queuing system disappeared, they had to pick up the phone.

Problem: I'm having the "not invented here" problem: People resist my idea because they say "We've never done it like that before."
Advice: **1.** Highlight identity: Is there some aspect of your idea that's consistent with the history of your organization? (E.g., *We've always been the pioneers in this industry.*) Or is your idea consistent with a professional identity that people share? **2.** Find a bright spot that *is* invented here and clone it.

Problem: We should be doing *something*, but we're getting bogged down in analysis.

Advice: **1.** Don't overanalyze and play to the weaknesses of the Rider. Instead, find a feeling that will get the Elephant moving. **2.** Create a destination post-card. That way, the Rider starts analyzing *how to get there* rather than *whether anything should be done.* **3.** Simplify the problem by scripting the critical moves: What's your equivalent of the 1% milk campaign?

Problem: The environment has shifted, and we need to over-come our old patterns of behavior.

Advice: **1.** Can you create a new habit so the Rider doesn't constantly have to wrestle the Elephant? **2.** Set an action trigger. Preload your decision by imagining the time and place where you're going to act differently. **3.** Use Natalie Elder's strategy of creating a routine for the morning that eliminates the old, bad behavior. **4.** The old pattern is powerful, so make sure to script the critical moves, because ambiguity is the enemy. ALL railroad came up with four simple rules to work its way out of financial distress.

Problem: People simply aren't motivated to change.

Advice: **1.** Is an identity conflict standing in the way? If so, you'll need to "sell" the new identity (think Brasilata's inventors). Encourage people to take a small step toward the new identity, as in the "Drive Safely" study. **2.** Create a destina-tion postcard that makes the change more attractive (like the teacher who told her first graders "You'll be third graders by the end of the year"). **3.** Lower the bar to get people moving, as with the 5-Minute Room Rescue. **4.** Use social pres-sure to encourage change (as when Gerard Cachon posted the review times for the operations journal). **5.** Can you smooth the Path so much that even an un-motivated person will slide along? Remember, even jerks in the dorm donated to the food drive when given a specific invitation and a map.

Problem: I'll change tomorrow.

Advice: **1.** Shrink the change so you can start today. **2.** If you can't start today, set an action trigger for tomorrow. **3.** Make yourself accountable to someone. Let your colleagues or loved ones know what you're trying to change, so their peer pressure will help you.

Problem: People keep saying, "It will never work."

Advice: **1.** Find a bright spot that shows it can work. There's no situation that's 100 percent failure. Like a solutions-focused therapist, look for the flashes of success. **2.** Think of Bill Parcells and the way he prods players for small victories in practice. Can you engineer a success that could change your team's attitude? **3.** Some people probably *do* think it will work. Carve out a free space for them where they can catalyze the change without facing direct opposition.

Problem: I know what I should be doing, but I'm not doing it.

Advice: **1.** Knowing isn't enough. You've got an Elephant problem. **2.** Think of the 5-Minute Room Rescue. Starting small can help you overcome dread. What is the most trivial thing that you can do—right at this moment—that would represent a baby step toward the goal? **3.** Look for Path solutions. How can you tweak your environment so that you're "forced" to change? **4.** Behavior is contagious. Get someone else involved with you so that you can reinforce each other.

Problem: You don't know my people. They absolutely hate change.

Advice: How many of your people are married or have a child? Whatever you're proposing is a less dramatic change. (And, by the way, reread the section on the Fundamental Attribution Error. You're committing it.)

Problem: People were excited at first, but then we hit some rough patches and lost momentum.

Advice: **1.** Focus on building habits. When you create habits, you get the new behavior "for free" (think of the stand-up meetings), and you're less likely to backslide. **2.** Motivate the Elephant by reminding people how much they've already accomplished (like putting two stamps on their car-wash cards). **3.** Teach the growth mindset. Every success is going to involve rough patches. Recall the IDEO example, which warned people not to panic when the going got tough.

Problem: It's just too much.

Advice: **1.** Shrink the change until it's not too much. Don't give the Elephant an excuse to give up. **2.** Start developing the growth mindset. Progress doesn't always come easily—achieving success requires some failures along the way. Don't beat yourself up when those failures occur.

Problem: Everyone seems to agree that we need to change, but nothing's happening.

Advice: **1.** Remember, what looks like resistance is often lack of clarity. Miner County residents really started moving when the high school students scripted the critical move of spending 10 percent more money in Miner County. **2.** Don't forget the Path. Are there obstacles to change that you can remove? **3.** Can you find a bright spot that can serve as a model for the right behavior? Think of the mothers in the Vietnamese village. They always wanted their kids to be better nourished, but they didn't change until two things happened: (1) They learned exactly what to do from the bright-spot moms (e.g., use brine shrimp and sweet-potato greens); (2) Seeing the success of the bright-spot moms made them hopeful and ready to move.

Next Steps

If you've finished *Switch* and are hungry for more, visit the book's website:

www.switchthebook.com/resources

On the site, you can find resources like these:

- **One-page overview.** Download and print the one-page overview (see page 259) and share it with your colleagues. [PDF format]
- **The *Switch* podcast series.** Listen to a series of short, tailored podcasts, in which the authors offer their thoughts about how to apply the book's concepts to different kinds of change.
  - *Switch for Business*
  - *Switch for Marketers*
  - *Switch for the Social Sector*
  - *Switch for Personal Change*
- ***Switch* book club materials.** Get access to a Facilitator's Guide designed to help lead book-club discussions on *Switch*. [PDF format]
- **Switch Your Organization outline**. Use this outline to guide your team's efforts to change your business or nonprofit. [PDF format]

Recommendations for Additional Reading

We read tons of books on change while writing *Switch*. Here are some of our favorites, in no particular order:

- *The Happiness Hypothesis*, by Jonathan Haidt [Psychology, Philosophy, Happiness]. Haidt came up with the Elephant/Rider analogy that we use in *Switch*. If you want to be happier and smarter, you should read his book.
- *Mindset*, by Carol Dweck [Psychology, Individual change]. If you found our discussion of the growth mindset (in Chapter 7) interesting, then please go to the source. Everyone should own this book.
- *The Heart of Change*, by John Kotter and Dan Cohen [Business and organizational change]. Our favorite book of Kotter's, this book will be useful if you are trying to change a big organization.

- *Mindless Eating*, by Brian Wansink [Dieting]. Do you want to lose a few pounds, or are you just curious about why everyone else is getting fatter? This book is filled with clever research like the popcorn study we described in the first chapter.
- *Nudge*, by Richard Thaler and Cass Sunstein [Decision making and public policy]. The authors argue that people can be "nudged" to make better decisions, and they propose some great Path solutions.
- *One Small Step Can Change Your Life*, by Robert Maurer [Individual and organizational change]. If you liked the chapter on shrinking the change, this is your book. Maurer shows how small steps can lead to great change.
- *Divorce Busting*, by Michele Weiner-Davis [Relationships]. Anyone in a relationship can benefit from this book by a practitioner of solutions-focused therapy.
- *Influencer*, by Kerry Patterson et al. [Societal and organizational change]. The authors behind *Crucial Conversations* wrote this excellent book on behavior change.
- *Unleashing Change*, by Steven Kelman [Government, Organizational change]. Kelman reviews his experience in leading procurement reform in the federal government. If you're looking for a change book that's rigorous and full of data, check out this one.

Notes

Chapter One

1 **Popcorn.** For dozens of clever studies of eating behavior, see Brian Wansink (2006), *Mindless Eating*, New York: Bantam Dell. The popcorn study is on pp. 16–19.

5 **Clocky.** Sales statistics come from this MIT online magazine: http://web.mit.edu/invent/iow/nanda.html (accessed June 20, 2009). Most of the sales came through Nanda's own website. According to the article, Nanda "was somewhat taken by surprise when the device attracted a great deal of attention after its description was posted, along with dozens of other student projects, on the Media Lab website. Several trend-watching blogs and websites such as Engadget took note of the Clocky concept and soon had introduced thousands of potential customers to the device through photos and links online." Gauri Nanda received an Ig Nobel Prize in Economics in 2005 for "theoretically adding many more hours to the workday."

7 **Jonathan Haidt.** See Haidt (2006), *The Happiness Hypothesis: Finding Modern Truth in Ancient Wisdom*, New York: Basic

Books, especially pp. 3–5. Haidt reviews metaphors presented by Buddha, Plato (including the quotation we include), and Freud and then presents his own metaphor. We love his Elephant/Rider metaphor—particularly the obvious imbalance in physical power between the two—and we're grateful to him for letting us use it here. In *The Happiness Hypothesis,* Haidt focuses not on change but rather on understanding what we can learn about being happy from the intersection of centuries of wisdom and modern psychology. If you want to be happier and smarter, read his book.

10 **Self-control is an exhaustible resource.** The papers we cite in this section are from an exciting area of research, started in the last fifteen years. The classic first paper, which includes the chocolate-chip cookie study, is Roy F. Baumeister, Ellen Bratslavsky, Mark Muraven, and Dianne M. Tice (1998), "Ego Depletion: Is the Active Self a Limited Resource?" *Journal of Personality and Social Psychology, 74,* 1252–1265. The sad-movie study is part of Mark Muraven, Dianne M. Tice, and Roy Baumeister (1998), "Self-Control as Limited Resource: Regulatory Depletion Patterns," *Journal of Personality and Social Psychology, 74,* 774–789. The experiments that show the self-control problems induced by too many choices are described in Kathleen D. Vohs, Roy F. Baumeister et al. (2008), "Making Choices Impairs Subsequent Self-Control: A Limited-Resource Account of Decision Making, Self-Regulation, and Active Initiative," *Journal of Personality and Social Psychology, 94,* 883–898. In the wedding-registry study, experimental participants spent only twelve minutes setting up a simulated registry, yet that short amount of time was sufficient to sap their self-control. Given that real brides spend months choosing invitations, place settings, reception venues, and music lists, it's no wonder that some turn into Bridezillas.

13 **424 kinds of gloves.** Jon Stegner's story and the quotations are from John P. Kotter and Dan S. Cohen (2002), *The Heart of Change,* Boston: Harvard Business School Press, pp. 29–30.

15 **1% milk.** For the story of the development of this campaign, see Steve Booth-Butterfield and Bill Reger (2004), "The Message Changes Belief and the Rest Is Theory: The '1% or Less' Milk

Campaign and Reasoned Action," *Preventive Medicine, 39,* 581–
588. The actual study is described in Bill, Reger, Margo G.
Wootan, Steven Booth-Butterfield, and Holli Smith (1998), "1%
or Less: A Community-Based Nutrition Campaign," *Public
Health Reports, 113,* 410–419.

19 **In 2004, Donald Berwick.** Berwick's 100,000 lives campaign is
the subject of a case study prepared by Chip's colleagues at Stanford University's Graduate School of Business. See Hayagreeva
Rao and David Hoyt (2008), "Institute for Healthcare Improvement: The Campaign to Save 100,000 Lives," Stanford Graduate
School of Business Case Study L-13. For additional insight into
this case, check out an article by Rao and Robert Sutton (September 2008), "The Ergonomics of Innovation," *The McKinsey
Quarterly,* http://www.mckinseyquarterly.com/The_ergonom-
ics_of_innovation_2197 (accessed May 17, 2009).

Chapter Two

27 **In 1990, Jerry Sternin.** The Vietnam story is compiled from various sources. An article by David Dorsey (December 2000), "Positive Deviant," *Fast Company,* p. 42, first introduced popular
audiences to Jerry and Monique Sternin's work on positive deviance. Other details are from Jerry Sternin's presentation at the
Boston College Center for Corporate Social Responsibility in
April 2008 and from interviews of Jerry Sternin by Chip Heath
in March and April 2008 and of Monique Sternin in May 2009.

27 **"We were like orphans."** Most of the direct quotations in this
section are from Dorsey, "Positive Deviant."

28 **Bright spots.** Sternin's term for these outliers is *positive deviants,*
which is based on a statistical analogy. Picture a statistical bell
curve on which most people have outcomes around average.
Sternin was looking for people on the positive tail of the bell
curve.

Although the positive deviance methodology pioneered by
Sternin is very useful, we found that the "deviance" terminology
tends to be confusing or off-putting to people who aren't familiar with statistics, so we use the "bright-spots" terminology. Later

in this chapter, we carry the term *bright spots* over to other situations that involve exceptional positive performance.

Jerry Sternin died in November 2008. His work lives on through the work of Monique Sternin and the Positive Deviance Initiative at Tufts University. For an overview of the large number of domains in which positive deviance methods have produced substantial change, see the bibliography of work at http://www.positivedeviance.org/materials/bib_subj.html. Positive deviance was one of the "Ideas of the Year" highlighted by *New York Times Magazine* in 2008.

32 **Emory University's School of Public Health.** See U. Agnes Trinh Mackintosh, David R. Marsh, and Dirk G. Schroeder (2002), "Sustained Positive Deviant Child Care Practices and Their Effects on Child Growth in Viet Nam," *Food and Nutrition Bulletin, 23,* 16–25.

33 **"School stinks," said Bobby.** Bobby's story is from John J. Murphy (1994), "Working with What Works: A Solution-Focused Approach to School Behavior Problems," *School Counselor, 42,* 59–66.

34 **Solutions-focused brief therapy.** A relatively new therapeutic approach, solutions-focused brief therapy (SFBT) was pioneered by therapists at the Palo Alto Mental Research Institute, where Steve de Shazer and Insoo Kim Berg did their training. De Shazer and Berg are known for their emphasis on solutions and on the Miracle Question, which we consider later. SFBT has been applied in many different arenas. Wallace J. Gingerich of Case Western Reserve keeps a list of SFBT studies on his website: http://www.gingerich.net/SFBT/2007_review.htm. For his 2007 review of the literature, Gingerich accumulated a list of 150 studies, most conducted since 1997, that investigated the effect of SFBT on behavior. SFBT has been applied to day-to-day situations such as couples therapy, bullying at school, and how kids perform in math. It also has been used with even more serious problems: domestic violence offenders, prisoners, substance abusers, individuals found guilty of DUI, and suicide prevention programs. See Steve de Shazer, Yvonne Dolan, Harry Korman, Terry Trepper, Eric McCollum, and Insoo Kim Berg (2007), *More*

than Miracles: The State of the Art of Solution-Focused Brief Therapy, New York: Haworth Press, p. 157.

35 **Marriage therapist Michele Weiner-Davis.** The quotations in this section and the golf example are from Weiner-Davis, *Divorce Busting* (1992), New York: Simon & Schuster, pp. 15–18. This is one of the most insightful and practical books on change we found in any domain. Even if your relationship is going well, you'll benefit from reading this book.

36 **Miracle Question.** This version of the question is from de Shazer et al., *More than Miracles,* the book that brought de Shazer and Berg, the founders of SFBT, together with four other experienced solutions-focused therapists to talk about current practice. SFBT therapists typically record their counseling sessions, with their clients' permission, for use in training new therapists and refining their own technique, and these authors spent time reviewing videotapes of therapy sessions and asking one another, "Why did you ask that there?" Reading *More than Miracles* is the therapy equivalent of sitting around reviewing game tapes with Super Bowl–winning football coaches. It's a great experience for a therapist or counselor.

36 **Brian Cade.** The two counseling sessions by Brian Cade are described in Kathryn Shine (March 24, 2002), "C'mon, get happy," *Sun Herald,* p. 38. Also see Cade and William Hudson, *A Brief Guide to Brief Therapy* (1993), New York: Norton.

37 **Man with a drinking problem.** The example is from the *Harvard Mental Health Letter* (September 1, 2006), "Solution-focused therapy (methods of psychotherapy)."

41 **Xolair.** The Xolair example is described in Richard Pascale and Jerry Sternin (May 2005), "Your Company's Secret Change Agents," *Harvard Business Reviews,* pp. 73–81.

45 **Learn English at home.** Go to http://www.english-at-home.com/vocabulary/english-word-for-emotions/ (accessed May 17, 2009).

46 **Bad is stronger than good.** This review paper is unusually long, thorough (233 references!), and depressing. See Roy F. Baumeister, Ellen Bratslavsky, Catrin Finkenauer, and Kathleen D. Vohs (2001), "Bad Is Stronger than Good," *Review of General*

Psychology, 5, 323–370. The final summary quotation is on p. 355.

47 **Marcus Buckingham.** Interested readers could start with this book: Buckingham (2007), *Go Put Your Strengths to Work: 6 Powerful Steps to Achieve Outstanding Performance,* New York: Free Press.

48 **A husband forgot his wife's birthday.** For an even freakier world, imagine that the husband had forgotten all but one of his wife's last fourteen birthdays, yet she, being a bright-spot aficionado, was *energized* because she knew success was possible.

48 **Solving problems versus scaling successes.** Another domain in which people have made progress following bright spots is the field called Appreciative Inquiry (AI), which focuses on analyzing successes rather than failures. For instance, an AI practitioner who is investigating customer-service problems wouldn't ask, "What can we do to minimize client anger and complaints?" Instead, she'd ask, "When have customers been most pleased with their service, and what can we apply from those moments of success?" Tom Krattenmaker, a practitioner of AI, says, "Positive stories, unlike data or lists, stir imaginations and generate excitement about the company and what it is capable of accomplishing in the future." See Tom Krattenmaker (2005), "Change Through Appreciative Inquiry," in *Managing Change to Reduce Resistance,* Boston: Harvard Business School Press, pp. 49–58; the quotation is on p. 55.

Chapter Three

49 **Chronic hip pain.** The study that showed physicians were more likely to refer a patient to surgery when confronted with two medication options is Donald A. Redelmeier and Eldar Shafir (1995), "Medical Decision Making in Situations That Offer Multiple Alternatives," *Journal of the American Medical Association,* 273, 302–305.

50 **Decision paralysis.** Some of the language in our discussion of decision paralysis first appeared in a column we wrote for *Fast Company* (November 2007), "Analysis of Paralysis," http://www

.fastcompany.com/magazine/120/analysis-of-paralysis.html (accessed May 17, 2009).

50 **Shopping is a lot more tiring.** Researchers have shown that the focused decisions you have to make while you're shopping actually deplete your self-control. What saps your control is not the time you spend shopping; it's the number of choices you have to make. That must be why Decembers are so bad for overindulging in food and drink. See Kathleen D. Vohs, Roy F. Baumeister et al. (2008), "Making Choices Impairs Subsequent Self-Control: A Limited-Resource Account of Decision Making, Self-Regulation, and Active Initiative," *Journal of Personality and Social Psychology, 94,* 883–898.

50 **Scene 1, 2, 3.** See Sheena S. Iyengar and Mark R. Lepper (2000), "When Choice Is Demotivating: Can One Desire Too Much of a Good Thing?" *Journal of Personality and Social Psychology, 79,* 995–1006. See Sheena Sethi-Iyengar, G. Huberman, and W. Jiang (2004), "How Much Choice Is Too Much? Contributions to 401(k) Retirement Plans," in O. S. Mitchell and S. Utkus (eds.), *Pension Design and Structure: New Lessons from Behavioral Finance* (pp. 83–97), Oxford: Oxford University Press. The dating study is Ray Fisman, Sheena S. Iyengar, E. Kamenica, and Itamar Simonson (2006), "Gender Differences in Mate Selection: Evidence from a Speed Dating Experiment," *Quarterly Journal of Economics, 121*(2), 673–697. Sheena S. Iyengar's book *How We Choose: The Subtext of Life* (New York: Twelve Publishers) is coming out around May 2010, and you should look for it.

52 **Barry Schwartz.** See Schwartz (2003), *The Paradox of Choice: Why More Is Less,* New York: Ecco, p. 2.

54 **America Latina Logistica (ALL).** The case of the Brazilian railroad is described in Donald N. Sull, Andre Delben Silva, and Fernando Martins (January 14, 2004), *America Latina Logistica,* Harvard Business School Case 9-804-139, Boston: Harvard Business School Press.

60 **Food Pyramid.** The Food Pyramid graphic and data are from the site http://mypyramid.gov/pyramid/index.html.

62 *The Critical Path.* See Michael Beer, Russell A. Eisenstat, and Bert Spector (1990), *The Critical Path to Corporate Renewal.*

Boston: Harvard Business School Press. The contrast between outcome goals and behavioral goals is on p. 244.

63 **110 parents who had abused their children.** The results of the study are described in Mark Chaffin, Jane F. Silovsky, Beverly Funderburk et al. (2004), "Parent-Child Interaction Therapy with Physically Abusive Parents: Efficacy for Reducing Future Abuse Reports," *Journal of Consulting and Clinical Psychology, 72,* 500–510. Most of the quotations are from an interview between Chip Heath and Beverly Funderburk in October 2008.

67 **Miner County.** The story of the revitalization of Miner County is based on two sources: (1) interviews between Chip Heath, Randy Parry, and Kathy Callies in May 2008 and May 2009 and (2) an article by Jonathan Eig (March 27, 2005), "As Farmers Dwindle, Towns Make Best of What's Left," *Wall Street Journal.* Eig's article is especially interesting because his editors originally sent him to write a "turn out the lights" story about the last years of Miner County. But the community didn't know that, and residents shared with him the remarkable changes of the previous few years. Eig was impressed, and the story he wrote was guardedly optimistic, not the bleak tale he'd originally envisioned. His editors were so shocked by his optimistic tone that they rejected his first few drafts because his story was so far from what they had been expecting.

Chapter Four

73 **Crystal Jones.** Jones's story is from a training manual for young teachers who are going to teach in some of the toughest school districts in the country. Jones's story is described on pp. 26, 50–51, and the other goal is quoted on p. 37 of *Teaching as Leadership* (2008), Washington, DC: Teach For America.

75 **BHAG.** See James C. Collins and Jerry I. Porras (1994), *Built to Last: Successful Habits of Visionary Companies,* New York: Harper Business. The examples of BHAGs are from James C. Collins and Jerry I. Porras (September–October 1996), "Building Your Company's Vision," *Harvard Business Review,* pp. 65–77.

76 **Laura Esserman.** For Esserman's story, see Victoria Chang and Jeffrey Pfeffer (2003), "Laura Esserman (A)," Stanford Graduate

School of Business Case Study OB-42A. Quotations not in the case study are from interviews that Chip Heath conducted with Laura Esserman and Meredithe Mendelsohn in May 2009.

82 **"15% return on equity."** See Michael Beer, Russell A. Eisenstat, and Bert Spector (1990), *The Critical Path to Organizational Renewal.* Boston: Harvard Business School Press, p. 85.

83 **Judy Samuelson.** This Clinic is from an interview between Dan Heath and Judy Samuelson in May 2009.

87 **BP's "No dry holes."** Industry history, quotations, and the description of BP's "No dry holes" goal are from interviews by Chip Heath with Pete Callagher, Jim Farnsworth, and Ian Vann in 2005.

94 **Jack Rivkin.** The turnaround of the Shearson Lehman research department is described in Ashish Nanda, Boris Groysberg, and Lauren Prusiner (January 23, 2006), *Lehman Brothers (A): Rise of the Equity Research Department,* Harvard Business School Case Study 9-906-034, Boston: Harvard Business School Press.

Chapter Five

102 **Robyn Waters, Target.** Waters's story is from an interview by Chip Heath with Robyn Waters in November 2008.

105 **In *The Heart of Change.*** See John P. Kotter and Dan S. Cohen (2002), *The Heart of Change,* Boston: Harvard Business School Press, p. x. The quote about the advantages of analytical tools is on p. 12.

108 **HopeLab Re-Mission.** The backstory of the Re-Mission game is from an interview by Chip Heath with HopeLab research director Steve Cole in November 2008. The HopeLab clinical test of the Re-Mission game is described in Pamela M. Kato, Steve W. Cole, Andrew S. Bradlyn, and Brad H. Pollock (2008), "A Video Game Improves Behavioral Outcomes in Adolescents and Young Adults with Cancer: A Randomized Trial," *Pediatrics, 122,* e305–e317. The doubling of odds for a 20 percent increase in compliance is indicated by Jean L. Richardson et al. (1990), "The Effect of Compliance with Treatment on Survival Among Patients with Hematologic Malignancies," *Journal of Clinical Oncology, 8*(2), 356–364.

110 **"Where'd you find six dumb people?"** See M. A. Cusumano and R. W. Selby (1995), *Microsoft Secrets*, New York: Free Press. The Microsoft usability test lab is described on p. 379. The problem of programmers having more advanced machines than their customers is discussed on p. 347.

113 **Fake Weatherman.** See Peter Borkenau and Anette Liebler (1993), "Convergence of Stranger Ratings of Personality and Intelligence with Self-Ratings, Partner Ratings, and Measured Intelligence," *Journal of Personality and Social Psychology*, 65, 546–553. The correlation between self-ratings and measured IQ was .29, accounting for 8 percent of the variance. The correlation between stranger ratings and IQ was .38, accounting for 14 percent of the variance. Strangers thus did about 66 percent better than people themselves.

114 **We're all lousy self-evaluators.** The research studies on self-evaluation and the examples of positive illusions are summarized in David Dunning, Chip Heath, and Jerry Suls (2004), "Flawed Self-Assessment: Implications for Health, Education, and the Workplace," *Psychological Science in the Public Interest*, 5, 69–106. David Dunning also has some interesting research on what he calls the "unskilled and unaware" phenomenon. The worst self-evaluators are people who lack skill. For instance, people who don't have a sense of humor are most likely to think their bad jokes are funny, and people who lack skill in grammar are most likely to confidently ignore a useful correction. When the research came out, dozens of newspaper articles appeared illustrating the "unskilled and unaware" phenomenon with a discussion of workplace bosses, a topic not covered in the original research article.

115 **Attila the Accountant.** Sim Sitkin, who is now a professor of management at Duke University's Fuqua School of Business, told this story to Chip Heath in May 2009.

119 **"In the absence of a dire threat."** See David A. Garvin and Michael A. Roberto (February 2005), "Change Through Persuasion," *Harvard Business Review*, pp. 1–8, reprinted in Harvard Business School Press (2006), *Harvard Business Review on Leading Through Change* (pp. 85–104), Boston: Harvard Business School

Press. The "dire threat" quote is on p. 86; the "deathbed" quote is on p. 87.

119 **Rock bottom.** See Ruth Maxwell (1986), *Breakthrough: What to Do When Alcoholism or Chemical Dependency Hits Close to Home,* New York: Ballantine Books; the conference incident is on pp. 4–5.

119 **The burning platform.** See William E. Smith and Helen Gibson (July 18, 1988), "Disaster 'Screaming like a Banshee,' " *Time,* http://www.time.com/time/magazine/article/0,9171,967917,00. html (accessed May 28, 2009).

120 *Glengarry Glen Ross.* See David Mamet (1984), *Glengarry Glen Ross: A Play,* New York: Grove Press.

121 **What Good Are Positive Emotions?** See Barbara L. Fredrickson (1998), "What Good Are Positive Emotions?" *Review of General Psychology, 2,* 300–319. Among the studies Frederickson cites: Doctors experiencing positive emotions solve a tricky medical dilemma more flexibly and quickly. Students in a positive mood devise more innovative solutions to a technical challenge. Negotiators in a positive state of mind are more successful and creative negotiators; they find "win-win" solutions more often. Positive emotion also makes it easier for people to make connections among dissimilar ideas, and it makes them less likely to slip into an "us versus them" mentality. All of these tendencies—flexible problem solving, innovative solutions, less political infighting— would be very useful in a change situation.

Chapter Six

124 **A study of hotel maids.** See Alia J. Crum and Ellen J. Langer (2007), "Mind-Set Matters: Exercise and the Placebo Effect," *Psychological Science, 18,* 165–171.

126 **Car-wash loyalty cards.** See J. C. Nunes and X. Dreze (2006), "The Endowed Progress Effect: How Artificial Advancement Increases Effort," *Journal of Consumer Research, 32,* 504–512.

127 **50 percent of the money in the bag.** This practice was discussed in an interview between Chip Heath and Jan Alfieri, of the Association of Fundraising Professionals, in February 2009.

Alfieri says that this money is usually raised in what fund-raising professionals call the "quiet period" before the campaign is announced publicly. Historically the amount was 50 percent, but some recent campaigns raised as much as 70 percent. Alfieri says, "All this is calculated to give donors the assurance the campaign will succeed."

129 **Shrink the change.** Thousands of studies in psychology indicate that people do better when they have high situational self-confidence, or self-efficacy. People with high self-efficacy perform better on sports, academic, and work tasks; they persevere longer; and they rebound better when they encounter a setback.

How do you build this kind of self-efficacy? Most research on self-efficacy is correlational so it can't distinguish (a) self-confidence as a mindset that can be grown from (b) self-confidence that arises for other reasons. Michael Jordan may report high self-efficacy in trying a new sport, but that self-efficacy may be due to his physical abilities, not to his mindset. The literature on self-efficacy suggests a couple of ways to build self-efficacy as a mindset—for example, by experiencing personal success in a difficult situation or by seeing a role model experience success. Those solutions, however, may be less available in a time of change when personal success and role models are in short supply.

Some research suggests that shrinking the change may provide a good game plan for building self-efficacy. Al Bandura and Dale Schunk tried to teach subtraction skills to elementary school kids who had been identified as having "gross deficits in arithmetic." On an initial 25-question subtraction test, two-thirds of their kids got less than one problem correct. The researchers developed seven modules to teach key subtraction skills (such as how to borrow from the next column). Each module outlined a principle, gave two examples, and provided six pages of problems to be worked by the students. All kids were brought in for seven 30-minute, self-paced sessions with no coaching from a teacher. One group was given a big, distant goal of completing the seven modules by the end of the seventh session. Another group was given a close-by, shrink-the-change goal of completing one module during each session. On the final test, the proximal-goals group solved 81 percent of the problems, and the distal-goals groups solved only 45 percent. Later, after the study sessions were over, kids were given a free play period and two sets of exercises to entertain themselves—some subtraction problems and some "solve the code" puzzles. The kids with distant goals did only one subtraction problem on average. But the kids who built self-efficacy through proximal goals—even though they initially hated math just as much—solved fourteen subtraction problems on average during the free play period. Stretch goals (or BHAGs) may be fine when you already have strong self-efficacy. But Bandura and Shunk's study suggests that when you're building self-efficacy, you might want to shrink the change. See Albert Bandura and Dale H. Schunk (1981), "Cultivating Competence, Self-Efficacy, and Intrinsic Interest Through Proximal Self-Motivation," *Journal of Personality and Social Psychology, 41,* 586–598.

130 **5-Minute Room Rescue.** Check out http://www.flylady.net/pages/FLYFaq.asp (accessed December 17, 2008).

131 **Personal finance guru Dave Ramsey.** Dave Ramsey describes the Farrars' situation and his debt-fighting techniques in Ramsey (2007), *The Total Money Makeover,* Nashville, Thomas Nelson. The Farrars' story is on pp. 116–117. We've looked at a lot of financial plans by various gurus, and Ramsey's strikes us as the most consistent with the psychological principles of change we review in *Switch.* Ramsey's own experience is on page 3, and the "motivation is more important than math" quote is on p. 114.

137 **Steve Kelman ... procurement reform.** See Steve Kelman (2005), *Unleashing Change: A Study of Organizational Renewal in Government,* Washington, DC: Brookings Institution Press. Kelman disputes the classic assumption in the organizational change literature that people resist change. He argues that in many situations there is a pent-up demand for change that merely needs to be "unleashed" by top leaders; he makes a compelling—and inspiring—argument that this is the case. The chocolate-chip cookie milspecs is on p. 4. The "set other changes in motion" quote is on p. 83. The story of the credit card and past performance pledges is on pp. 82–88. The A grade from the Brookings Institution is on p. 4.

138 **$320 billion in discetionary purchases.** The dollar amount is
from Kelman, *Unleashing Change,* p. 3. The comparison is from
the *Statistical Abstract of the United States, 2004–2005,* Washington, DC; U.S. Census Bureau. Table 642 reports the 2002 output of "computer and electronic products" as $139.9 billion and
the output of "motor vehicles, trailers, & parts" as $119.3 bil-
lion. So there's actually room left over.

141 **A *miracle scale* ranging from 0 to 10.** See also the discussion of
the miracle scale in Steve de Shazer, Yvonne Dolan, Harry Korman, Terry Trepper, Eric McCollum, and Insoo Kim Berg (2007),
*More than Miracles: The State of the Art of Solution-Focused Brief
Therapy,* New York: Haworth Press, pp. 61–72. There's a great
example of the scaling question in practice in the case study of Lee
the dock manager in Scott D. Miller and Insoo Kim Berg (1995),
*The Miracle Method: A Radically New Approach to Problem Drink-
ing,* New York: Norton, pp. 39–59.

142 **Track patients' self-reported progress.** Once the 0 to 10 scale is
set up, it becomes easier for clients to notice and start talking
about even small improvements toward their goal. When a therapist identifies a substantial change on the scale—say, a half-point
improvement toward the goal—the therapist will ask, "How
did you do it?" Therapists are trained to be persistent in asking
the *how* question several times: "It's important to be persistent
even if, and oftentimes particularly if, the client seems to be struggling a bit at first to formulate an answer. The question implies
the client did something that was helpful; things didn't get better without a reason." Some therapists call this process *positive
blaming.* Try it with your kids when they make an improvement. See discussion around p. 63 of de Shazer et al., *More than
Miracles.*

143 **NFL coach Bill Parcells.** See Bill Parcells (2001), "The Tough
Work of Turning Around a Team," reprinted in *Harvard Business
Review on Turnarounds* (pp. 105–114), Boston: Harvard Business
School Press; the quotation is on pp. 111–112.

144 **UCLA coach John Wooden.** Quoted in Robert Maurer (2004),
One Small Step Can Change Your Life: The Kaizen Way, New York:
Workman, p. 11.

144 **Small wins.** See Weick (1984), "Small Wins: Redefining the Scale of Social Problems," *American Psychologist, 39*(1), p. 46.

145 **David Allen.** See Allen (2001), *Getting Things Done,* New York: Viking Penguin, p. 239.

146 **Al-Anon.** See Al-Anon Family Groups (1995), *How Al-Anon Works for Families and Friends of Alcoholics,* Virginia Beach, VA: Al-Anon Family Groups; the quotation is on p. 73.

147 **George kissed Paula.** See Michele Weiner-Davis (1992), *Divorce Busting,* New York: Simon & Schuster, p. 92.

Chapter Seven

149 **College student Paul Butler.** The facts of the Butler story are from an interview Dan Heath conducted with Butler in October 2008. For a short version of the story and a photo of Butler, go to http://rareconservation.org/about/page.php?subsection=History (accessed May 28, 2009).

152 **Pride campaigns.** Information about Rare's Pride campaigns is available on Rare's website: http://www.rareconservation.org. Rare now focuses more on protecting precious areas, such as reefs and forests, than on preserving particular species. But Rare conservationists continue to work on precious areas by rallying the public around what they call a "charismatic species" that symbolizes specific areas that need protection. For instance, the Napoleon wrasse fish was the charismatic species in the waters surrounding the Togian Islands of Indonesia, which contain 262 species of coral and countless other species that depend on the coral.

153 **James March . . . identity model.** See March (1994), *A Primer on Decision Making: How Decisions Happen,* New York: Free Press, especially ch. 2, where March provides a beautiful contrast of consequence-based decision making and decision making through identity. For a longer treatment of this topic, see Chip Heath and Dan Heath, *Made to Stick: Why Some Ideas Survive and Others Die,* New York: Random House, 2007, pp. 182–199, including the story of the hugely successful "Don't Mess with Texas" antilittering campaign, which was a textbook application of identity.

154 **Concerned about the rapid turnover among its nurses.** For more on this story and on Appreciative Inquiry, see Tom Krattenmaker (2005), "Change Through Appreciative Inquiry," in *Managing Change to Reduce Resistance* (pp. 49–58), Boston: Harvard Business School Press. The Wood quotation is on p. 57. The improvement statistics are from Diana Whitney, Amanda Trosten-Bloom, and David Cooperrider (2003), *The Power of Appreciative Inquiry: A Practical Guide to Positive Change,* New York: Berrett-Koehler, pp. 94–95.

156 **Brasilata.** Background information comes from the Brasilata website (accessed February 13, 2009). Revenue in 2007 was 384,102,000 Brazilian reals, per this page: http://www .brasilata.com.br/en/financas_resultados.php. The number of ideas per inventor is from http://www.brasilata.com.br/en/ projeto_historico.php. For the car-bumper inspired can, go to http://www.brasilata.com.br/en/prod_18un_b.php. For the energy-saving idea stories, go to http://www.brasilata.com.br/en/ projecto_fatos_relevantes.php. All conversions between U.S. dollars and Brazilian reals were calculated on February 13, 2009.

158 **Citizens for Safe Driving.** See Jonathan L. Freedman and Scott C. Fraser (1966), "Compliance Without Pressure: The Foot-in-the-Door Technique," *Journal of Personality and Social Psychology, 4,* 195–203. This study started a whole field that investigates "foot-in-the-door" techniques. Most of these techniques seem to work because they form (or re-form) people's identity. For an insightful analysis of these techniques, under the label "commitment and consistency," see Robert Cialdini (2000), *Influence: Science and Practice,* 4th ed., New York: Allyn & Bacon, ch. 3. For the "Once [the home owner] has agreed . . ." quote, see Freedman and Fraser, "Compliance Without Pressure," p. 201.

163 **"Fixed mindset" . . . "growth mindset."** This quiz and all the fixed/growth-mindset material come from Carol S. Dweck (2006), *Mindset: The New Psychology of Success,* New York: Random House. The quiz is on p. 13. Every teacher, coach, manager, and parent should read Dweck's book.

166 **The brain is like a muscle.** See Lisa S. Blackwell, Kali H. Trzesniewski, and Carol S. Dweck (2007), "Implicit Theories

of Intelligence Predict Achievement Across an Adolescent Transition: A Longitudinal Study and an Intervention," *Child Development, 78,* 246–263.

167 **Dramatic transformations.** The quotation is from Dweck, *Mindsets,* p. 59.

168 **"Failure in the middle."** See Rosabeth Moss Kanter (November 23, 2003), *Leadership for Change: Enduring Skills for Change Masters,* Harvard Business School Note 9-304-06, Boston: Harvard Business School Press, p. 11, based on her 2001 book *Evolve! Succeeding in the Digital Culture of Tomorrow,* Boston: Harvard Business School Press.

168 **"Three steps forward and two steps back."** See Michele Weiner-Davis (1992), *Divorce Busting,* New York: Simon & Schuster, p. 212.

170 **Amy Edmondson.** See Edmondson (2003), "Framing for Learning: Lessons in Successful Technology Implementation," *California Management Review, 45,* 34–54. To protect her research participants, Edmondson used pseudonyms for the hospitals and the medical personnel.

171 **Recover fully in three weeks instead of two months.** The MICS recovery statistics are from Barbara Kuhn Timby and Nancy E. Smith (2006), *Introductory Medical-Surgical Nursing,* 9th ed., New York: Lippincott Williams & Wilkins, p. 532.

173 **A famous story about IBM.** See Paul B. Carroll (1993), *Big Blues,* New York: Crown; the quotation is on p. 51.

173 **Molly Howard.** Dan Heath interviewed Molly Howard in August 2008. The Principal of the Year award is described in Del Jones (March 16, 2008), "USA's Top Principal Could Teach CEOs a Thing or Two," *USA Today,* http://www.usatoday.com/money/companies/management/2008-03-16-principal-advice_N.htm (accessed February 6, 2009). Howard told Heath, "Companies can pick and choose the raw materials. Public education accepts all. We are a zero-reject business. That's a big, big difference."

Chapter Eight

180 **W. Edwards Deming.** See Deming (1982), *Out of the Crisis.* Boston: Massachusetts Institute of Technology Center for Advanced Engineering Study. The fires story is on p. 325.

180 **Fundamental Attribution Error.** See Lee Ross (1977), "The Intuitive Psychologist and His Shortcomings: Distortions in the Attribution Process," in L. Berkowitz (ed.), *Advances in Experimental Social Psychology* (vol. 10), New York: Academic Press. Echoes of the Fundamental Attribution Error are found in the conventional wisdom of many fields. Marketers talk about finding the right psychographic for a consumer good. Health psychologists talk about the importance of targeting people who are "ready" to stop smoking. Human resources people talk about getting the right people on the bus. Change experts talk about classifying the three types of people in any change effort: Believers, Fence Sitters, and Resisters. But social psychology is filled with examples that show situations trump personal attributes. For example, the food-drive study discussed in section 2 of this chapter says that you're three times better-off with a food-drive Resister with a map than with a true Believer without one.

180 **Marriage therapist Michele Weiner-Davis.** See Weiner-Davis (1992), *Divorce Busting,* New York: Simon & Schuster, p. 42. The kind of thinking fostered by the Fundamental Attribution Error has been shown to hurt marriages. Research has shown that couples experience more distress when they insist on attributing their relationship problems to traitlike characteristics of their partner that are global and stable. These attributions lead to more negative conversations and serious fights when couples try to work through their problems. See Norman Epstein, Donald H. Baucom, and Lynn A. Rankin (1993), "Treatment of Marital Conflict: A Cognitive-Behavioral Approach," *Clinical Psychology Review, 13,* 45–57.

182 **Distinguish "saints" from "jerks."** The food-drive study is described in L. Ross and R. E. Nisbett (1991), *The Person and the*

Situation: Perspectives of Social Psychology, New York: McGraw-Hill, pp. 132–133.

184 **Peter Bregman.** The source of this account is Bregman's blog, "The Easiest Way to Change People's Behavior" (March 11, 2009), http://blogs.harvardbusiness.org/bregman/2009/03/the-easiest-way-to.html, and an interview between Chip Heath and Bregman in May 2009.

187 **Becky Richards . . . "medication vests."** This story is based on an interview between Chip Heath and Becky Richards in June 2008 and a conference presentation by Richards at the BEACON collaborative in San Francisco in April 2008.

191 **"Sterile cockpit" rule.** See http://en.wikipedia.org/wiki/Sterile_Cockpit_Rule (accessed July 23, 2009). The rule was developed by the FAA in 1981 after investigations showed that some aircraft crashes during the 1970s were caused when flight crews were distracted from their instruments by idle chatter in the cockpit.

191 **The IT group . . . "sterile cockpit."** See Leslie A. Perlow (1997), *Finding Time: How Corporations, Individuals, and Families Can Benefit from New Work Practices,* Ithaca, NY: Cornell University Press. The quotations about the results of the "quiet hours" experiment are on p. 126. Perlow conducted this study for her graduate school dissertation. As an outsider to the company, and only a student at the time (she's now a senior professor at Harvard), Perlow was responsible for a simple intervention that the division vice president declared "a new benchmark"!

193 **Amanda Tucker.** This story is based on an example Tucker recounted in May 2009 in a Stanford Graduate School of Business class on "How to Change Things When Change Is Hard." Used with her permission.

197 **Haddon Matrix.** For an overview of the Haddon Matrix, see a presentation online produced by the San Francisco Department of Health (which in turn draws on work by Carolyn Fowler at Johns Hopkins University's Bloomberg School of Public Health): http://www.ccsf.edu/Resources/Faculty/jeskinne/documents/HAD2Complete.pdf (accessed June 14, 2009). Our thanks to Carolyn Fowler and Eric Tash for their insights on the Haddon Matrix.

199　**Rackspace.** The Rackspace story and quotations are from two interviews between Dan Heath and Graham Weston, conducted October 2007 and February 2009. Revenue growth data from internal company data were supplied to the authors.

Chapter Nine

203　**Mike Romano.** Mike's name and a few irrelevant details were altered to protect his identity. The information comes from an interview between the soldier and research assistant Elaine Bartlett in January 2009.

204　**The White House was so troubled.** The case study of drug use by soldiers before and after the Vietnam War is in Lee N. Robins, John E. Helzer, and Darlene H. Davis (1975), "Narcotic Use in Southeast Asia and Afterward," *Archives of General Psychiatry, 32,* 955–961.

208　**36 percent of the successful changes.** See Todd F. Heatherton and Patricia A. Nichols (1994), "Personal Accounts of Successful Versus Failed attempts at Life Change," *Personality and Social Psychology Bulletin, 20,* 664–675.

209　**Peter Gollwitzer.** Gollwitzer's summary of his work on triggers— Gollwitzer calls them "implementation intentions"—can be found in Gollwitzer (1999), "Implementation Intentions: Strong Effects of Simple Plans," *American Psychologist, 54,* 493–503. Most of the studies described in this section are referenced in that article. The quotation about "passing control to the environment" is on p. 495.

211　**Recovering from hip- or knee-replacement surgery.** See Sheina Orbell and Paschal Sheeran (2000), "Motivational and Volitional Processes in Action Initiation: A Field Study of the Role of Implementation Intentions," *Journal of Applied Social Psychology, 30,* 780–797.

212　**Recent meta-study.** Peter M. Gollwitzer, Paschal Sheeran, and Thomas L. Webb (2005), "Implementation Intentions and Health Behaviors," in M. Conner and P. Norman (eds.), *Predicting Health Behavior: Research and Practice with Social Cognition Models* (2nd edition). Buckingham, UK: Open University Press.

215 **Stand-up meeting.** See William G. Pagonis with Jeffrey L. Cruik-shank (1992), *Moving Mountains: Lessons in Leadership and Logistics from the Gulf War,* Boston: Harvard Business School Press; the quotation is on pp. 185–186. For the use of stand-up meetings in software development, see http://en.wikipedia.org/wiki/Stand-up_meeting (accessed May 27, 2009). Agile programmers disdain the typical IT style of delivering a whole program all at once (and typically late). Instead, they collaborate on a series of quick prototypes, each of which receives customer input, in the hope of catching problems early and preventing costly rework later.

217 **Two cups of soup each day.** See Barbara J. Rolls, Liane S. Roe, Amanda M. Beach, and Panny M. Kris-Etherton (2005), "Provision of Foods Differing in Energy Density Affects Long-Term Weight Loss," *Obesity Research, 13,* 1052–1060.

217 **Natalie Elder.** Dan Heath interviewed Natalie Elder in August 2008.

220 **The humble checklist.** Parts of the section on checklists originally appeared in our *Fast Company* column (March 2008), "The Heroic Checklist," http://www.fastcompany.com/magazine/123/heroic-checklist.html.

220 **Holy Grail of checklists.** See Atul Gawande (December 10, 2007), "The Checklist: If Something So Simple Can Transform Intensive Care, What Else Can It Do?" *New Yorker,* pp. 86–101.

221 **Checklists educate people about what's best.** We're not advocating the kind of checklists that are associated with some quality improvement processes—for example, the elaborate procedure manuals compiled for ISO 9000 certification. To educate people about what's best and to help them avoid blind spots, a checklist has to be simple enough that people will actually *use* it. The pre-flight checklist for a 747 is less than one page long. If your checklist requires more than one sheet of paper, you need to simplify it.

222 **Chronic parking problem.** For the parking study, see C. F. Gettys et al. (1987), "An Evaluation of Human Act Generation Performance," *Organizational Behavior and Human Decision Processes, 39,* 23–51.

223 **"Standardize on the mission-critical elements."** Dan Heath interviewed Dr. Pronovost in January 2008.

Chapter Ten

226 **A stream of smoke.** See Latané and Darley (1968), "Group Inhibition of Bystander Intervention in Emergencies," *Journal of Personality and Social Psychology, 10,* 215–221. Latané and Darley's work on bystander nonintervention is one of the cleverest streams of research in social psychology. Because it's a classic, professors of social psychology teach it often, and they recommend to their students a simple technique to overcome nonintervention: Point to someone and give that person a specific instruction such as "*You* call 911." It's not that people aren't willing to help. It's just that the Rider is caught in an infinite loop, trying to look at everyone else for cues about how to behave, and those cues aren't coming.

227 **Obesity is contagious.** See Nicholas A. Christakis and James H. Fowler (2007). "The Spread of Obesity in a Large Social Network over 32 Years," *New England Journal of Medicine, 357,* 370–379. The quotation is from Gina Kolata (June 25, 2007), "Study Says Obesity Can Be Contagious," *New York Times.* Be on the lookout for Christakis and Fowler's book *Connected: The Surprising Power of Our Social Networks and How They Shape Our Lives,* New York: Little, Brown and Company (2009).

227 **Drinking is contagious.** See Michael Kremer and Dan Levy (2005), "Peer Effects and Alcohol Use Among College Students," Working paper, Harvard University.

229 **Guests at the hotel reuse their towels.** See Noah J. Goldstein, Steve J. Martin, and Robert B. Cialdini (2008), *Yes! 50 Scientifically Proven Ways to Be Persuasive,* New York: Free Press, ch. 1.

229 **Gerard Cachon.** Chip Heath interviewed Gerard Cachon in August 2008 and May 2009.

233 **Designated driver.** Statistics are from Harvard University's School of Public Health, http://www.hsph.harvard.edu/research/chc/harvard-alcohol-project/ (accessed June 14, 2009). The Grant Tinker quotations are from Nikki Finke (December 29,

1988), "A TV Crusade on Drunken Driving," *Los Angeles Times,* p. 5E.

234 **"Sugar-daddy" relationships.** Statistics about cross-generational relationships are from Population Reference Bureau (2007), *Addressing Cross-Generational Sex: A Desk Review of Research and Programs.* The American teens statistic is on p. 16; the statistic for sub-Saharan Africa is on p. 9.

237 **Fataki.** We led the workshop that developed the Fataki idea and the first three radio commercials. A video of Chip Heath talking about the work on the day the first radio spots were recorded is on *The NewsHour with Jim Lehrer* website: http://www.pbs.org/ newshour/bb/africa/july-dec07/aids_11-30.html. Dan Heath was, at that moment, Photoshopping a prototype of the first Fataki billboards.

242 **Lou Gerstner . . . "Culture . . . *is* the game."** See Louis V. Gerstner (2002), *Who Says Elephants Can't Dance?,* New York: HarperBusiness, p. 182.

242 **Katherine Kellogg.** Thanks to Kellogg's careful work, this is one of the most closely observed change efforts in the entire organizational behavior literature. See Katherine C. Kellogg (2008), "Not Faking It: Making Real Change in Response to Regulation at Two Surgical Teaching Hospitals," Working paper, MIT.

Chapter Eleven

251 **Skateboarding monkey.** Parts of the section on Amy Sutherland and exotic-animal training originally appeared in our *Fast Company* column (April 2008), "Your Boss Is a Monkey," http://www .fastcompany.com/magazine/124/your-boss-is-a-monkey.html (accessed June 14, 2009).

251 **"What Shamu Taught Me."** The *New York Times* article is from June 25, 2006, and can be found at http://www.nytimes.com/ 2006/06/25/fashion/25love.html (accessed May 17, 2009). Also see Amy Sutherland (2008), *What Shamu Taught Me About Life, Love, and Marriage: Lessons for People from Animals and Their Trainers,* New York: Random House. The "verbal grooming"

quotation and other details are from an interview between Dan Heath and Amy Sutherland in January 2008.

253 **Psychologist Alan Kazdin.** See Kazdin (2008), *The Kazdin Method for Parenting the Defiant Child: With No Pills, No Therapy, No Contest of Wills,* New York: Houghton Mifflin. The quotations are from p. 34.

253 **Change isn't an event; it's a process.** Chip Heath thanks Bo Brockman for teaching this idea.

254 **Steven Kelman.** On pp. 22–24, Kelman explains why mere exposure and cognitive dissonance may cause people to resist change. Then, in an insightful analysis on pp. 123–127, he shows how the same factors make change hard to stop once they get going. See Kelman (2005), *Unleashing Change: A Study of Organizational Renewal in Government,* Washington, DC: Brookings Institution Press.

Acknowledgments

Some readers gave us feedback on an early draft of the text. You helped us separate the wheat from the chaff and also saved us from a major Clocky miscue. Thanks to Hans van Alebeek, Elissa R. Allen, Lance Andersen, Cassie Anderson, Mark Dyar, Alex Estrada, Bruce Fuller, Lisa Hoashi, Tom Jansen, Brett Jenks, Anne Kennedy, Ray Kilmer, Ken Kozek, Russ Krieger, Ron Misak, Timothy J. Moreau, Shashank Patel, Andre Piazza, Joanne Quan, John Sankovich, Sam Sears, Karla Shearer, Mike Short, Jim Spina, Happy Webberman, and Patty Williams.

A special thanks to some people who gave us in-depth advice on the manuscript: Fred and Brenda Heath, Brian Lanahan, Justin Osofsky, Mark Schlueter, Sim Sitkin, and Glenn Sommer.

A special thank-you to Jon Haidt for sharing his analogy with us. (Imagine the horror of a framework calling for people to "direct the reflective system" and "motivate the unconscious system.") Thanks to Chip's students in the "How to Change Things When Change Is Hard" course at Stanford for helping refine the framework (and showing us how to talk about bright spots and finding the feeling), and to the people who attended Dan's workshop at Wake Forest University (and a shout-out to Bill Davis for making that happen). Thank you to Elaine Bartlett for her reporting on the Mike Romano story.

We work with such wonderful partners and friends—we cannot thank you enough: Bob Safian, David Lidsky, and Chris Osekoski and the team at *Fast Company;* Les Tuerk and Tom Neilssen and everyone at BrightSight; Kevin Small and his team at ResultSource; and Mark Fortier and Liz Hazelton at Fortier PR. Eternal gratitude to Christy Fletcher (for making us authors and for "Switch"), as well as her fabulous team at Fletcher & Co.

The team at Broadway Books has been incredible: Tara Gilbride, Meredith McGinnis, Whitney Cookman, Songhee Kim, and Robert Siek. And a special authorial love letter to Michael Palgon and our editor, Roger Scholl—you're the best.

And finally, no thank-you would seem adequate for all that our family has done to support us, but we'll thank them anyway: Mom, Dad, and Susan, and our wives, Susan and Amanda.

Index